Indian Stock Market Anomalies

Dr. J. Sudarvel

Dr.R. Velmurugan

Published by

BONFRING®
Intellectual Integrity

Indian Stock Market Anomalies

9 789386 638410 >

ISBN 978-93-86638-41-0

Authors

Dr. J. Sudarvel

Dr.R. Velmurugan

Bonfring

309, 2nd Floor, 5th Street Extension, Gandhipuram,

Coimbatore-641 012.

Tamilnadu, India.

E-mail: info@bonfring.org | Website: www.bonfring.org

Phone: 0422 4213231

Table of Contents

CHAPTER I

INDIAN STOCK MARKET ANOMALIES

1.1. Introduction

Stock market plays a vital role for the economic development of a country, by properly channeling the funds for productive purpose. The proposition that a well-regulated stock market extends significant economic services is now widely accepted and recognized by various academicians. Stock market assists economy as well as individual investors by mobilizing the scarce resources and allocation in those sectors, which employ them optimally. Stock market assists individual investors by providing continuous market for securities. From economic point of view, a well-developed stock market has been considered requisite for economic growth as well as improvements in country's productivity. The progress of a country can be judged by ascertaining the stock market indicators like liquidity, asset pricing and turnover. In addition, by ensuring a free and fair trading of stocks and performance of pricing mechanism, by ensuring a suitable return on investment will ensure viable investment opportunities, in the stock markets acts as a driving force for channeling savings into profitable investment and hence, ensures an optimal allocation of capital. In recent years, there has been greater distress in the midst of shareholders, portfolio managers and researchers concerning about the behaviour of stock market prices. The investors are eager to earn a higher rate of return on their investments. Hence, in order to satisfy investor's expectations, the portfolio managers have to look at the stock market conditions keenly and accordingly advise investors and to construct a sound portfolio. Our country is believed to be as one of the fastest up-and-coming markets in the world with a well established stock market with a long history of organized trading in securities. Over the last few years, advanced technology and online based transactions have modernized the stock exchanges whereas, in terms of the number of companies listed and total market capitalization, the Indian capital market is considered large relative to the country's stage of economic development.

The subject of anomaly in the stock market has attracted the attention of researchers for a long time due to its potential of producing abnormal returns during certain periods of the year. Anomaly refers to the regular and repetitive fluctuation in a time series which occur periodically over a span of less than a year. The existence of a pronounced seasonal behaviour in the market might suggest some form of market inefficiency. The existence of seasonality in stock returns, however, violates an important hypothesis in finance, i.e. Efficient Market Hypothesis (EMH) because equity prices are no longer random and can be predicted based on past pattern. The proposition, "Stock returns are not predictable" was until very recently regarded as one of the most firmly established empirical researchers on the behaviour of stock returns. However, the non-predictability proposition has been questioned recently and consequently certain anomalies in the behaviour of returns such as Week-of-the Month Effect, Day-of-the Week Effect, Intra-day Effect, Size Effect, Tax-year Effect, Turn-of-the Year Effect, January Effect, Monthly Effect, Turn-of-the Month Effect and Price-Earning Ratio Effect and some others have been observed. These anomalies disprove the existence of Efficient Market Hypothesis. Thus, in the present study an earnest attempt has been made to ascertain whether Anomalies exists in BSE Sensex, NSE Index, BSE and NSE Sectoral indices and if exists, nature of anomaly exists in Indian Stock Market.

1.2. Statement of the Problem

If the market is not efficient, there will exists some market efficiency anomalies, then the investors can gain some abnormal returns by using well planned strategies within the market. A big boom has been witnessed in Stock Markets in recent times. A large number of new players have entered the market and trying to gain market share in this fast improving market. Study of anomalies assist the investors in taking advantage of the irregularity of information in the market. Investors may have chances to make use of the calendar anomalies to earn abnormal return. The movements of stocks during particular times of the year, in particular stock markets can be observed and investments can be done accordingly. The anomalies could be identified by studying the price movements of the stock and the investors can invest cleverly during these times to earn abnormal returns. Hence, the present study has been carried out to ascertain (i) Whether stock market anomalies prevails in BSE Sensex, 19 BSE sectoral indices, NSE Nifty and 12 NSE sectoral indices and (ii) If anomaly exists, what type of anomalies prevails in BSE Sensex, 19 BSE sectoral indices, NSE Nifty and 12 NSE sectoral indices.

1.3. Objectives of the Study

The present study has been carried out with the following objectives

1. To identify the existence of the Day of the Week Effect in Indian stock market.
2. To ascertain the presence of Semi- Month Effect in Indian stock market.
3. To examine the presence of Turn-of-the- Month effect in Indian stock market.
4. To identify the existence of Monthly/January Effect and Annual Effect in Indian stock market.
5. To identify the seasonality effect in Shariah index.
6. To study the Volatility Persistence in Indian Stock Market.

7. To offer Suggestions to the investors in timing their Investments.

1.4. Research Methodology

1.4.1. Data

The data required for the study is secondary in nature. Daily returns of BSE Sensex and 19 BSE sectoral indices, NSE CNX Nifty and 12 NSE sectoral indices have been collected from the website of BSE historical data and NSE historical data, respectively.

1.4.2. Study Period

The study period ranges between April 01st 2004 and March 31st 2015.

1.4.3. Sampling Design

By adopting purposive sampling method, data required for the study has been collected. The study period ranges between 1stApril 2004 and 31st March 2015. Hence, BSE and NSE sectoral indices, whose data available for the above mentioned period alone considered for analysis.

1.4.4. Framework of Analysis

The collected data have been analyzed by applying Descriptive statistics like Mean, Standard Deviation, Variance, Skewness, Kurtosis test, Ordinary Least Square(OLS) Regression, paired 't' test, Generalized Auto Regressive Conditional Heteroscedasticity (GARCH) and Shapiro-Wilk test are employed for analysis of data.

1.5. Significance of the Study

The present study would be useful to the Government, Investors, Fund Managers and stock brokers. This study is useful for Government of India to identify the market integration, functions and efficiency of stock market (efficient or not efficient) to make changes their rules and regulations.

This study is of great use to investor in predicting the share price behavior, if Anomalies are properly understood. Timing is one of the most important factors in investing in the stock market, who could have expected returns by altering the timing of trades which include delaying buy or sell their shares for certain days or month. The existence of Calendar Anomalies in stock markets across the country is widely described and these Anomalies should be examined in India. The detailed study of this Calendar Anomaly would help all the stakeholders in India and outside India to plan their investment.

1.6. Limitation of the Study

The present study was restricted only to equity segment of the stock market and doesn't examine the debt and derivative segments of the Indian stock market. The study is based on only secondary data. Hence, limitations applicable to secondary data are applicable to the present study too. The study covers only closing values of index whereas open, high and low values can also be used to test the efficiency of Indian securities market. While extending the results of the study, one should be careful to use the same judiciously by taking the limitations into consideration.

1.7. Chapter Scheme

The report of the study is presented in eleven chapters.

First Chapter introduces the theme of the study, Statement of the problem, Objectives of the study, Research methodology, Significance of the study and Limitation of the study.

Studies conducted abroad and in India are reviewed and the important findings are highlighted in *Chapter Two*.

Chapter Three deals with theoretical aspect on stock market anomalies.

Day of the week effect in Indian stock market are discussed in detail at *Chapter Four.*

Chapter Five deals with the Semi Month effect in Indian stock market.

Prevalence of Turn-of-the Month Effect in Indian Stock Market is ascertained in *Chapter Six.*

Chapter Seven consolidates the Monthly effect and April effect in Indian stock market.

Annual Effect in Indian stock market is ascertained in *Chapter Eight.*

Chapter Nine discuss with the seasonality effect in Shariah Index in Indian stock market.

Volatility in Indian stock market is diagrammatically represented in *Chapter Ten.*

Last Chapter summarizes the findings and Suggestions of the study.

CHAPTER II

REVIEW OF LITERATURE

2.1. Introduction

In the absence of the empirical evidence, it would be difficult to know the price of the shares in stock market. While empirical tests of return-volatility behaviour are plentiful for developed stock markets, the focus on developing and emerging stock markets has only begun in recent years the interest in these emerging markets has arisen from the increased globalization and integration of the world economy in general and that of financial markets in particular. Market Anomalies are market patterns that do seem to lead to abnormal returns more often than not, and since some of these patterns are based on information in financial reports, market anomalies present a challenge to the semi-strong form of the EMH, and indicate that fundamental analysis does have some value for the individual investor. Several studies have been conducted to analyse the Calendar Anomaly of Indian as well as Global Capital Market. This study investigates the existing literature in the field of Indian Stock Market Anomalies. The focus of the literature survey is to review these various stock market anomalies that were experimental over time in different stock indices in India and foreign. The Anomalies analysed in this literature review include the Day-of-the week-effect, Turn of the Month Effect, Semi-Month Effect, January Effect and turn of the year effect.

2.2. Day of the Week Effect

Ankur Singhal, Vikram Bahure (2009) in their study entitled "Week End Effect of Stock Returns in the Indian Market"founds that delay between the trading and settlement period, complex effects of holidays on daily returns and effect of investor expectations leads to day of the week effect.

Ash Narayan Sah (2009) in his study entitled "Stock Market Seasonality: A Study of the Indian Market" confirmed that the day of the week effect present in Nifty and Junior Nifty returns.

Ashish Garg, B.S.Bodla and Sangeetha Chhabra (2010) in their study entitled "Seasonal Anomalies in Stock Returns: A Study Developed and Emerging Markets" found that day of the week effect exists in Indian stock market and not exists in US market.

Allan Muchemi Kuria and Dr. George Kamau Riro (2013) in their study entitled "Stock Market Anomalies: A Study of Seasonal Effects on Average Returns of Nairobi Securities Exchange" found that the existence of day of the week effect in Nairobi Securities Exchange.

Archana. S, Mohammed Safeer and Dr.S. Kevin (2014) in their study entitled "A Study on Market Anomalies in Indian Stock Market" proves that the day of the week effect does exists in Indian stock market (i.e.) stock prices tend to decrease on Monday, then closing stock prices on previous Friday.

Catherine Kalayaan S. Almonte (2004) in his study entitled "The Day-of-the-week effect in the Philippine Stock Market" observed that the day-of-the-week effect exists in the Philippine stock market as confirmed by result of the Kruskal-Wallis H test. Therefore, the Philippine stock market showed some form of market inefficiency.

Daniel Cohen and Robert Taylor (2012) in their study entitled "The Disappearance of the Day of the Week Effect: Evidence from the London Stock Exchange" confirmed there was a day of the week effect on the London Stock Exchange. Volatility has increased on Monday then the disappearance of the day of the week effect and volatility decreased on Thursday. The reason for the disappearance is not known but it may have been caused by more sophisticated trading practices, which allowed investors to exploit opportunities caused by the day of the week effect leading to their disappearance.

Dragan Tevdovski, Martin Mihajlov and Igor Sazdovski (2012) in their study entitled "The Day of the Week Effect in South Eastern Europe Stock Markets" proves that the day of the week effect is found only in Croatian and Bulgarian Stock Market. The day of the week effect does not exist in Bosnia, Herzegovina, Macedonia and Serbia.

Elena Valentina Ilica and Drago Opreaa (2014) in their study entitled "Seasonality in the Romanian stock market: the-day-of-the-week effect" confirmed that the day of the week effect is present on the Romanian stock market due to the existence of seasonality in the risk-return relationship.

Faryad Hussain, Kashif Hamid, Rana Shahid Imdad Akash and Majid Imdad Khan (2011) in their study entitled "Day of the Week Effect and Stock Returns: (Evidence from Karachi Stock Exchange-Pakistan)" proves that day of the week effect does exist in Karachi stock exchange–Pakistan. Returns on Tuesday are more volatile over other days. Empirical results of the study show that the assumption of the "EMH" is violated in different days' domain.

Hakan Berument and Halil Kiymaz (2001) in their study entitled **"The Day of the Week Effect on Stock Market Volatility"** found that the day of the week effect is present in both volatility and the return calculation. While the highest and lowest returns are perceived on Wednesday and

Monday, the highest and the lowest volatility are observed on Friday and Wednesday, correspondingly. The highest volatility on Friday may be a result of several macroeconomic news releases taking place on Thursday and Friday.

HooiHooi Lean and Veronica Kah Min Tan (2010) in their study entitled "Existence of the Day-of-the-week Effect in FTSE Bursa Malaysia"found that that the day-of-the-week effect exist for the FTSE Bursa Malaysia MESDAQ Index.

Manish. R. Pathak (2013) in his study entitled "Stock Market Seasonality: A Study of the Indian Stock Market (NSE)" observes that day of the week effect not noticed in Indian stock market due to the increased volatility, increased awareness among Indian investors, Globalization of Indian Economy, Reach of Media, Emergence of Derivatives segment and increase in disposable Income.

Marcus Davidsson, Per-Olof Bjuggren, Daniel Wiberg and Helena Bohman (2006) in their study entitled "Stock Market Anomalies A Literature Review and Estimation of Calendar effects on the S&P 500 index" found support of the weekend effect that returns on Friday is higher than returns on Mondays however, this weekend effects may have been given too much attention and appear to be rather overrated.

Mohamed Khaled Al-Jafari (2012) in his study entitled "An Empirical Investigation of the Day-of- the-Week Effect on Stock Returns and Volatility: Evidence from Muscat Securities Market" proves that the day-of-the-week effect is not present at Muscat Securities Market. As Muscat stock market seems to start positive and ends also positive with downturn during the rest of the trading days.

Muhammad Arshad Haroon and Nida Shah (2013) in their study entitled "Investigating Day-of-the-Week Effect in Stock Returns: Evidence from Karachi Stock Exchange-Pakistan" found mixed results for both Sub Periods. Sub Period I (2004 – 2007) negates the prevalence of Day-of-the-Week Effect due to political instability. Day-of-the-Week Effect exists in Sub Period II. The argument to support this result might be that the period after election in 2008 - 2011 comprised of democracy and political stability in terms of government and fairly consistent policies.

Nikolas L. Hourvouliades and Nick Kourkoumelis (2009) in their study entitled "New Evidence for the Day-of-the-Week Effect in the Financial Crisis" found that the day of the week effect does not exists in Cyprus, Romania and Ukraine but opposite results holds from Greece and Turkey. The contradictory evidence in each market's efficiency pattern is probably due to a different level of maturity and interdependence.

Naliniprava Tripathy (2010) in her study entitled "Expiration and Week Effect: Empirical Evidence from the Indian Derivative Market" proves that the day-of-the week effect does not persist in Indian derivative market, as there are no price distortions on the expiration day.

Nik Maheran Nik Muhammad and Nik Muhd Naziman Abd. Rahman (2010) in their study entitled "Efficient Market Hypothesis and Market Anomaly: Evidence from Day-of-the Week Effect of Malaysian Exchange" founds that Financial crisis leads to day of the week-effect in Malaysian Exchange.

Nageswari and Dr.M.Selvam (2011) in their study entitled "An Empirical Study on Seasonal Analysis in the Indian Stock Market" found that there is no day of the week effect in Indian stock market.

Nikunj R. Patel, Nitesh Radadia and Juhi Dhawan (2012) in their study entitled "Day of the Week Effect of Asian Stock Markets" found that the Asian stock market are not normally distributed. The efficiency in the market indicates the succeeding price variation should be autonomous to each other. Further there is no evidence of day of the week effect in Asian countries, as investor cannot predict market behaviour and may not have opportunities to improve their returns by timing their investments during whole period and all the three sub-periods for any of markets understudy of Asian region.

Nabaghan Mallick and Dr.Sathya Swaroop Debasish (2013) in their study entitled "Day of the Week Effect on National Stock Exchange with respect to Gas, Oil and Refineries Industries in India" proves that the day of the week effect does exists in all selected companies BRPL, GAIL, HPCL, IOCL, IPCL, ONGC and Reliance India Limited.

Neeraj Amarnani and Parth Vaidya (2014) in their study entitled "Study of Calendar Anomalies in Indian Stock Markets" proves that the day of the week effect does not exists in BSE Sensex returns.

Phaisarn Sutheebanjard and Wichian Premchaiswadi (2010) in their study entitled "Analysis of Calendar Effects: Day-of-the-Week Effect on the Stock Exchange of Thailand" found that the day-of-the-week effect was present in the Thailand Stock Exchange.

Papia Mitra and Gholam Syedain Khan (2014) in their study entitled "An Analysis of Day-of-the-Week and Intraday Effects in the Indian Stock Market: Evidence from National Stock Exchange" found that the presence of reverse weekend effect in the Indian stock market (i.e) "Friday's return lowest from other days called reverse week end effect". Friday's return is found lower than other day's return.

Ricky Chee-Jiun Chia and Venus Khim-Sen Liew (2010) in their study entitled "Evidence on the Day of the Week effect and Asymmetric Behavior in the Bombay Stock Exchange" proves that the day of the week effect does exists in Bombay Stock Exchange, India. BSE regardless of sub periods, after controlling for time varying variance and asymmetrical market behaviour revealed to the positive and negative news.

Ritesh Patel and Mitesh Patel (2011) in their study entitled "An Econometric Analysis of Bombay Stock Exchange: Annual Returns Analysis, Day-of-the-Week Effect and Volatility of Returns" confirms that the day of the week effect does not exists by Bombay Stock Exchange, India.

Sunil Poshakwale (1996) in his study entitled "Evidence on Weak Form Efficiency and Day of the Week Effect in the Indian Stock Market" found that the day of the week effect observed on the BSE. This study has presented evidence concentrating on the weak form efficiency and on the day of week effect in the Bombay Stock Exchange under the consideration that variance is time dependent.

Sarma S.N (2004) in his study entitled "Stock Market Seasonality in an Emerging Market" proves that the presence of day of the week effect in Indian stock market returns during the post liberalization period. The study period is characteristic of a highly unsettled economic environment and the fact that the indices underwent frequent shuffling and reshuffling unconnected to the religiously advocated principles of diversification.

SiqiGuo and Zhiqiang Wang (2007) in their study entitled "Market efficiency anomalies A study of seasonality effect on the Chinese stock exchange" found that the Day of the week effect does exists in Chinese stock market.

Srinivasan P. and Kalaivani M(2013) in their study entitled "Day-of-the-Week Effects in the Indian stock market" confirmed that day of the week effect exists in Indian stock market during 1st July, 1997 to 29th June, 2012 Indian stock markets are weak-form inefficient.

Truong Dong Loc (2012) in his study entitled "Day-of-the-week effect on stock returns and volatility: The case of Ho Chi Minh Stock Exchange, Vietnam" proves that the day-of-the-week effects on stock returns and volatility are exists in the Ho Chi Minh Stock Exchange, Vietnam.

Umar Bida Ndako (2013) in his study entitled "The Day of the Week effect on stock market returns and volatility: Evidence from Nigeria and South Africa" found that day of the week effect does exists in both Nigeria and South Africa between pre and post liberalisation period. This clearly indicates that investors in the Nigerian equity market react more to positive news than the negative news and this is at odds with most empirical findings.

Wing-Keung Wong, Aman Agarwal and Nee-Tat Wong (2006) in their study entitled "The Disappearing Calendar Anomalies in the Singapore Stock Market" found that the day-of-the-week effect may no longer exist in the Singapore market.

Werner Kristjanpoller Rodriguez (2012) in his study entitled "Day of the Week Effect in Latin American Stock Markets" found that the Day of the Week Effect is fairly prevalent during the period across the markets in Latin America. Supporting the notion that Mondays are "negative" days while Fridays are "positive" days, and volatility is higher on Mondays and is lower on Fridays.

Yeliz Yalcin and Eray M. Yucel (2006) in their study entitled "The Day-of-the-Week Effect on Stock-Market Volatility and Return: Evidence from Emerging Markets" proves that the day of the week effect is not strongly present in their study period. Consequently, the DOW effects estimated for a set of countries and the reasons behind the DOW effects do not necessarily display a one-to-one correspondence, which makes the recognition of common patterns even harder.

2.3. Semi Month Effect

Ashish Garg, B.S. Bodla and Sangeeta Chhabra (2010) in their study entitled "Seasonal Anomalies in Stock Returns: A Study of Developed and Emerging Markets" found that the semi month effect does exists both in Indian stock market as well as US stock market. Semi-Monthly Effect, the mean return of the First Half Month has been compared with the average return of the rest half of the month.

Ercan Balaban and Meliha Bulu (1996) in their study entitled "Is There a Semi-Monthly Effect in the Turkish Stock Market?" found that the semi-monthly or intra-month effects do not exists in the Turkish Stock Market. Their study results imply that aggregate stock returns in Turkey appear to be generated by different factors compared to those in the developed markets where semi-monthly effects have been present in almost all. Therefore, international portfolio diversification works. 3 This is of particular importance to foreign investors who already full access to the Turkish stock market and hold approximately 25 percent of total tradable shares in Turkey.

Eleftherios Giovanis (2009) in his study entitled "Calendar Effects and Seasonality on Returns and Volatility" found that the semi-month effect, where in 7 and 2 cases accept for both first and second half of the month returns are significant lower and higher, both India and Canada first half of the month noticed higher returns and lower returns noticed in the second half of the month.

Nageswari. P and Dr.M. Selvam (2011) in their study entitled "Calendar Anomalies in the Indian Stock Market" found that the Semi Month Effect did exist in the Indian Stock Market returns during the study period (2002 - 2010).

Nageswari. P, Dr.M. Selvam and Dr.J. Gayathri (2011) in their study entitled "An Empirical Analysis of Semi-Month and Turn of the Month Effects in Indian Stock Market" found that higher mean returns was recorded for the first half month than the rest of the day of the month. It is found that the semi month effect does not exist in BSE Sensex and S&P CNX Nifty index returns during the study period.

SiqiGuo and Zhiqiang Wang (2007) in his study entitled "Market efficiency anomalies A study of seasonality effect on the Chinese stock exchange" found that the semi-month effect does not exist in Chinese stock market.

Ushad Subadar Agathee (2009) in his study entitled "Semi-Monthly Effect: Evidence from the Maurtian Official Stock Market" found that the semi month does exists in The Maurtian Official Stock Market.

2.4. Turn of the Month Effect

Amy Dickinson and David R. Peterson (1995) in their study entitled "Expectations of weekend and Turn-of-the-Month Mean Return Shifts Implicit in Index Call Option Prices" proves turn-of-the-month effect are at least partially anticipated in United States."

Ashish Garg, B.S. Bodla and Sangeeta Chhabra (2010) in their study entitled "Seasonal Anomalies in Stock Returns: A Study of Developed and Emerging Markets" found that the turn of the month effect does exists both at Indian stock market and US market. Efficiency of the stock markets is closely related to the allocation of scarce capital resources. The allocation of capital resources to their most productive use can only be achieved in the presence of an efficient pricing mechanism, which requires an efficient dissemination of the information.

Archana. S, Mohammed Safeer and Dr.S. Kevin (2014) in their study entitled "A Study on Market Anomalies in Indian Stock Market" found that the Turn of the month effect are minimally visible but not statistically proven for the analysed period. Due to their timely actions prices of stocks quickly adjust to the new information, and reflect all the available information. So no investor can beat the market by generating abnormal returns.

Eleftherios Giovanis (2009) in his Study entitled "Calendar Effects and Seasonality on Returns and Volatility" found that the turn-of-the-month effect is still persistent only in two stock indices, in Yugoslavia and Sweden. Reason for turn-of-the-month effect the transaction cost, which are too high for the investors to profit from this calendar anomaly, as the investors cannot exploit the pattern.

Erhard Reschenhofer (2010) in his study entitled "Further Evidence on the Turn-of-the-Month Effect" strongly corroborate the existence of the turn-of-the-month effect in the S&P 500 index.

FiroozehKolahi (2006) in his Study entitled "Turn-of-the-Month Effect for the European Stock Market" Confirmed that the Turn-of-the-Month Effect does exists in MSCI Euro indices January 2001 to December 2005.

Idries M. Al-Jarrah, Basheer A. Khamees and Ibrahim Hashem Qteishat (2011) in their study entitled "The "Turn of the Month Anomaly" in Amman Stock Exchange: Evidence and Implications" found that the turn of the month effect does not significantly exhibit in the Amman Stock Exchange, Jordan.

Lan Liu (2013) in his study entitled "The Turn-of-the-Month Effect in the S&P 500 (2001-2011)" found that the turn of month does exists in US. Investment made on days before the turn-of-the-month performs better than those made during the turn-of-the-month. However, they show that even without the foresight or perfect predicting ability, investors can still achieve a better performance by spreading the investment throughout the month.

Polina Heininen and Vesa Puttonen (2008) in their study entitled "Stock Market Efficiency in the Transition Economies through the Lens of Calendar Anomalies" found that the stock returns of predictable based on the turn-of-the-month effect exists in Croatia, Hungary, Poland, Romania, Russia and Slovenia.

Nageswari. P and Dr.M. Selvam (2011) in their study entitled "Calendar Anomalies in the Indian Stock Market" found that the Turn of the Month Effect did exist in returns of the Indian Stock Market during the study period (2002 - 2010).

Nageswari. P, Dr.M. Selvam and Dr.J. Gayathri (2011) in their study entitled "An Empirical Analysis of Semi-Month and Turn of the Month Effects in Indian Stock Market" proves that the turn of the Month Effect does not exists in Indian Stock Market. Most of the cash flows come in to the Indian Stock Market in the first few days of the month, which induces stock prices to move upward. Hence, the Indian Stock Market cannot be treated as fully efficient till now.

Neeraj Amarnani and Parth Vaidya (2014) in their study entitled "Study of Calendar Anomalies in Indian Stock Markets" found that the Turn of the month effect does exists in both Sensex and Nifty in India.

Prajapati. B. A, Ashwin Modi and Jay Desai (2013) in their study entitled "A Survey of Day of the Month Effect in World Stock Markets" proves that the turn of the month does exists in selected indices, also confirms that all the markets tested in the research are not efficient and there exists opportunities for superior returns. The average of the return on the last two trading days of the preceding month, and the first three days of the subsequent month were computed and compared with the mean return for the rest of the days in the subsequent month.

Silva. PM (2010) in his study entitled "Calendar "Anomalies" in the Portuguese stock market" found that the Turn of the month effect does exists in the Portuguese stock market.

Van der Gugten. T and D. J. C. Smant (2010) in their study entitled "Stock Market Calendar Anomalies and Macroeconomic News Announcements" found that turn-of-the-month effect still present when macro-economic news announcement days are not considered. The significance of the turn-of-the-month effect is practically the same for non-announcement days and for all trading days.

Vesna Karadzic and Tamara Backovic Vulic (2011) in their study entitled "The Montenegrin capital market: Calendar anomalies" proves that turn of the month effect does exists in Montenegrin capital market. the results of our investigation show the opposite. The disappearance of at least one of three tested calendar anomalies from the Montenegrin capital market suggests that this market is becoming more efficient.

2.5. Monthly Effect or Month of the Year Effect

Denis O. Boudreaux (1995) in his study entitled "The Monthly Effect in International Stock Markets: Evidence and Implications" observed that monthly effect was found in the Danish, Norwegian and German markets, and the monthly effect (negative effect) does not exist in the Pacific basin market of Singapore/Malaysia.

Mihir Dash, Anirban Dutta and Mohit Sabharwal (2011) in their study entitled "Seasonality and Market Crashes in Indian Stock Markets" found that the month-of-the-year effect does exists in Indian stock markets. The results of the study also indicate a highly significant negative impact of market crashes on stock market returns, as would be expected, and that the incidence of market crashes reduces the seasonal effects.

Manish. R. Pathak (2013) in his study entitled "Stock Market Seasonality: A Study of the Indian Stock Market" (NSE) observes that month of the year effect is not noticed in Indian stock market due to the increased volatility, increased awareness among Indian investors, Globalization of Indian Economy, reach of Media, emergence of Derivatives segment and Increase in disposable Income.

Nageswari. P, M. Selvam, S. Vanitha and M. Babu (2013) in their study entitled "An Empirical Analysis of January Anomaly in the Indian Stock Market" proves that the monthly effect and tax loss hypothesis does exists in Indian stock market. The Study also provides evidence that the market was not able to price the risk appropriately as higher returns were possible by taking less risk and this indicates market inefficiency.

Pandey. IM (2002) in his study entitled "Is There Seasonality in the Sensex Monthly Returns?" confirms the January effect of stock return does exist in India. The result of the study indicates that stock returns in India are not entirely random. This study confirms that the Indian stock market may not be an efficient. This could result from several social, economic and political factors. These results of the study could be attributed to the 'information' hypothesis.

Paul Alagidede (2013) in his study entitled "Month of the Year and Pre-Holiday Effects in African Stock Markets" found that the January seasonality is evident in Egypt, Nigeria, Zimbabwe, Kenya, Morocco and South Africa and not at Tunisia.

Sarbapriya (2012) in her study entitled "Investing Seasonal Behaviour in the Monthly Returns: Evidence from BSE Sensex of India" proves that the month of year effect is noticed in Indian stock market, whereas an investor may dispose the shares in the month of March for availing income tax benefits.

Shyam Lal Dev Pandey and Gopi Prachetas (2012) in his study entitled "Testing of Risk Anomalies in Indian Equity Market by Using Monthly Average Risk & Return" proves that low volatile stocks offer higher average rate of return than high volatile stocks, which proves the existence of inefficiency in Indian Stock Market.

2.6. Volatility

Eleftherios Giovanis (2009) in his study entitled "Calendar Effects and Seasonality on Returns and Volatility" found that Periodic- GARCH model or the Periodic Stochastic Volatility Model are the appropriate models for measuring volatility.

Halil Kiymaz, and Hakan Berument (2003) in their study entitled "The Day of the Week Effect on Stock Market Volatility and Volume: International Evidence" proves that the day of the week effect anomaly is noticed both in equity and non-equity markets. High volatility would be accompanied by low trading volume because of the unwillingness of liquidity traders to trade in periods of high stock market volatility.

2.7. Conclusion

From the above studies, it is ascertained that stock market anomalies are the result of fundamental factors, cyclical factors, macroeconomic news, investor expectation and sentiments, etc. There are a number of factors besides investor expectations and trade settlement cycle that can be related to the seasonality in equity market returns, and why the performance of fund managers may vary across calendar days. For example, unfavourable news releases on the weekend and overreaction as a result of human psychology have an effect stock price performance. Day-of-the Week-Effect, Semi Month Effect, Turn of the Month Effect, Monthly Effect and Volatility prevails in various countries. Day-of-the Week-Effect was mostly prevailing in foreign countries and India.In previous studies researchers have concentrated on the macro level BSE–Sensex and NSE-Nifty as a whole but no researcher concentrated sectorial indices. In order to fill this vacuum, the present study considers both macro and sectoral indices. The third chapter discuss on Theoretical aspect of stock market anomalies.

Chapter III

Stock Market Anomalies

3.1. Introduction

Stock market anomalies are cross-sectional and time series patterns in security returns that are not predicted by a central paradigm or theory. The following paragraph discuss on calender based anomalies

3.2. Types of Calender Based Anomalies

Calender based anomalies are broadly classified as (i) Day-of-the-week Effect, (ii) Semi Month Effect, (iii) Turn of the Month Effect, (iv) Monthly Effect and (v) Tax-Year Effect (April Effect).

3.2.1. Day-of-the-Week Effect

The standard assumption in financial theory is that the distribution of stock returns are identical for all weekdays, however, stock market shuts down during Saturday and Sunday. This break provides the possibility of day-of-the-week effect, i.e. some weekday is different from other weekdays in the stock market. If the day-of-the-week effect exists, some investors can take an advantage from it to make arbitrage.

3.2.2. Semi-Month Effect

Semi-month Effect, the mean return of the First Half Month has been compared to the rest of the day of the month. The return of the first 15 days has been compared to rest of the day's return of the month. The purpose of studying Semi-Month Effect is to find appropriate investment time during fortnight month.

3.2.3. Turn-of-the- Month Effect

The trend of stock prices to increase during the last two days and the first three days of each month, is called Turn of the Month Effect. For the purpose of this study, the average of the return on the last two trading days of the preceding month, and the first three days of the subsequent month were computed and compared with the mean return for the rest of the days in the subsequent month.

3.2.4. Monthly Effect

The Monthly Effect is also known as the month of the year effect. The Monthly effect is one of the most important calendar anomalies. The month-of-the-year effect would be present when returns in some months are higher than other months. It is caused normally by a significant low return in March.

3.2.5. *Tax-Year Effect (April Effect)*

The prices tend to rise as the selling pressure disappears at the end of the tax year and the investors tend to buy back those securities This, in turn, encourages the investor's portfolio decisions by motivating them for sale of declining securities. Thus, as a result, resultant short-term capital losses could be offset against taxable income. It further indicates that selling pressure before the expiry of tax year might depress prices of securities. In the US, the tax year coincides with Calendar year but the situation is different in India, as the tax-year commences on April 1st and ends on March 31st. It is most evident in the securities which have experienced recent price declines.

3.3. Reason for Anomalies

The following are the factors that contributes towards anomalies

3.3.1. *Emotional Factors*

Emotion often overrules intelligence in decisions and can filter facts, where the investor may give too much weight to facts that are agreeable and may tend to ignore or underweight facts that are antithetical to one's predisposition.

There is the **fear of regret**, or **regret avoidance**, which causes investors to hold losing positions too long in the hope that they will become profitable or sell winners too soon to lock in profits lest they turn into losses.

3.3.2. *Overconfidence*

Overconfidence in one's abilities can lead to higher portfolio turnover and to lower returns. Despite the fact that few investors or even professional portfolio managers beat the market over an extended time, there is still a considerable amount of active portfolio management. One study has shown, on the average, that men have lower returns than women because they trade more actively, presumably because they have greater confidence in their abilities.

3.3.3. *Conservatism*

Conservatism is the hesitation of many investors to act on new information, where such information should dictate an action or a change to one's strategy. This hesitation to news, for instance, eventually leads to action at different times for different investors, leading to momentum as more investors start reacting to the news.

3.3.4. Belief Perseverance

Belief perseverance is the persistence of one's selection process and investment strategies even when such strategies are failing or are suboptimal, causing the investors to ignore new information that may contradict one's decisions.

3.3.5. Loss Aversion

Loss aversion is the propensity for people to avoid losses even for possible gains. Hence, people often hang onto losing stocks longer than they should, since selling would actualize the loss; otherwise, it is still just a "paper loss". Loss aversion is related to the marginal utility of money, where the 1st dollars are more valuable than additional dollars. For instance, most investors would avoid an investment where there was a 50% chance of either earning $50,000 on a $100,000 investment, or an equal chance of losing the same amount, because the $50,000 lost would have greater marginal utility, and therefore be more valuable to the investor, than the $50,000 potentially gained.

3.3.6. Misinformation and Thinking Errors

Misinformation and thinking errors probably account for most market inefficiencies, since no one knows everything and, even if they did, they may not make the best decisions based on that information.

3.3.7. Forecasting Errors

Forecasting errors are a typical example, since even stock analysts are frequently wrong about future earnings and prospects for the companies that they cover.

3.3.8. Representativeness

Representativeness is the extrapolation of future results based on a limited set of observations or facts; hence, this is sometimes known as small sample neglect. This is best illustrated by investors seeking a fund in which to invest, and basing their decision on the fund's most recent performance rather than covering a longer duration, especially during bear markets. Often, this is the result of the lack of due diligence, where the investor relies on brochures or other advertising materials put out by the company or fund instead of doing independent research.

3.3.9. Narrow Framing

Narrow framing is the evaluation of too few factors that may affect an investment. For instance, an investor may buy a security because of its past performance without considering economic factors that may be changing that could change the performance of the security. Mental accounting is a specific kind of narrow framing in which different investments are mentally segregated, applying different criteria and due diligence to different investments where the different consideration may be unwarranted. For example, treating separate investments as if they were the only investment rather than as part of one's portfolio. Biased information gathering and thinking is the distortion of personal bias on facts and thinking to conform with one's current opinions or actions.

3.3.10. Limits to Arbitrage

First, there is the risk that the mispricing will get worse, and, therefore, present a risk to arbitraging. The market influence of behavioral bias may be greater than the influence of arbitrageurs, especially since arbitraging behavioral bias is not risk-free. And even if prices do trend toward their intrinsic prices, it may take longer than arbitrageurs think—maybe longer than their investment horizon.

Secondly, financial models may be inaccurate, making arbitrage risky.

Thirdly, much of the arbitrage activity would require short selling, which, with stocks, is very risky, and many institutional investors are not permitted to sell short.

3.4. Conclusion

In India too, stock market anomalies prevails. The following chapters discuss about nature of anomalies prevails in Indian stock market.

CHAPTER IV

DAY OF THE WEEK EFFECT IN INDIAN STOCK MARKET

4.1. Introduction

The standard assumption in financial theory is that the distribution of stock returns is identical for all weekdays, however, stock market does not function during Saturday and Sunday. This break provides the possibility of day-of-the-week effect, i.e. some weekday is different from other weekdays in the stock market. If the day-of-the-week effect exists, some investors can take an advantage from it to make arbitrage.

Different models explain the variation in the stock returns with the help of fundamental factors. But there still exists a component of unexplained variation that can be explained by trends in the fundamental factors, cyclical factors, macroeconomic news, investor expectation and sentiments, etc. In this chapter, the effect of cyclical factors on stock returns in the form of day of the week effect is considered. The form caused by macroeconomic news can only partially subsume the weekend effects of stock returns. There are a number of factors besides investor expectations and trade settlement cycle that can be related to the seasonality in equity market returns, and why the performance of fund managers may vary across calendar days. For example, unfavorable news releases on the weekend and overreaction as a result of human psychology have an effect on stock price performance. In addition, the day of the week pattern returns and volumes are empirically found to be more pronounced for securities in which institutional investors play a greater role.

4.2. Tools for Analysis

The collected data have been analyzed by making use of Returns, Descriptive statistics such as Mean, Standard Deviation, Variance, Skewness, Kurtosis, Shapiro-Wilk test and OLS Regression.

4.2.1. Return

The gain or loss of a security in a particular period. The return consists of the income and the capital gains relative on an investment. The total return of the period can be calculated as

$$= (P1 - P0)/P0 \times 100$$

4.2.2. *Mean*

Mean is the average value of the series, obtained by adding up the series and dividing by the number of observations.

4.2.3. *Standard Deviation*

Standard deviation is a measure of the dispersion of a set of data from its mean. The more spread apart the data, the higher the deviation. Standard deviation is calculated as the square root of variance.

4.2.4. *Variance*

Variance is a measurement of the spread between numbers in a data set. The variance measures how far each number in the set is from the mean. Variance is calculated by taking the differences between each number in the set and the mean, squaring the differences and dividing the sum of the squares by the number of values in the set.

4.2.5. *Skewness*

This is a measure of the distribution tilt. In other words, the skewness measures asymmetry. A symmetric distribution has a '0' skewness, a distribution skewed to the right has positive skewness, and a distribution skewed to the left has negative skewness.

4.2.6. *Kurtosis*

This is a measure of the distribution "tailedness" relative to the normal distribution. A light-tailed distribution has fewer values in the tails than the normal distribution, and will have negative Kurtosis. A heavy-tailed distribution has more values in the tails than the normal distribution, and will have positive kurtosis.

4.2.7. *Shapiro-Wilk test*

The Shapiro-Wilk test, whether a random sample, $X^1, X^2, ..., X^n$ comes from (specifically) a normal distribution. Stats requires a random sample of between 3 and 2,000 for the Shapiro-Wilk test.

4.2.8. *Ordinary Least Squares Regression (OLS)*

Ordinary Least Squares (OLS) is a statistical technique which efforts to find the function which most closely approximates the data (a "best fit").

4.3. Day of the Week Effect

The following subsections discuss about the day of the week effect of BSE Sensex, 19 BSE sectoral indices, NSE Nifty and 12 NSE sectoral indices.

4.3.1. BSE Sensex Index

The following table tries to ascertain, whether Day of the week effect prevails in BSE Sensex Index.

Table 4.1: Day of the Week Effect – BSE Sensex Index

	MONDAY	TUESDAY	WEDNESDAY	THURSDAY	FRIDAY
Mean	.0585	.0571	.1119	.0517	.0701
Median	.1361	.0736	.0724	.1238	.0885
Std. Deviation	1.84093	1.42805	1.42813	1.41268	1.66770
Variance	3.389	2.039	2.040	1.996	2.781
Skewness	.866	.226	-.050	-.153	-.401
Kurtosis	17.664	4.510	3.633	3.069	5.877
Shapiro-Wilk	.000	.000	.000	.000	.000

Source – Database collected from BSE web portal and computed.

High mean returns were noticed during Wednesday (.1119) and low mean returns were found during Thursday (.0517). While comparing to variance, high level of volatility was noticed on Monday (3.389) and low level of volatility was noticed on Thursday (1.996).

Result of the Skewness test disclosed that positive value and it was noticed during Monday returns (.866) and Tuesday returns (.226), which implies that most of the Monday and Tuesday returns were more than the average returns. The other day's returns were found negative skewness, which implies that most of the other day's returns were less than the average returns. The Kurtosis result of the BSE SENSEX index returns were found leptokurtic on all the days of the week. Since, Kurtosis values are greater than 3, thus, it is inferred that the level of risk associated with the day's returns of the BSE Sensex index was high, which means investors may obtain either high level of profit or loss.

As the calculated P value of the Shapiro-Wilk test is less than 0.01, it is clearly proved that the data are not normally distributed. Hence, anomaly exists in the BSE SENSEX index returns.

To measure day of the week effect, OLS is employed. Friday return is introduced as dependent variable and the rest of the day, namely Monday, Tuesday, Wednesday and Thursday are considered as independent variables. The following table illustrates the determinants of Day of the week effect of BSE Sensex Index.

Table 4.2: Determinants of Day of the Week Effect- BSE Sensex Index

	Coefficient	*Std. Error*	*t-ratio*	*p-value*	
Constant	0.0634003	0.0715935	0.8856	0.37626	
Monday	0.12291	0.0386308	3.1817	0.00155	**
Tuesday	0.0990964	0.0497762	1.9908	0.04701	*
Wednesday	-0.0507541	0.050164	-1.0118	0.31211	
Thursday	-0.0211469	0.0508809	-0.4156	0.67786	
R-squared	0.27797	Adjusted R-squared		0.20487	
F (4, 532)	3.802657	P-value(F)		0.004649	

Source – Database collected from BSE web portal and computed.

The result of OLS disclose that Monday return is found to be significant at 1 per cent level and Tuesday return is found to be significant at 5 per cent level. Variables which are significant are discussed below.

Monday

The regression coefficient indicates that Monday returns positively influences Friday returns. The value of the regression coefficient indicates that a unit of increase in Monday return shall increase Friday return by 0.122 units. Higher rate of return on Monday leads to a higher rate of return on Friday.

Tuesday

The regression coefficient indicates that Tuesday returns positively influences Friday returns. The value of the regression coefficient indicates that a unit of increase in Tuesday return shall increase Friday return by 0.099 units. Higher rate of return on Tuesday leads to a higher rate of return on Friday.

The value of R^2 is found to be significant at one per cent level. This shows that the regression equation framed is a good fit. Around 27.79 per cent of variation in Friday return is due to select variables.

4.3.2. BSE Auto Index

The following table tries to ascertain, whether Day of the week effect prevails in BSE Auto Index.

Table 4.3: Day of the Week Effect – BSE Auto Index

	MONDAY	TUESDAY	WEDNESDAY	THURSDAY	FRIDAY
Mean	.0584	.0659	.0973	.1051	.0976
Median	.1721	.0769	.1198	.1313	.1223
Std. Deviation	1.70189	1.49992	1.41087	1.47332	1.62413
Variance	2.896	2.250	1.991	2.171	2.638
Skewness	-.423	.198	-.054	-.353	-.411
Kurtosis	6.228	2.374	.974	3.026	4.597
Shapiro-Wilk	.000	.000	.000	.000	.000

Source – Database collected from BSE web portal and computed.

High mean returns were noticed during Thursday (.1051) and low mean returns were found during Monday (.0584). While comparing to variance, high level of volatility was noticed on Monday (2.896) and low level of volatility was noticed on Wednesday (1.991).

Result of the Skewness test disclosed the positive value and it was noticed during Tuesday (.198), which implies that most of the Tuesday returns were more than the average returns. The other day's returns were found negative skewness, which implies that most of the other day's returns were less than the average returns. The Kurtosis result of the BSE AUTO index returns were found leptokurtic on Monday returns (6.228), Thursday returns (3.026) and Friday returns (4.597). Since, Kurtosis values are greater than 3, thus, it is inferred that the level of risk associated with the Monday, Thursday and Friday returns of the BSE Automobile sector was high, which means investors may obtain either high level of profit or loss. The other day's returns were found platykurtic. Since, Kurtosis values are less than 3, thus, it is inferred that the level of risk associated with the other day's returns of the BSE Automobile sector was low, which means investors may obtain either low level of profit or loss.

As the calculated P value of the Shapiro-Wilk test is less than 0.01, it is clearly proved that the data are not normally distributed. Hence, there exists anomaly in the BSE AUTO index returns.

The following table illustrates the determinants of Day of the week effect of BSE Auto Index.

Table 4.4: Determinants of Day of the Week Effect – BSE Auto Index

	Coefficient	*Std. Error*	*t-ratio*	*p-value*	
Constant	0.0897237	0.069969	1.2823	0.20028	
Monday	0.0724479	0.041009	1.7666	0.07786	
Tuesday	0.135451	0.0461511	2.9349	0.00348	**
Wednesday	-0.044944	0.0498848	-0.9010	0.36802	
Thursday	-0.0113476	0.0478231	-0.2373	0.81253	
R-squared	0.22926	Adjusted R-squared		0.15579	
F (4, 532)	3.120692	P-value(F)		0.014855	

Source – Database collected from BSE web portal and computed.

The result of OLS disclose that Tuesday return is found to be significant at 1 per cent level.

Tuesday

The regression coefficient indicates that Tuesday returns positively influences Friday returns. The value of the regression coefficient indicates that a unit of increase in Tuesday return shall increase Friday return by 0.135 units. Higher rate of return on Tuesday leads to a higher rate of return on Friday.

The value of R^2 is found to be significant at five per cent level. This shows that the regression equation framed is a good fit. Around 22.92 per cent of variation in Friday return is due to the select variable.

4.3.3. BSE Bank Index

The following table tries to ascertain, whether Day of the week effect prevails in BSE Bank Index.

Table 4.5: Day of the Week Effect – BSE Bank Index

	MONDAY	TUESDAY	WEDNESDAY	THURSDAY	FRIDAY
Mean	.0683	.0727	.1227	.0721	.1204
Median	.1519	.1236	.0627	.1119	.1234
Std. Deviation	2.38137	1.99156	1.85940	1.90484	2.13469
Variance	5.671	3.966	3.457	3.628	4.557
Skewness	.522	.382	.310	.086	-.446
Kurtosis	11.102	4.263	2.799	2.200	4.183
Shapiro-Wilk	.000	.000	.000	.000	.000

Source – Database collected from BSE web portal and computed.

High mean returns were noticed during Wednesday (.1227) and low mean returns were found during Monday (.0683). While comparing to variance, high level of volatility was noticed on Monday (5.671) and low level of volatility was noticed on Wednesday (3.457).

Result of the Skewness test disclosed that negative value and it was noticed during Friday (-.446), which implies that most of the Friday returns were less than the average returns. The other day's returns were found positive skewness, which implies that most of the other day's returns were more than the average returns. The Kurtosis result of the BSE Bank index returns were found leptokurtic on Monday returns (11.102), Tuesday returns (4.263) and Friday returns (4.183). Since, Kurtosis values are greater than 3, thus, it is inferred that the level of risk associated with the Monday, Tuesday and Friday returns of the BSE Banking sector was high, which means investors may obtain either high level of profit or loss. The other day's returns were found platykurtic. Since, Kurtosis values are less than 3, thus, it is inferred that the level of risk associated with the other day's returns of the BSE Banking sector was low, which means investors may obtain either low level of profit or loss.

As the calculated P value of the Shapiro-Wilk test is less than 0.01, it is clearly proved that the data are not normally distributed. Hence, there exists anomaly in the BSE BANK index returns.

The following table illustrates the determinants of Day of the week effect of BSE Bank Index.

Table 4.6: Determinants of Day of the Week Effect - BSE Bank Index

	Coefficient	*Std. Error*	*t-ratio*	*p-value*	
Constant	0.10149	0.0915191	1.1089	0.26795	
Monday	0.127439	0.0381335	3.3419	0.00089	**
Tuesday	0.0914666	0.045588	2.0064	0.04532	*
Wednesday	-0.0122795	0.0489504	-0.2509	0.80202	
Thursday	0.0484001	0.0479133	1.0102	0.31288	
R-squared	0.28990	Adjusted R-squared		0.21690	
F (4, 532)	3.970849	P-value(F)		0.003480	

Source – Database collected from BSE web portal and computed.

The result of OLS disclose that Monday return is found to be significant at 1 per cent level and Tuesday return is found to be significant at 5 per cent level.

Monday

The regression coefficient indicates that Monday returns positively influences Friday returns. The value of the regression coefficient indicates that a unit of increase in Monday return shall increase Friday return by 0.127 units. Higher rate of return on Monday leads to a higher rate of return on Friday.

Tuesday

The regression coefficient indicates that Tuesday returns positively influences Friday returns. The value of the regression coefficient indicates that a unit of increase in Tuesday return shall increase Friday return by 0.091 units. Higher rate of return on Tuesday leads to a higher rate of return on Friday.

The value of R^2 is found to be significant at one per cent level. This shows that the regression equation framed is a good fit. Around 28.99 per cent of variation in Friday return is due to the select variables.

4.3.4. BSE Basic Materials Index

The following table tries to ascertain, whether Day of the week effect prevails in BSE Basic Materials Index.

Table 4.7: Day of the Week Effect – BSE Basic Materials Index

	MONDAY	TUESDAY	WEDNESDAY	THURSDAY	FRIDAY
Mean	.0813	.0019	.2064	-.0527	.0033
Median	.0996	.0908	.1422	.0389	.0145
Std. Deviation	2.13651	1.70596	1.84995	1.80503	1.88432
Variance	4.565	2.910	3.422	3.258	3.551
Skewness	-.200	-.224	.451	-.582	-.259
Kurtosis	6.201	1.649	4.847	4.055	4.035
Shapiro-Wilk	.000	.000	.000	.000	.000
Source – Database collected from BSE web portal and computed.					

High mean returns were noticed during Wednesday (.2064) and low mean returns were found during Thursday (-.0527). While comparing to variance, high level of volatility was noticed on Monday (4.565) and low level of volatility was noticed on Tuesday (2.910).

Result of the Skewness test disclosed that positive value and it was noticed during Wednesday returns (0.451), which implies that most of the Wednesday returns were more than the average returns. The other day's returns were found negative skewness, which implies that most of the other day's returns were less than the average returns. The Kurtosis result of the BSE Material Index returns were found platykurtic on Tuesday returns (1.649). Since, Kurtosis values are less than 3, thus, it is inferred that the level of risk associated with the Tuesday returns of the BSE Material sector was low, which means investors may obtain either low level of profit or loss. The other day's returns were found leptokurtic. Since, Kurtosis values are greater than 3, thus, it is inferred that the level of risk associated with the other day's returns of the BSE Material index was high, which means investors may obtain either high level of profit or loss.

As the calculated P value of the Shapiro-Wilk test is less than 0.01, it is clearly proved that the data are not normally distributed. Hence, there exists anomaly in the BSE Material Index returns.

The following table illustrates the determinants of Day of the week effect of BSE Basic Materials Index.

Table 4.8: Determinants of Day of the Week Effect – BSE Basic Materials Index

	Coefficient	*Std. Error*	*t-ratio*	*p-value*	
Constant	0.00386178	0.085265	0.0453	0.96389	
Monday	0.14122	0.03996	3.5340	0.00045	**
Tuesday	0.0201911	0.0494198	0.4086	0.68305	
Wednesday	0.0998182	0.0460195	2.1690	0.03059	*
Thursday	0.186673	0.0471651	3.9579	0.00009	**
R-squared	0.61838	Adjusted R-squared		0.53750	
F(4, 464)	7.645958	P-value(F)		0.01106	

Source – Database collected from BSE web portal and computed.

The result of OLS disclose that Monday and Thursday return is found to be significant at 1 per cent level and Wednesday return is found to be significant at 5 per cent level.

Monday

The regression coefficient indicates that Monday returns positively influences Friday returns. The value of the regression coefficient indicates that a unit of increase in Monday return shall increase Friday return by 0.141 units. Higher rate of return on Monday leads to a higher rate of return on Friday.

Wednesday

The regression coefficient indicates that Wednesday returns positively influences Friday returns. The value of the regression coefficient indicates that a unit of increase in Wednesday return shall increase Friday return by 0.099 units. Higher rate of return on Wednesday leads to a higher rate of return on Friday.

Thursday

The regression coefficient indicates that Thursday returns positively influences Friday returns. The value of the regression coefficient indicates that a unit of increase in Thursday return shall increase Friday return by 0.186 units. Higher rate of return on Thursday leads to a higher rate of return on Friday.

The value of R^2 is found to be significant at five per cent level. This shows that the regression equation framed is a good fit. Around 61.83 per cent of variation in Friday return is due to the select variables.

4.3.5. BSE Consumer Durables Index

The following table tries to ascertain, whether Day of the week effect prevails in BSE Consumer Durables Index.

Table 4.9: Day of the Week Effect – BSE Consumer Durables Index

	MONDAY	TUESDAY	WEDNESDAY	THURSDAY	FRIDAY
Mean	.1500	.0902	.1096	.0540	.0941
Median	.1623	.1843	.2462	-.0058	.1582
Std. Deviation	2.26117	1.86371	1.85466	1.78696	1.80870
Variance	5.113	3.473	3.440	3.193	3.271
Skewness	-.066	.157	-.158	-.094	-.625
Kurtosis	6.650	3.072	3.798	2.893	4.060
Shapiro-Wilk	.000	.000	.000	.000	.000

Source – Database collected from BSE web portal and computed.

High mean returns were noticed during Monday (.1500) and low mean returns were found during Thursday (.0540). While comparing to variance, high level of volatility was noticed on Monday (5.113) and low level of volatility was noticed on Thursday (3.193).

Result of the Skewness test disclosed that positive value and it was noticed during Tuesday returns (0.157), which implies that most of the Tuesday returns were more than the average returns. The other day's returns were found negative skewness, which implies that most of the other day's returns were less than the average returns. The Kurtosis result of the BSE Consumer Durables index returns were found platykurtic on Thursday returns (2.893). Since, Kurtosis values are less than 3, thus, it is inferred that the level of risk associated with the Thursday returns of the BSE Consumer Durables sector was low, which means investors may obtain either low level of profit or loss. The other day's returns were found leptokurtic. Since, Kurtosis values are greater than 3, thus, it is inferred that the level of risk associated with the other day's returns of the BSE Consumer Durables sector was high, which means investors may obtain either high level of profit or loss. As the calculated P value of the Shapiro-Wilk test is less than 0.01, it is clearly proved that the data are not normally distributed. Hence, there exists anomaly in the BSE Consumer Durables index returns.

The following table illustrates the determinants of Day of the week effect of BSE Consumer Durables Index.

Table 4.10: Determinants of Day of the Week Effect – BSE Consumer Durables Index

	Coefficient	*Std. Error*	*t-ratio*	*p-value*
Constant	0.0922355	0.0784633	1.1755	0.24031
Monday	0.0509721	0.0345937	1.4735	0.14122
Tuesday	0.0077732	0.0417716	0.1861	0.85245
Wednesday	-0.0378047	0.042403	-0.8916	0.37303
Thursday	-0.0456303	0.0437339	-1.0434	0.29725
R-squared	0.07404	Adjusted R-squared		0.0059
F (4, 532)	0.992058	P-value(F)		0.411320
Source – Database collected from BSE web portal and computed.				

The result of OLS regression analysis disclose that the select independent variables collectively contribute to 7.40 per cent variation in Friday returns.

4.3.6. BSE Consumer Goods Index

The following table tries to ascertain, whether Day of the week effect prevails in BSE Consumer Goods Index.

Table 4.11: Day of the Week Effect – BSE Consumer Goods Index

	MONDAY	TUESDAY	WEDNESDAY	THURSDAY	FRIDAY
Mean	.0858	.0746	.0684	.0742	.1549
Median	.1888	.1047	.0040	.1043	.1708
Std. Deviation	2.36121	1.78332	1.77358	1.81757	2.01443
Variance	5.575	3.180	3.146	3.304	4.058
Skewness	.937	.158	-.007	.228	-.338
Kurtosis	16.593	2.402	2.990	3.546	2.639
Shapiro-Wilk	.000	.000	.000	.000	.000
Source – Database collected from BSE web portal and computed.					

High mean returns were noticed during Friday (.1549) and low mean returns were found during Wednesday (.0684). While comparing to variance, high level of volatility was noticed on Monday (5.575) and low level of volatility was noticed on Wednesday (3.146).

Result of the Skewness test disclosed that positive value and it was noticed during Monday returns (.937), Tuesday returns (.158) and Thursday returns (.228), which implies that most of the Monday, Tuesday and Thursday returns were more than the average returns. The other day's returns were found negative skewness, which implies that most of the other day's returns were less than the average returns. The Kurtosis result of the BSE Consumer Goods index returns were found leptokurtic on Monday returns (16.593) and Thursday returns (3.546). Since, Kurtosis values are greater than 3, thus, it is inferred that the level of risk associated with the Monday and Thursday returns of the BSE Consumer Goods sector was high, which means investors may obtain either high level of profit or loss. The other day's returns were found platykurtic. Since, Kurtosis values are less than 3, thus, it is inferred that the level of risk associated with the other day's returns of the BSE Consumer Goods sector was low, which means investors may obtain either low level of profit or loss.

As the calculated P value of the Shapiro-Wilk test is less than 0.01, it is clearly proved that the data are not normally distributed. Hence, there exists anomaly in the BSE Consumer Goods index returns.

The following table illustrates the determinants of Day of the week effect of BSE Consumer Goods Index.

Table 4.12: Determinants of Day of the Week Effect – BSE Consumer Goods Index

	Coefficient	*Std. Error*	*t-ratio*	*p-value*	
Constant	0.142317	0.0862695	1.6497	0.09960	
Monday	0.134994	0.0364667	3.7018	0.00024	**
Tuesday	0.0637318	0.0483235	1.3189	0.18778	
Wednesday	-0.0109882	0.0486315	-0.2259	0.82133	
Thursday	-0.0390026	0.0476374	-0.8187	0.41330	
R-squared	0.28926	Adjusted R-squared		0.21625	
F(4, 532)	3.961772	P-value(F)		0.003535	

Source – Database collected from BSE web portal and computed.

The result of OLS disclose that Monday return is found to be significant at 1 per cent level.

Monday

The regression coefficient indicates that Monday returns positively influences Friday returns. The value of the regression coefficient indicates that a unit of increase in Monday return shall increase Friday return by 0.134 units. Higher rate of return on Monday leads to a higher rate of return on Friday.

The value of R^2 is found to be significant at one per cent level. This shows that the regression equation framed is a good fit. Around 28.92 per cent of variation in Friday return is due to the select variable.

4.3.7. BSE Energy Index

The following table tries to ascertain, whether Day of the week effect prevails in BSE Energy Index.

Table 4.13: Day of the Week Effect – BSE Energy Index

	MONDAY	TUESDAY	WEDNESDAY	THURSDAY	FRIDAY
Mean	.2167	-.0357	.1456	-.1175	.0846
Median	.1680	.0000	.0684	-.0155	.0000
Std. Deviation	1.87573	1.69099	1.69083	1.96091	2.03819
Variance	3.518	2.859	2.859	3.845	4.154
Skewness	.247	-.036	.035	-1.541	1.543
Kurtosis	3.538	4.558	1.997	10.097	17.874
Shapiro-Wilk	.000	.000	.000	.000	.000

Source – Database collected from BSE web portal and computed.

High mean returns were noticed during Monday (.2167) and low mean returns were found during Thursday (-0.1175). While comparing to variance, high level of volatility was noticed on Friday (4.154) and low level of volatility was noticed on Tuesday and Wednesday (2.859).

Result of the Skewness test disclosed that positive value and it was noticed during Monday returns (.247), Wednesday returns (.035) and Friday returns (1.543), which implies that most of the Monday, Wednesday and Friday returns were more than the average returns. The other day's returns were found negative skewness, which implies that most of the other day's returns were less than the average returns. The Kurtosis result of the BSE Energy Index returns were found platykurtic on Wednesday returns (1.997). Since, Kurtosis values are less than 3, thus, it is inferred that the level of risk associated with the Wednesday returns of the BSE Energy Index sector was low, which means investors may obtain either low level of profit or loss. The other day's returns were found leptokurtic. Since, Kurtosis values are greater than 3, thus, it is inferred that the level of risk associated with the other day's returns of the BSE Energy Index sector was high, which means investors may obtain either high level of profit or loss.

As the calculated P value of the Shapiro-Wilk test is less than 0.01, it is clearly proved that the data are not normally distributed. Hence, there exists anomaly in the BSE Energy Sector Unit Index returns.

The following table illustrates the determinants of Day of the week effect of BSE Energy Index.

Table 4.14: Determinants of Day of the Week Effect – BSE Energy Index

	Coefficient	*Std. Error*	*t-ratio*	*p-value*
Constant	0.0775899	0.0956398	0.8113	0.41763
Monday	0.00543811	0.0503204	0.1081	0.91399
Tuesday	-0.0458475	0.0560355	-0.8182	0.41367
Wednesday	0.0361372	0.0557751	0.6479	0.51736
Thursday	0.0146481	0.0486047	0.3014	0.76327
R-squared	0.02706	Adjusted R-squared		-0.05891
F(4, 464)	0.314767	P-value(F)		0.868113
Source – Database collected from BSE web portal and computed.				

The result of OLS regression analysis disclose that the select independent variables collectively contribute to 2.76 per cent variation in Friday returns.

4.3.8. BSE Finance Index

The following table tries to ascertain, whether Day of the week effect prevails in BSE Finance Index.

Table 4.15: Day of the Week Effect – BSE Finance Index

	MONDAY	TUESDAY	WEDNESDAY	THURSDAY	FRIDAY
Mean	.2335	.0225	.0833	.1333	-.1080
Median	.1168	.1017	.1070	.1910	-.0428
Std. Deviation	1.84194	2.01920	2.12980	1.98702	1.77778
Variance	3.393	4.077	4.536	3.948	3.160
Skewness	.125	-.496	1.307	.182	-.073
Kurtosis	2.540	4.807	14.196	3.272	2.200
Shapiro-Wilk	.000	.000	.000	.000	.000
Source – Database collected from BSE web portal and computed.					

High mean returns were noticed during Monday (.2335) and low mean returns were found during Friday (-0.1080). While comparing to variance, high level of volatility was noticed on Wednesday (4.536) and low level of volatility was noticed on Friday (3.160).

Result of the Skewness test disclosed that positive value and it was noticed during Monday returns (.125), Wednesday returns (1.307) and Thursday returns (.182), which implies that most of the Monday, Wednesday and Thursday returns were more than the average returns. The other day's returns were found negative skewness, which implies that most of the other day's returns were less than the average returns. The Kurtosis result of the BSE Finance Index returns were found platykurtic on Monday returns (2.540) and Friday returns (2.200). Since, Kurtosis values are less than 3, thus, it is inferred that the level of risk associated with the Monday and Friday returns of the BSE Finance Index sector was low, which means investors may obtain either low level of profit or loss. The other day's returns were found leptokurtic. Since, Kurtosis values are greater than 3, thus, it is inferred that the level of risk associated with the other day's returns of the BSE Finance Index sector was high, which means investors may obtain either high level of profit or loss.

As the calculated P value of the Shapiro-Wilk test is less than 0.01, it is clearly proved that the data are not normally distributed. Hence, there exists anomaly in the BSE Finance Index returns.

The following table illustrates the determinants of Day of the week effect of BSE Finance Index.

Table 4.16: Determinants of Day of the Week Effect – BSE Finance Index

	Coefficient	*Std. Error*	*t-ratio*	*p-value*	
Constant	-0.111409	0.0823038	-1.3536	0.17651	
Monday	-0.0433037	0.0444968	-0.9732	0.33097	
Tuesday	0.0684081	0.040388	1.6938	0.09098	
Wednesday	-0.0409894	0.0381309	-1.0750	0.28295	
Thursday	0.107855	0.0415114	2.5982	0.00967	**
R-squared	0.27993	Adjusted R-squared		0.19613	
F(4, 464)	3.340681	P-value(F)		0.010329	
Source – Database collected from BSE web portal and computed.					

The result of OLS disclose that Thursday return is found to be significant at 1 per cent level.

Thursday

The regression coefficient indicates that Thursday returns positively influences Friday returns. The value of the regression coefficient indicates that a unit of increase in Thursday return shall increase Friday return by 0.107 units. Higher rate of return on Thursday leads to a higher rate of return on Friday.

The value of R^2 is found to be significant at five per cent level. This shows that the regression equation framed is a good fit. Around 27.99 per cent of variation in Friday return is due to the select variable.

4.3.9. BSE Fast Moving Consumer Goods Index

The following table tries to ascertain, whether Day of the week effect prevails in BSE Fast Moving Consumer Goods index.

Table 4.17: Day of the Week Effect – BSE Fast Moving Consumer Goods Index

	MONDAY	TUESDAY	WEDNESDAY	THURSDAY	FRIDAY
Mean	.0994	.0775	.1203	.0650	.0399
Median	.0808	.1394	.1196	.0831	.0837
Std. Deviation	1.52315	1.28874	1.23058	1.26617	1.34153
Variance	2.320	1.661	1.514	1.603	1.800
Skewness	.330	-.556	-.039	-.190	-.036
Kurtosis	5.283	4.943	2.463	3.497	3.081
Shapiro-Wilk	.000	.000	.000	.000	.000

Source – Database collected from BSE web portal and computed.

High mean returns were noticed during Wednesday (.1203) and low mean returns were found during Friday (.0399). While comparing to variance, high level of volatility was noticed on Monday (2.320) and low level of volatility was noticed on Wednesday (1.514).

Result of the Skewness test disclosed that positive value and it was noticed during Monday returns (.330), which implies that most of the Monday returns were more than the average returns. The other day's returns were found negative skewness, which implies that most of the other day's returns were less than the average returns.

The Kurtosis result of the BSE Fast Moving Consumer Goods index returns were found platykurtic in Wednesday returns (2.463). Since, Kurtosis values are less than 3, thus, it is inferred that the level of risk associated with the Wednesday returns of the BSE Fast Moving Consumer Goods sector was low, which means investors may obtain either low level of profit or loss. The other day's returns were found leptokurtic. Since, Kurtosis values are greater than 3, thus, it is inferred that the level of risk associated with the other day's returns of the BSE Fast Moving Consumer Goods sector was high, which means investors may obtain either high level of profit or loss.

As the calculated P value of the Shapiro-Wilk test is less than 0.01, it is clearly proved that the data are not normally distributed. Hence, there exists anomaly in the BSE Fast Moving Consumer Goods index returns.

The following table illustrates the determinants of Day of the week effect of BSE Fast Moving Consumer Goods Index.

Table 4.18: Determinants of Day of the Week Effect – BSE Fast Moving Consumer Goods Index

	Coefficient	*Std. Error*	*t-ratio*	*p-value*	
Constant	0.0413489	0.0717417	0.5764	0.56462	
Monday	0.189842	0.0363808	5.2182	<0.00001	**
Tuesday	0.104616	0.0466761	2.2413	0.02542	*
Wednesday	0.102819	0.0478109	2.1505	0.03196	*
Thursday	-0.0437762	0.0473255	-0.9250	0.35538	
R-squared	0.68967	Adjusted R-squared		0.61966	
F(4, 532)	3.981772	P-value(F)		0.003235	

Source – Database collected from BSE web portal and computed.

The result of OLS disclose that Monday return is found to be significant at 1 per cent level and Tuesday and Wednesday return is found to be significant at 5 per cent level.

Monday

The regression coefficient indicates that Monday returns positively influences Friday returns. The value of the regression coefficient indicates that a unit of increase in Monday return shall increase Friday return by 0.189 units. Higher rate of return on Monday leads to a higher rate of return on Friday.

Tuesday

The regression coefficient indicates that Tuesday returns positively influences Friday returns. The value of the regression coefficient indicates that a unit of increase in Tuesday return shall increase Friday return by 0.104 units. Higher rate of return on Tuesday leads to a higher rate of return on Friday.

Wednesday

The regression coefficient indicates that Wednesday returns positively influences Friday returns. The value of the regression coefficient indicates that a unit of increase in Wednesday return shall increase Friday return by 0.102 units. Higher rate of return on Wednesday leads to a higher rate of return on Friday.

The value of R^2 is found to be significant at one per cent level. This shows that the regression equation framed is a good fit. Around 68.96 per cent of variation in Friday return is due to the select variables.

4.3.10. BSE Health Care Index

The following table tries to ascertain, whether Day of the week effect prevails in BSE Health Care Index.

Table 4.19: Day of the Week Effect – BSE Healthcare Index

	MONDAY	TUESDAY	WEDNESDAY	THURSDAY	FRIDAY
Mean	.1370	.0144	.1434	.0125	.0941
Median	.1374	-.0043	.1761	.0932	.0718
Std. Deviation	1.15890	1.09946	1.07333	1.22824	1.24499
Variance	1.343	1.209	1.152	1.509	1.550
Skewness	-.213	-.244	-.474	-1.756	-.103
Kurtosis	2.596	1.985	3.397	10.778	6.428
Shapiro-Wilk	.000	.000	.000	.000	.000

Source – Database collected from BSE web portal and computed.

High mean returns were noticed during Wednesday (.1434) and low mean returns were found during Thursday (.0125). While comparing to variance, high level of volatility was noticed on Friday (1.550) and low level of volatility was noticed on Wednesday (1.152).

Result of the Skewness test disclosed that negative value and it was noticed all the days of the week, which implies that all the days of the week returns were less than the average returns. The Kurtosis result of the BSE Health Care Index returns were found platykurtic in Monday returns (2.596) and Tuesday returns (1.985).

Since, Kurtosis values are less than 3, thus, it is inferred that the level of risk associated with the Monday and Tuesday returns of the BSE Health Care Index sector was low, which means investors may obtain either low level of profit or loss. The other day's returns were found leptokurtic. Since, Kurtosis values are greater than 3, thus, it is inferred that the level of risk associated with the other day's returns of the BSE Health Care Index sector was high, which means investors may obtain either high level of profit or loss.

As the calculated P value of the Shapiro-Wilk test is less than 0.01, it is clearly proved that the data are not normally distributed. Hence, there exists anomaly in the BSE Health Care Index returns.

The following table illustrates the determinants of Day of the week effect of BSE Health Care Index.

Table 4.20: Determinants of Day of the Week Effect – BSE Healthcare Index

	Coefficient	*Std. Error*	*t-ratio*	*p-value*
Constant	0.0918883	0.0583129	1.5758	0.11576
Monday	-0.0305531	0.0501922	-0.6087	0.54301
Tuesday	0.0711561	0.0526214	1.3522	0.17696
Wednesday	0.0403017	0.05374	0.7499	0.45367
Thursday	0.0425424	0.0473934	0.8976	0.36984
R-squared	0.07354	Adjusted R-squared		-0.01203
F(4, 464)	0.859383	P-value(F)		0.488258
Source – Database collected from BSE web portal and computed.				

The result of OLS regression analysis disclose that the select independent variables collectively contribute to 7.35 per cent variation in Friday returns.

4.3.11. BSE Industrial Index

The following table tries to ascertain, whether Day of the week effect prevails in BSE Industrial Index.

Table 4.21: Day of the Week Effect – BSE Industrial Index

	MONDAY	TUESDAY	WEDNESDAY	THURSDAY	FRIDAY
Mean	.1756	.0094	.0857	.1581	-.1252
Median	.1818	.1096	.0927	.2446	.0073
Std. Deviation	1.75994	1.81729	1.98704	1.78385	1.75126
Variance	3.097	3.303	3.948	3.182	3.067
Skewness	-.046	-.468	1.394	-.039	-.376
Kurtosis	3.009	4.279	16.518	2.921	1.474
Shapiro-Wilk	.000	.000	.000	.000	.000
Source – Database collected from BSE web portal and computed.					

High mean returns were noticed during Monday (.1756) and low mean returns were found during Friday (-0.1252). While comparing to variance, high level of volatility was noticed on Wednesday (3.948) and low level of volatility was noticed on Friday (3.067).

Result of the Skewness test disclosed that positive value and it was noticed during Wednesday returns (1.394), which implies that most of the Wednesday returns were more than the average returns. The other day's returns were found negative skewness, which implies that most of the other day's returns were less than the average returns. The Kurtosis result of the BSE Industrial Index returns were found platykurtic on Thursday returns (2.921) and Friday returns (1.474). Since, Kurtosis values are less than 3, thus, it is inferred that the level of risk associated with the Thursday returns and Friday returns of the BSE Industrial Index sector was low, which means investors may obtain either low level of profit or loss. The other day's returns were found leptokurtic. Since, Kurtosis values are greater than 3, thus, it is inferred that the level of risk associated with the other day's returns of the BSE Industrial Index sector was high, which means investors may obtain either high level of profit or loss.

As the calculated P value of the Shapiro-Wilk test is less than 0.01, it is clearly proved that the data are not normally distributed. Hence, there exists anomaly in the BSE Industrial Index returns.

The following table illustrates the determinants of Day of the week effect of BSE Industrial Index.

Table 4.22: Determinants of Day of the Week Effect – BSE Industrial Index

	Coefficient	*Std. Error*	*t-ratio*	*p-value*	
Constant	-0.162121	0.0802944	-2.0191	0.04405	
Monday	0.0573002	0.0454517	1.2607	0.20806	
Tuesday	0.0915727	0.0441188	2.0756	0.03848	*
Wednesday	-0.0108862	0.0399223	-0.2727	0.78522	
Thursday	0.164645	0.0451342	3.6479	0.00029	**
R-squared	0.44101	Adjusted R-squared		0.35861	
F(4, 464)	5.351788	P-value(F)		0.000321	

Source – Database collected from BSE web portal and computed.

The result of OLS disclose that Tuesday return is found to be significant at 5 per cent level and Thursday return is found to be significant at 1 per cent level.

Tuesday

The regression coefficient indicates that Tuesday returns positively influences Friday returns. The value of the regression coefficient indicates that a unit of increase in Tuesday return shall increase Friday return by 0.091 units. Higher rate of return on Tuesday leads to a higher rate of return on Friday.

Thursday

The regression coefficient indicates that Thursday returns positively influences Friday returns. The value of the regression coefficient indicates that a unit of increase in Thursday return shall increase Friday return by 0.164 units. Higher rate of return on Thursday leads to a higher rate of return on Friday.

The value of R^2 is found to be significant at one per cent level. This shows that the regression equation framed is a good fit. Around 44.10 per cent of variation in Friday return is due to the select variables.

4.3.12. BSE IT Index

The following table tries to ascertain, whether Day of the week effect prevails in BSE IT Index.

Table 4.23: Day of the Week Effect – BSE IT Index

	MONDAY	TUESDAY	WEDNESDAY	THURSDAY	FRIDAY
Mean	.1278	-.0220	.1777	.1071	-.0586
Median	.1734	.0000	.0664	.0480	-.0075
Std. Deviation	1.71385	1.70409	1.82479	1.72010	1.63621
Variance	2.937	2.904	3.330	2.959	2.677
Skewness	-.262	.060	.355	-.113	-.197
Kurtosis	5.636	3.259	5.362	3.249	3.268
Shapiro-Wilk	.000	.000	.000	.000	.000

Source – Database collected from BSE web portal and computed.

High mean returns were noticed during Wednesday (.1777) and low mean returns were found during Friday (-0.0586). While comparing to variance, high level of volatility was noticed on Wednesday (3.330) and low level of volatility was noticed on Friday (2.677).

Result of the Skewness test disclosed that positive value and it was noticed during Tuesday returns (.060) and Wednesday returns (.355), which implies that most of the Tuesday and Wednesday returns were more than the average returns. The other day's returns were found negative skewness, which implies that most of the other day's returns were less than the average returns. The Kurtosis result of the BSE IT index returns were found leptokurtic on all the days of the week. Since, Kurtosis values are greater than 3, thus, it is inferred that the level of risk associated with the day's returns of the BSE IT index was high, which means investors may obtain either high level of profit or loss.

As the calculated P value of the Shapiro-Wilk test is less than 0.01, it is clearly proved that the data are not normally distributed. Hence, there exists anomaly in the BSE IT Index returns.

The following table illustrates the determinants of Day of the week effect of BSE IT Index.

Table 4.24: Determinants of Day of the Week Effect – BSE IT Index

	Coefficient	*Std. Error*	*t-ratio*	*p-value*	
Constant	-0.0697638	0.0756717	-0.9219	0.35705	
Monday	0.00908305	0.0435676	0.2085	0.83495	
Tuesday	0.106468	0.0437722	2.4323	0.01538	*
Wednesday	-0.0130123	0.0411009	-0.3166	0.75170	
Thursday	0.137952	0.0438194	3.1482	0.00175	**
R-squared	0.34976	Adjusted R-squared		0.26584	
F	4.167985	P-value(F)		0.002513	

Source – Database collected from BSE web portal and computed.

The result of OLS disclose that Thursday return is found to be significant at 1 per cent level and Tuesday return is found to be significant at 5 per cent level.

Thursday

The regression coefficient indicates that Thursday returns positively influences Friday returns. The value of the regression coefficient indicates that a unit of increase in Thursday return shall increase Friday return by 0.137 units. Higher rate of return on Thursday leads to a higher rate of return on Friday.

Tuesday

The regression coefficient indicates that Tuesday returns positively influences Friday returns. The value of the regression coefficient indicates that a unit of increase in Tuesday return shall increase Friday return by 0.106 units. Higher rate of return on Tuesday leads to a higher rate of return on Friday. The value of R^2 is found to be significant at one per cent level. This shows that the regression equation framed is a good fit. Around 34.97 per cent of variation in Friday return is due to the select variables.

4.3.13. BSE Metal Index

The following table tries to ascertain, whether Day of the week effect prevails in BSE Metal Index.

Table 4.25: Day of the Week Effect – BSE Metal Index

	MONDAY	TUESDAY	WEDNESDAY	THURSDAY	FRIDAY
Mean	.0724	.0631	.0995	.1016	.1056
Median	.1751	.0619	.1477	.0879	.1033
Std. Deviation	1.73542	1.47630	1.38935	1.45059	1.59347
Variance	3.012	2.179	1.930	2.104	2.539
Skewness	.298	.165	-.078	-.323	-.451
Kurtosis	12.337	2.211	.753	2.803	4.078
Shapiro-Wilk	.000	.000	.000	.000	.000

Source – Database collected from BSE web portal and computed.

High mean returns were noticed during Friday (.1056) and low mean returns were found during Tuesday (0.0631). While comparing to variance, high level of volatility was noticed on Monday (3.012) and low level of volatility was noticed on Wednesday (1.930).

Result of the Skewness test disclosed that positive value and it was noticed during Monday returns (.298) and Tuesday returns (.165), which implies that most of the Monday and Tuesday returns were more than the average returns. The other day's returns were found negative skewness, which implies that most of the other day's returns were less than the average returns. The Kurtosis result of the BSE Metal Index returns were found leptokurtic on Monday returns (12.337) and Friday returns (4.078). Since, Kurtosis values are greater than 3, thus, it is inferred that the level of risk associated with the Monday and Friday returns of the BSE Metal Index sector was high, which means investors may obtain either high level of profit or loss. The other day's returns were found platykurtic. Since, Kurtosis values are less than 3, thus, it is inferred that the level of risk associated with the other day's returns of the BSE Metal Index sector was low, which means investors may obtain either low level of profit or loss.

As the calculated P value of the Shapiro-Wilk test is less than 0.01, it is clearly proved that the data are not normally distributed. Hence, there exists anomaly in the BSE Metal Index returns.

The following table illustrates the determinants of Day of the week effect of BSE Metal Index.

Table 4.26: Determinants of Day of the Week Effect – BSE Metal Index

	Coefficient	*Std. Error*	*t-ratio*	*p-value*	
Constant	0.0987262	0.0688007	1.4350	0.15189	
Monday	0.0675323	0.0395214	1.7088	0.08808	
Tuesday	0.119395	0.0460792	2.5911	0.00983	**
Wednesday	-0.0464702	0.0497387	-0.9343	0.35058	
Thursday	-0.012656	0.0477713	-0.2649	0.79117	
R-squared	0.19556	Adjusted R-squared		0.12184	
F(4, 532)	2.652786	P-value(F)		0.032435	
Source – Database collected from BSE web portal and computed.					

The result of OLS disclose that Tuesday return is found to be significant at 1 per cent level.

Tuesday

The regression coefficient indicates that Tuesday returns positively influences Friday returns. The value of the regression coefficient indicates that a unit of increase in Tuesday return shall increase Friday return by 0.119 units. Higher rate of return on Tuesday leads to a higher rate of return on Friday.

The value of R^2 is found to be significant at five per cent level. This shows that the regression equation framed is a good fit. Around 19.56 per cent of variation in Friday return is due to the select variable.

4.3.14. BSE Oil and Gas Index

The following table tries to ascertain, whether Day of the week effect prevails in BSE OIL & GAS Index.

Table 4.27: Day of the Week Effect – BSE Oil & Gas Index

	MONDAY	TUESDAY	WEDNESDAY	THURSDAY	FRIDAY
Mean	.0371	.0456	.1430	-.0299	.0768
Median	.0490	.0305	.0774	-.0076	.1009
Std. Deviation	2.10509	1.64774	1.74884	1.68646	2.02107
Variance	4.431	2.715	3.058	2.844	4.085
Skewness	.478	-.258	.049	-.338	-.950
Kurtosis	16.507	4.277	5.441	2.229	9.242
Shapiro-Wilk	.000	.000	.000	.000	.000
Source – Database collected from BSE web portal and computed.					

High mean returns were noticed during Wednesday (.1430) and low mean returns were found during Thursday (-0.0299). While comparing to variance, high level of volatility was noticed on Monday (4.431) and low level of volatility was noticed on Tuesday (2.715).

Result of the Skewness test disclosed that positive value and it was noticed during Monday returns (.478) and Wednesday returns (.049), which implies that most of the Monday and Wednesday returns were more than the average returns. The other day's returns were found negative skewness, which implies that most of the other day's returns were less than the average returns. The Kurtosis result of the BSE Oil & Gas Index returns were found platykurtic on Thursday returns (2.229). Since, Kurtosis values are less than 3, thus, it is inferred that the level of risk associated with the Thursday returns of the BSE Oil & Gas Index sector was low, which means investors may obtain either low level of profit or loss. The other day's returns were found leptokurtic. Since, Kurtosis values are greater than 3, thus, it is inferred that the level of risk associated with the other day's returns of the BSE Oil & Gas sector was high, which means investors may obtain either high level of profit or loss.

As the calculated P value of the Shapiro-Wilk test is less than 0.01, it is clearly proved that the data are not normally distributed. Hence, there exists anomaly in the BSE Oil & Gas Index returns.

The following table illustrates the determinants of Day of the week effect of BSE Oil & Gas Index.

Table 4.28: Determinants of Day of the Week Effect – BSE Oil & Gas Index

	Coefficient	*Std. Error*	*t-ratio*	*p-value*	
Constant	0.0756762	0.0863363	0.8765	0.38114	
Monday	0.160959	0.0407546	3.9495	0.00009	**
Tuesday	0.0852805	0.0524628	1.6255	0.10464	
Wednesday	-0.077784	0.0492326	-1.5799	0.11472	
Thursday	-0.0210442	0.0510262	-0.4124	0.68020	
R-squared	0.35901	Adjusted R-squared		0.28652	
F(4, 532)	4.952669	P-value(F)		0.000630	

Source – Database collected from BSE web portal and computed.

The result of OLS disclose that Monday return is found to be significant at 1 per cent level.

Monday

The regression coefficient indicates that Monday returns positively influences Friday returns. The value of the regression coefficient indicates that a unit of increase in Monday return shall increase Friday return by 0.160 units. Higher rate of return on Monday leads to a higher rate of return on Friday.

The value of R^2 is found to be significant at one per cent level. This shows that the regression equation framed is a good fit. Around 35.90 per cent of variation in Friday return is due to the select variable.

4.3.15. BSE Power Index

The following table tries to ascertain, whether Day of the week effect prevails in BSE Power sector.

Table 4.29: Day of the Week Effect – BSE Power Index

	MONDAY	TUESDAY	WEDNESDAY	THURSDAY	FRIDAY
Mean	.0553	.0503	.0633	-.0204	.0714
Median	.1569	.1055	.0540	.0650	.0489
Std. Deviation	2.12782	1.72128	1.65935	1.65997	1.87573
Variance	4.528	2.963	2.753	2.756	3.518
Skewness	.893	.142	.418	-.094	-.605
Kurtosis	13.874	4.046	4.365	3.505	5.076
Shapiro-Wilk	.000	.000	.000	.000	.000

Source – Database collected from BSE web portal and computed.

High mean returns were noticed during Friday (.0714) and low mean returns were found during Thursday (-0.0204). While comparing to variance, high level of volatility was noticed on Monday (4.528) and low level of volatility was noticed on Wednesday (2.753).

Result of the Skewness test disclosed that negative value and it was noticed during Thursday returns (-0.094) and Friday returns (-.605), which implies that most of the Thursday and Friday returns were less than the average returns. The other day's returns were found positive skewness, which implies that most of the other day's returns were more than the average returns. The Kurtosis result of the BSE Power index returns were found leptokurtic on all the days of the week. Since, Kurtosis values are greater than 3, thus, it is inferred that the level of risk associated with the day's returns of the BSE Power index was high, which means investors may obtain either high level of profit or loss.

As the calculated P value of the Shapiro-Wilk test is less than 0.01, it is clearly proved that the data are not normally distributed. Hence, there exists anomaly in the BSE Power Index returns.

The following table illustrates the determinants of Day of the week effect of BSE Power Index.

Table 4.30: Determinants of Day of the Week Effect – BSE Power Index

	Coefficient	*Std. Error*	*t-ratio*	*p-value*
Constant	0.072083	0.0842458	0.8556	0.39262
Monday	-0.0356754	0.0394886	-0.9034	0.36673
Tuesday	-0.0266348	0.0487961	-0.5458	0.58542
Wednesday	0.0386501	0.0505956	0.7639	0.44529
Thursday	-0.00475733	0.0510559	-0.0932	0.92580
R-squared	0.03607	Adjusted R-squared		-0.04444
F(4, 495)	0.448036	P-value(F)		0.773851
Source – Database collected from BSE web portal and computed.				

The result of OLS regression analysis disclose that the select independent variables collectively contribute to 3.60 per cent variation in Friday returns.

4.3.16. BSE Public Sector Unit Index

The following table tries to ascertain, whether Day of the week effect prevails in BSE Public sector unit index.

Table 4.31: Day of the Week Effect – BSE Public Sector Unit Index

	MONDAY	TUESDAY	WEDNESDAY	THURSDAY	FRIDAY
Mean	.0372	.0058	.0684	.0206	.0415
Median	.1808	.0947	.0763	.1326	.0532
Std. Deviation	1.95907	1.53312	1.50383	1.52207	1.71372
Variance	3.838	2.350	2.261	2.317	2.937
Skewness	.074	-.030	.270	-.124	-1.460
Kurtosis	14.963	3.552	4.486	2.968	12.095
Shapiro Wilk	.000	.000	.000	.000	.000
Source – Database collected from BSE web portal and computed.					

High mean returns were noticed during Wednesday (.0684) and low mean returns were found during Tuesday (0.0058). While comparing to variance, high level of volatility was noticed on Monday (3.838) and low level of volatility was noticed on Wednesday (2.261).

Result of the Skewness test disclosed that positive value and it was noticed during Monday returns (.074) and Wednesday returns (.270), which implies that most of the Monday and Wednesday returns were more than the average returns. The other day's returns were found negative skewness, which implies that most of the other day's returns were less than the average returns. The Kurtosis result of the BSE Public Sector Unit Index returns were found platykurtic on Thursday returns (2.968). Since, Kurtosis values are less than 3, thus, it is inferred that the level of risk associated with the Thursday returns of the BSE Public Sector Unit Index sector was low, which means investors may obtain either low level of profit or loss. The other day's returns were found leptokurtic. Since, Kurtosis values are greater than 3, thus, it is inferred that the level of risk associated with the other day's returns of the BSE Public Sector Unit Index sector was high, which means investors may obtain either high level of profit or loss.

As the calculated P value of the Shapiro-Wilk test is less than 0.01, it is clearly proved that the data are not normally distributed. Hence, there exists anomaly in the BSE Public Sector Unit Index returns. The following table illustrates the determinants of Day of the week effect of BSE Public Sector Unit Index.

Table 4.32: Determinants of Day of the Week Effect – BSE Public Sector Unit Index

	Coefficient	*Std. Error*	*t-ratio*	*p-value*	
Constant	0.0413489	0.0717417	0.5764	0.56462	
Monday	0.189842	0.0363808	5.2182	<0.00001	**
Tuesday	0.104616	0.0466761	2.2413	0.02542	*
Wednesday	0.102819	0.0478109	2.1505	0.03196	*
Thursday	-0.0437762	0.0473255	-0.9250	0.35538	
R-squared	0.68967	Adjusted R-squared		0.61966	
F(4, 532)	9.852031	P-value(F)		0.00213	

Source – Database collected from BSE web portal and computed.

The result of OLS disclose that Monday return is found to be significant at 1 per cent level and Tuesday and Wednesday return is found to be significant at 5 per cent level.

Monday

The regression coefficient indicates that Monday returns positively influences Friday returns. The value of the regression coefficient indicates that a unit of increase in Monday return shall increase Friday return by 0.189 units. Higher rate of return on Monday leads to a higher rate of return on Friday.

Tuesday

The regression coefficient indicates that Tuesday returns positively influences Friday returns. The value of the regression coefficient indicates that a unit of increase in Tuesday return shall increase Friday return by 0.104 units. Higher rate of return on Tuesday leads to a higher rate of return on Friday.

Wednesday

The regression coefficient indicates that Wednesday returns positively influences Friday returns. The value of the regression coefficient indicates that a unit of increase in Wednesday return shall increase Friday return by 0.102 units. Higher rate of return on Wednesday leads to a higher rate of return on Friday.

The value of R^2 is found to be significant at one per cent level. This shows that the regression equation framed is a good fit. Around 68.96 per cent of variation in Friday return is due to the select variables.

4.3.17. BSE Realty Index

The following table tries to ascertain, whether Day of the week effect prevails in BSE Realty Index.

Table 4.33: Day of the Week Effect – BSE Realty Index

	MONDAY	TUESDAY	WEDNESDAY	THURSDAY	FRIDAY
Mean	-.0261	.0679	.1673	.0569	-.0286
Median	.2088	.0807	.1264	.1144	-.0353
Std. Deviation	3.13172	2.96789	2.98122	2.73983	2.91379
Variance	9.808	8.808	8.888	7.507	8.490
Skewness	.449	.254	-.009	-.069	-1.213
Kurtosis	7.452	2.203	3.823	2.186	11.244
Shapiro-Wilk	.000	.000	.000	.000	.000

Source – Database collected from BSE web portal and computed.

High mean returns were noticed during Wednesday (.1673) and low mean returns were found during Friday (-0.0286). While comparing to variance, high level of volatility was noticed on Monday (9.808) and low level of volatility was noticed on Wednesday (7.507).

Result of the Skewness test disclosed that positive value and it was noticed during Monday returns (0.449) and Tuesday returns (.254), which implies that most of the Monday and

Tuesday returns were more than the average returns. The other day's returns were found negative skewness, which implies that most of the other day's returns were less than the average returns. The Kurtosis result of the BSE Realty Index returns were found platykurtic on Tuesday returns (2.203) and Thursday returns (2.186). Since, Kurtosis values are less than 3, thus, it is inferred that the level of risk associated with the Tuesday and Thursday returns of the BSE Realty sector was low, which means investors may obtain either low level of profit or loss. The other day's returns were found leptokurtic. Since, Kurtosis values are greater than 3, thus, it is inferred that the level of risk associated with the other day's returns of the BSE Realty index was high, which means investors may obtain either high level of profit or loss.

As the calculated P value of the Shapiro-Wilk test is less than 0.01, it is clearly proved that the data are not normally distributed. Hence, there exists anomaly in the BSE Realty Index returns.

The following table illustrates the determinants of Day of the week effect of BSE Real Estate Index.

Table 4.34: Determinants of Day of the Week Effect – BSE Realty Index

	Coefficient	*Std. Error*	*t-ratio*	*p-value*	
Constant	-0.0484722	0.1361	-0.3562	0.72190	
Monday	0.0664758	0.043567	1.5258	0.12776	
Tuesday	0.0849389	0.0458885	1.8510	0.04483	*
Wednesday	0.106328	0.0454592	2.3390	0.001978	**
Thursday	-0.038031	0.0496135	-0.7665	0.44376	
R-squared	0.28806	Adjusted R-squared		0.20096	
F(4, 446)	3.307117	P-value(F)		0.0010962	

Source – Database collected from BSE web portal and computed.

The result of OLS disclose that Tuesday return is found to be significant at 5 per cent level and Wednesday return is found to be significant at 1 per cent level.

Tuesday

The regression coefficient indicates that Tuesday returns positively influences Friday returns. The value of the regression coefficient indicates that a unit of increase in Tuesday return shall increase Friday return by 0.084 units. Higher rate of return on Tuesday leads to a higher rate of return on Friday.

Wednesday

The regression coefficient indicates that Wednesday returns positively influences Friday returns. The value of the regression coefficient indicates that a unit of increase in Wednesday return shall increase Friday return by 0.106 units. Higher rate of return on Wednesday leads to a higher rate of return on Friday.

The value of R^2 is found to be significant at one per cent level. This shows that the regression equation framed is a good fit. Around 28.80 per cent of variation in Friday return is due to the select variables.

4.3.18. BSE Teck Index

The following table tries to ascertain, whether Day of the week effect prevails in BSE Teck Index.

Table 4.35: Day of the Week Effect – BSE Teck Index

	MONDAY	TUESDAY	WEDNESDAY	THURSDAY	FRIDAY
Mean	.0849	.0648	.1259	.0395	.0515
Median	.1703	.0590	.1272	.1065	.0386
Std. Deviation	1.81286	1.50437	1.51512	1.47632	1.72259
Variance	3.286	2.263	2.296	2.180	2.967
Skewness	.563	.517	-.282	-.151	-.458
Kurtosis	9.468	4.442	2.800	2.142	4.328
Shapiro-Wilk	.000	.000	.000	.000	.000

Source – Database collected from BSE web portal and computed.

High mean returns were noticed during Wednesday (.1259) and low mean returns were found during Thursday (.0395). While comparing to variance, high level of volatility was noticed on Monday (3.286) and low level of volatility was noticed on Wednesday (2.180).

Result of the Skewness test disclosed that positive value and it was noticed during Monday returns (0.563) and Tuesday returns (.517), which implies that most of the Monday and Tuesday returns were more than the average returns. The other day's returns were found negative skewness, which implies that most of the other day's returns were less than the average returns. The Kurtosis result of the BSE Teck Index returns were found platykurtic on Wednesday returns (2.800) and Thursday returns (2.142). Since, Kurtosis values are less than 3, thus, it is inferred that the level of risk associated with the Wednesday and Thursday returns of the BSE TECK sector was low, which means investors may obtain either low level of profit or loss. The other day's returns were found leptokurtic. Since, Kurtosis values are greater than 3, thus, it is inferred that the level of risk associated with the other day's returns of the BSE TECK index was high, which means investors may obtain either high level of profit or loss. As the calculated P value of the Shapiro-Wilk test is less than 0.01, it is clearly proved that the data are not normally distributed. Hence, there exists anomaly in the BSE TECK Index returns.

The following table illustrates the determinants of Day of the week effect of BSE Teck Index.

Table 4.36: Determinants of Day of the Week Effect – BSE Teck Index

	Coefficient	*Std. Error*	*t-ratio*	*p-value*	
Constant	0.0543954	0.0744369	0.7308	0.46525	
Monday	0.0846138	0.0407329	2.0773	0.03825	*
Tuesday	0.0371366	0.0491007	0.7563	0.44978	
Wednesday	-0.0851183	0.0490422	-1.7356	0.08321	
Thursday	-0.0458849	0.050523	-0.9082	0.36419	
R-squared	0.16198	Adjusted R-squared		0.08801	
F(4, 532)	2.189845	P-value(F)		0.048930	

Source – Database collected from BSE web portal and computed.

The result of OLS disclose that Monday return is found to be significant at 5 per cent level.

Monday

The regression coefficient indicates that Monday returns positively influences Friday returns. The value of the regression coefficient indicates that a unit of increase in Monday return shall increase Friday return by 0.084 units. Higher rate of return on Monday leads to a higher rate of return on Friday. The value of R^2 is found to be significant at five per cent level. This shows that the regression equation framed is a good fit. Around 16.19 per cent of variation in Friday return is due to the select variable.

4.3.19. BSE Telecom Index

The following table tries to ascertain, whether Day of the week effect prevails in BSE Telecom Index.

Table 4.37: Day of the Week Effect – BSE Telecom Index

	MONDAY	TUESDAY	WEDNESDAY	THURSDAY	FRIDAY
Mean	.1813	.0141	.1091	.0689	-.1895
Median	.0941	.0005	.0000	.0079	-.1697
Std. Deviation	1.94048	2.14104	2.21059	2.03210	2.02728
Variance	3.765	4.584	4.887	4.129	4.110
Skewness	-.145	-.376	1.078	-.116	-.171
Kurtosis	2.204	5.135	8.381	1.436	1.766
Shapiro-Wilk	.000	.000	.000	.000	.000

Source – Database collected from BSE web portal and computed.

High mean returns were noticed during Monday (.1813) and low mean returns were found during Friday (-.1895). While comparing to variance, high level of volatility was noticed on Wednesday (4.887) and low level of volatility was noticed on Monday (3.765).

Result of the Skewness test disclosed that positive value and it was noticed during Wednesday returns (1.078), which implies that most of the Wednesday returns were more than the average returns. The other day's returns were found negative skewness, which implies that most of the other day's returns were less than the average returns. The Kurtosis result of the BSE Telecom Index returns were found leptokurtic on Tuesday returns (5.135) and Wednesday returns (8.381). Since, Kurtosis values are greater than 3, thus, it is inferred that the level of risk associated with the Tuesday and Wednesday of the BSE Telecom sector was high, which means investors may obtain either high level of profit or loss. The other day's returns were found platykurtic. Since, Kurtosis values are less than 3, thus, it is inferred that the level of risk associated with the other day's returns of the BSE Telecom index was low, which means investors may obtain either low level of profit or loss.

As the calculated P value of the Shapiro-Wilk test is less than 0.01, it is clearly proved that the data are not normally distributed. Hence, there exists anomaly in the BSE Telecom Index returns.

The following table illustrates the determinants of Day of the week effect of BSE Telecom Index.

Table 4.38: Determinants of Day of the Week Effect – BSE Telecom Index

	Coefficient	*Std. Error*	*t-ratio*	*p-value*	
Constant	-0.183065	0.0939735	-1.9481	0.05201	
Monday	-0.0685867	0.0488398	-1.4043	0.16089	
Tuesday	0.0373735	0.0437603	0.8541	0.39352	
Wednesday	-0.00666715	0.0424261	-0.1571	0.87520	
Thursday	0.081681	0.0462461	1.7662	0.04802	*
R-squared	0.13356	Adjusted R-squared		0.04851	
F(4, 464)	1.570317	P-value(F)		0.018106	

Source – Database collected from BSE web portal and computed.

The result of OLS disclose that Thursday return is found to be significant at 5 per cent level.

Thursday

The regression coefficient indicates that Thursday returns positively influences Friday returns. The value of the regression coefficient indicates that a unit of increase in Thursday return shall increase Friday return by 0.082 units. Higher rate of return on Thursday leads to a higher rate of return on Friday. The value of R^2 is found to be significant at five per cent level. This shows that the regression equation framed is a good fit. Around 13.35 per cent of variation in Friday return is due to the select variable.

4.3.20. BSE Utilities Index

The following table tries to ascertain, whether Day of the week effect prevails in BSE Utilities Index.

Table 4.39: Day of the Week Effect – BSE Utilities Index

	MONDAY	TUESDAY	WEDNESDAY	THURSDAY	FRIDAY
Mean	.0779	.0040	.1339	-.0543	.0364
Median	.1423	.0715	.1227	-.0198	.1365
Std. Deviation	2.17823	1.66777	1.74127	1.60592	1.87288
Variance	4.745	2.781	3.032	2.579	3.508
Skewness	-.090	-.033	.767	-.268	-.609
Kurtosis	14.810	4.350	9.310	2.824	5.331
Shapiro-Wilk	.000	.000	.000	.000	.000

Source – Database collected from BSE web portal and computed.

High mean returns were noticed during Wednesday (.1339) and low mean returns were found during Thursday (-.0543). While comparing to variance, high level of volatility was noticed on Monday (4.745) and low level of volatility was noticed on Thursday (2.579).

Result of the Skewness test disclosed that positive value and it was noticed during Wednesday returns (0.767), which implies that most of the Wednesday returns were more than the average returns. The other day's returns were found negative skewness, which implies that most of the other day's returns were less than the average returns. The Kurtosis result of the BSE Utilities Index returns were found platykurtic on Thursday returns (2.824). Since, Kurtosis values are less than 3, thus, it is inferred that the level of risk associated with the Thursday returns of the BSE Utilities sector was low, which means investors may obtain either low level of profit or loss. The other day's returns were found leptokurtic. Since, Kurtosis values are greater than 3, thus, it is inferred that the level of risk associated with the other day's returns of the BSE Utilities index was high, which means investors may obtain either high level of profit or loss.

As the calculated P value of the Shapiro-Wilk test is less than 0.01, it is clearly proved that the data are not normally distributed. Hence, there exists anomaly in the BSE Utilities Index returns.

The following table illustrates the determinants of Day of the week effect of BSE Utilities Index.

Table 4.40: Determinants of Day of the Week Effect – BSE Utilities Index

	Coefficient	*Std. Error*	*t-ratio*	*p-value*	
Constant	0.0431415	0.085968	0.5018	0.61602	
Monday	0.104526	0.0395808	2.6408	0.00855	**
Tuesday	-0.0419332	0.0518277	-0.8091	0.41888	
Wednesday	0.0616157	0.0493531	1.2485	0.21249	
Thursday	0.125925	0.0543962	2.3150	0.02105	*
R-squared	0.29866	Adjusted R-squared		0.21502	
F(4, 464)	3.571057	P-value(F)		0.006986	

Source – Database collected from BSE web portal and computed.

The result of OLS disclose that Monday return is found to be significant at 1 per cent level and Thursday return is found to be significant at 5 per cent level.

Monday

The regression coefficient indicates that Monday returns positively influences Friday returns. The value of the regression coefficient indicates that a unit of increase in Monday return shall increase Friday return by 0.104 units. Higher rate of return on Monday leads to a higher rate of return on Friday.

Thursday

The regression coefficient indicates that Thursday returns positively influences Friday returns. The value of the regression coefficient indicates that a unit of increase in Thursday return shall increase Friday return by 0.125 units. Higher rate of return on Thursday leads to a higher rate of return on Friday. The value of R^2 is found to be significant at one per cent level. This shows that the regression equation framed is a good fit. Around 29.86 per cent of variation in Friday return is due to the select variables.

4.3.21. NSE Nifty Index

The following table tries to ascertain, whether Day of the week effect prevails in NSE Nifty index.

Table 4.41: Day of the Week Effect – NSE Nifty Index

	MONDAY	TUESDAY	WEDNESDAY	THURSDAY	FRIDAY
Mean	.0748	.0718	.0334	.0677	.1087
Median	.0878	.1094	.0681	.1689	.0838
Std. Deviation	1.87722	1.46589	1.51220	1.39901	1.57862
Variance	3.524	2.149	2.287	1.957	2.492
Skewness	.267	.155	.040	-.494	-.126
Kurtosis	21.336	4.320	3.080	2.938	3.463
Shapiro-Wilk	.000	.000	.000	.000	.000

Source – Database collected from NSE web portal and computed.

High mean returns were noticed during Friday (.1087) and low mean returns were found during Wednesday (.0334). While comparing to variance, high level of volatility was noticed on Monday (3.524) and low level of volatility was noticed on Thursday (1.957).

Result of the Skewness test disclosed that negative value and it was noticed during Thursday returns (-0.494) and Friday returns (-0.126), which implies that most of the Thursday and Friday returns were less than the average returns. The other day's returns were found positive skewness, which implies that most of the other day's returns were more than the average returns. The Kurtosis result of the NSE Nifty Index returns were found platykurtic on Thursday returns (2.938). Since, Kurtosis values are less than 3, thus, it is inferred that the level of risk associated with the Thursday returns of the NSE Nifty was low, which means investors may obtain either low level of profit or loss. The other day's returns were found leptokurtic. Since, Kurtosis values are greater than 3, thus, it is inferred that the level of risk associated with the other day's returns of the NSE Nifty index was high, which means investors may obtain either high level of profit or loss.

As the calculated P value of the Shapiro-Wilk test is less than 0.01, it is clearly proved that the data are not normally distributed. Hence, there exists anomaly in the NSE Nifty index returns.

The following table illustrates the determinants of Day of the week effect of NSE Nifty Index.

Table 4.42: Determinants of Day of the Week Effect – NSE Nifty Index

	Coefficient	*Std. Error*	*t-ratio*	*p-value*	
Constant	0.0981439	0.0681235	1.4407	0.15026	
Monday	0.0715209	0.0363453	1.9678	0.04961	*
Tuesday	-0.0292852	0.0465169	-0.6296	0.52925	
Wednesday	0.00424789	0.0447662	0.0949	0.92444	
Thursday	0.0938243	0.0490914	1.9112	0.05651	
R-squared	0.12768	Adjusted R-squared		0.05359	
F(4, 533)	1.723337	P-value(F)		0.0143364	

Source – Database collected from NSE web portal and computed.

The result of OLS disclose that Monday return is found to be significant at 5 per cent level.

Monday

The regression coefficient indicates that Monday returns positively influences Friday returns. The value of the regression coefficient indicates that a unit of increase in Monday return shall increase Friday return by 0.071 units. Higher rate of return on Monday leads to a higher rate of return on Friday. The value of R^2 is found to be significant at five per cent level. This shows that the regression equation framed is a good fit. Around 12.76 per cent of variation in Friday return is due to the select variable.

4.3.22. NSE Auto Index

The following table tries to ascertain, whether Day of the week effect prevails in NSE Auto Index.

Table 4.43: Day of the Week Effect – NSE Auto Index

	MONDAY	TUESDAY	WEDNESDAY	THURSDAY	FRIDAY
Mean	.0752	.0631	.0987	.1016	.1065
Median	.1752	.0619	.1477	.0879	.1056
Std. Deviation	1.73511	1.47630	1.38725	1.45059	1.59212
Variance	3.011	2.179	1.924	2.104	2.535
Skewness	.294	.165	-.077	-.323	-.453
Kurtosis	12.319	2.211	.762	2.803	4.090
Shapiro-Wilk	.000	.000	.000	.000	.000

Source – Database collected from NSE web portal and computed.

High mean returns were noticed during Friday (.1065) and low mean returns were found during Tuesday (.0631). While comparing to variance, high level of volatility was noticed on Monday (3.011) and low level of volatility was noticed on Wednesday (1.924).

Result of the Skewness test disclosed that positive value and it was noticed during Monday returns (0.294) and Tuesday returns (.165), which implies that most of the Monday and Tuesday returns were more than the average returns. The other day's returns were found negative skewness, which implies that most of the other day's returns were less than the average returns. The Kurtosis result of the NSE Auto Index returns were found leptokurtic on Monday returns (12.319) and Friday returns (4.090). Since, Kurtosis values are greater than 3, thus, it is inferred that the level of risk associated with the Monday and Friday returns of the NSE Automobile sector was high, which means investors may obtain either high level of profit or loss. The other day's returns were found platykurtic. Since, Kurtosis values are less than 3, thus, it is inferred that the level of risk associated with the other day's returns of the NSE Auto index was low, which means investors may obtain either low level of profit or loss.

As the calculated P value of the Shapiro-Wilk test is less than 0.01, it is clearly proved that the data are not normally distributed. Hence, there exists anomaly in the NSE Auto index returns.

The following table illustrates the determinants of Day of the week effect of NSE Auto Index.

Table 4.44: Determinants of Day of the Week Effect – NSE Auto Index

	Coefficient	*Std. Error*	*t-ratio*	*p-value*	
Constant	0.0996118	0.0686779	1.4504	0.14753	
Monday	0.0677461	0.0394812	1.7159	0.08676	
Tuesday	0.119237	0.0460367	2.5900	0.00986	**
Wednesday	-0.0465074	0.049696	-0.9358	0.34978	
Thursday	-0.0127342	0.0477298	-0.2668	0.78973	
R-squared	0.19559	Adjusted R-squared		0.12201	
F(4, 533)	2.658264	P-value(F)		0.032141	

Source – Database collected from NSE web portal and computed.

The result of OLS disclose that Tuesday return is found to be significant at 1 per cent level.

Tuesday

The regression coefficient indicates that Tuesday returns positively influences Friday returns. The value of the regression coefficient indicates that a unit of increase in Tuesday return shall increase Friday return by 0.119 units. Higher rate of return on Tuesday leads to a higher rate of return on Friday.

The value of R^2 is found to be significant at five per cent level. This shows that the regression equation framed is a good fit. Around 19.55 per cent of variation in Friday return is due to the select variable.

4.3.23. NSE Bank Index

The following table tries to ascertain, whether Day of the week effect prevails in NSE Bank Index.

Table 4.45: Day of the Week Effect – NSE Bank Index

	MONDAY	TUESDAY	WEDNESDAY	THURSDAY	FRIDAY
Mean	.1383	.0516	.0463	.0786	.1531
Median	.1951	.0914	-.0211	.1243	.0858
Std. Deviation	2.36374	2.01611	1.99726	1.88710	2.11204
Variance	5.587	4.065	3.989	3.561	4.461
Skewness	.281	.287	.196	-.252	-.130
Kurtosis	11.574	4.163	2.574	1.518	3.760
Shapiro-Wilk	.000	.000	.000	.000	.000

Source – Database collected from NSE web portal and computed.

High mean returns were noticed during Friday (.1531) and low mean returns were found during Wednesday (.0463). While comparing to variance, high level of volatility was noticed on Monday (5.587) and low level of volatility was noticed on Thursday (3.561).

Result of the Skewness test disclosed that negative value and it was noticed during Thursday returns (-0.252) and Friday returns (-0.130), which implies that most of the Thursday and Friday returns were less than the average returns. The other day's returns were found positive skewness, which implies that most of the other day's returns were more than the average returns. The Kurtosis result of the NSE Bank Index returns were found platykurtic on Wednesday returns (2.574) and Thursday returns (1.518). Since, Kurtosis values are less than 3, thus, it is inferred that the level of risk associated with the Wednesday and Thursday returns of the NSE Banking sector was low, which means investors may obtain either low level of profit or loss. The other day's returns were found leptokurtic. Since, Kurtosis values are greater than 3, thus, it is inferred that the level of risk associated with the other day's returns of the NSE Bank index was high, which means investors may obtain either high level of profit or loss.

As the calculated P value of the Shapiro-Wilk test is less than 0.01, it is clearly proved that the data are not normally distributed. Hence, there exists anomaly in the NSE Bank index returns. The following table illustrates the determinants of Day of the week effect of NSE Banking Index.

Table 4.46: Determinants of Day of the Week Effect – NSE Bank Index

	Coefficient	*Std. Error*	*t-ratio*	*p-value*	
Constant	0.133439	0.0910234	1.4660	0.14324	
Monday	0.0871831	0.0387485	2.2500	0.02486	*
Tuesday	0.0684474	0.0451966	1.5144	0.13051	
Wednesday	0.0100372	0.0452915	0.2216	0.82470	
Thursday	0.0313634	0.0484895	0.6468	0.51804	
R-squared	0.15765	Adjusted R-squared		0.08378	
F(4, 533)	2.134267	P-value(F)		0.045335	

Source – Database collected from NSE web portal and computed.

The result of OLS disclose that Monday return is found to be significant at 5 per cent level.

Monday

The regression coefficient indicates that Monday returns positively influences Friday returns. The value of the regression coefficient indicates that a unit of increase in Monday return shall increase Friday return by 0.087 units. Higher rate of return on Monday leads to a higher rate of return on Friday. The value of R^2 is found to be significant at five per cent level. This shows that the regression equation framed is a good fit. Around 15.76 per cent of variation in Friday return is due to the select variable.

4.3.24. NSE Energy Index

The following table tries to ascertain, whether Day of the week effect prevails in NSE Energy Index.

Table 4.47: Day of the Week Effect – NSE Energy Index

	MONDAY	TUESDAY	WEDNESDAY	THURSDAY	FRIDAY
Mean	.0386	.0773	.0255	.0024	.0734
Median	.0532	.0648	-.0487	.1110	.1150
Std. Deviation	2.02307	1.58855	1.60250	1.54708	1.71597
Variance	4.093	2.523	2.568	2.393	2.945
Skewness	-.506	-.099	.227	-.388	-.448
Kurtosis	17.441	4.001	4.215	2.251	6.182
Shapiro-Wilk	.000	.000	.000	.000	.000

Source – Database collected from NSE web portal and computed.

High mean returns were noticed during Tuesday (.0773) and low mean returns were found during Thursday (.0024). While comparing to variance, high level of volatility was noticed on Monday (4.093) and low level of volatility was noticed on Thursday (2.393).

Result of the Skewness test disclosed that positive value and it was noticed during Wednesday returns (.227), which implies that most of the Wednesday returns were more than the average returns. The other day's returns were found negative skewness, which implies that most of the other day's returns were less than the average returns. The Kurtosis result of the NSE Energy Index returns were found platykurtic on Thursday returns (2.251). Since, Kurtosis values are less than 3, thus, it is inferred that the level of risk associated with the Thursday returns of the NSE Energy sector was low, which means investors may obtain either low level of profit or loss. The other day's returns were found leptokurtic. Since, Kurtosis values are greater than 3, thus, it is inferred that the level of risk associated with the other day's returns of the NSE Energy index was high, which means investors may obtain either high level of profit or loss.

As the calculated P value of the Shapiro-Wilk test is less than 0.01, it is clearly proved that the data are not normally distributed. Hence, there exists anomaly in the NSE Energy index returns.

The following table illustrates the determinants of Day of the week effect of NSE Energy Index.

Table 4.48: Determinants of Day of the Week Effect – NSE Energy Index

	Coefficient	*Std. Error*	*t-ratio*	*p-value*	
Constant	0.0675438	0.0733602	0.9207	0.35762	
Monday	0.130029	0.0362005	3.5919	0.00036	**
Tuesday	-0.00463815	0.04626	-0.1003	0.92017	
Wednesday	-0.0162971	0.0455426	-0.3578	0.72060	
Thursday	0.082974	0.0476727	1.7405	0.08235	
R-squared	0.27385	Adjusted R-squared		0.20085	
F(4, 533)	3.751738	P-value(F)		0.005073	

Source – Database collected from NSE web portal and computed.

The result of OLS disclose that Monday return is found to be significant at 1 per cent level.

Monday

The regression coefficient indicates that Monday returns positively influences Friday returns. The value of the regression coefficient indicates that a unit of increase in Monday return shall increase Friday return by 0.130 units. Higher rate of return on Monday leads to a higher rate of return on Friday.

The value of R^2 is found to be significant at one per cent level. This shows that the regression equation framed is a good fit. Around 27.38 per cent of variation in Friday return is due to the select variable.

4.3.25. NSE Finance Index

The following table tries to ascertain, whether Day of the week effect prevails in NSE Finance Index.

Table 4.49: Day of the Week Effect – NSE Finance Index

	MONDAY	TUESDAY	WEDNESDAY	THURSDAY	FRIDAY
Mean	.1467	.0669	.0476	.0817	.1370
Median	.2394	.0720	.0854	.1343	.0973
Std. Deviation	2.29690	1.91631	1.94061	1.78499	2.06041
Variance	5.276	3.672	3.766	3.186	4.245
Skewness	.476	.327	.186	-.316	-.112
Kurtosis	13.575	5.407	3.313	1.950	3.126
Shapiro-Wilk	.000	.000	.000	.000	.000

Source – Database collected from NSE web portal and computed.

High mean returns were noticed during Monday (.1467) and low mean returns were found during Wednesday (.0476). While comparing to variance, high level of volatility was noticed on Monday (5.276) and low level of volatility was noticed on Thursday (3.186).

Result of the Skewness test disclosed that negative value and it was noticed during Thursday returns (-0.316) and Friday returns (-0.112), which implies that most of the Thursday and Friday returns were less than the average returns. The other day's returns were found positive skewness, which implies that most of the other day's returns were more than the average returns. The Kurtosis result of the NSE Finance Index returns were found platykurtic on Thursday returns (1.950). Since, Kurtosis values are less than 3, thus, it is inferred that the level of risk associated with the Thursday returns of the NSE Finance sector was low, which means investors may obtain either low level of profit or loss. The other day's returns were found leptokurtic. Since, Kurtosis values are greater than 3, thus, it is inferred that the level of risk associated with the other day's returns of the NSE Finance index was high, which means investors may obtain either high level of profit or loss.

As the calculated P value of the Shapiro-Wilk test is less than 0.01, it is clearly proved that the data are not normally distributed. Hence, there exists anomaly in the NSE Finance index returns.

The following table illustrates the determinants of Day of the week effect of NSE Finance Index.

Table 4.50: Determinants of Day of the Week Effect – NSE Finance Index

	Coefficient	*Std. Error*	*t-ratio*	*p-value*	
Constant	0.121187	0.0891734	1.3590	0.17472	
Monday	0.0738472	0.0389625	1.8953	0.04859	*
Tuesday	0.0365231	0.0466834	0.7824	0.43435	
Wednesday	0.00883097	0.0455962	0.1937	0.84650	
Thursday	0.0171229	0.0502035	0.3411	0.73318	
R-squared	0.2760	Adjusted R-squared		0.01321	
F(4, 533)	1.177644	P-value(F)		0.0319636	

Source – Database collected from NSE web portal and computed.

The result of OLS disclose that Monday return is found to be significant at 5 per cent level.

Monday

The regression coefficient indicates that Monday returns positively influences Friday returns. The value of the regression coefficient indicates that a unit of increase in Monday return shall increase Friday return by 0.073 units. Higher rate of return on Monday leads to a higher rate of return on Friday. The value of R^2 is found to be significant at five per cent level. This shows that the regression equation framed is a good fit. Around 27.60 per cent of variation in Friday return is due to the select variable.

4.3.26. NSE Fast Moving Consumer Goods Index

The following table tries to ascertain, whether Day of the week effect prevails in NSE Fast Moving Consumer Goods Index.

Table 4.51: Day of the Week Effect – NSE Fast Moving Consumer Goods Index

	MONDAY	TUESDAY	WEDNESDAY	THURSDAY	FRIDAY
Mean	.0731	.1020	.0669	.1374	.0565
Median	.0896	.1207	.0695	.2002	.0845
Std. Deviation	1.50736	1.38534	1.28043	1.31304	1.33914
Variance	2.272	1.919	1.640	1.724	1.793
Skewness	-.963	-.185	.217	-.367	.203
Kurtosis	9.863	5.084	2.297	3.048	2.121
Shapiro-Wilk	.000	.000	.000	.000	.000

Source – Database collected from NSE web portal and computed.

High mean returns were noticed during Thursday (.1374) and low mean returns were found during Friday (.0565). While comparing to variance, high level of volatility was noticed on Monday (2.272) and low level of volatility was noticed on Wednesday (1.640).

Result of the Skewness test disclosed that positive value and it was noticed during Wednesday returns (.217) and Friday returns (0.203), which implies that most of the Wednesday and Friday returns were more than the average returns. The other day's returns were found negative skewness, which implies that most of the other day's returns were less than the average returns. The Kurtosis result of the NSE FMCG Index returns were found platykurtic on Wednesday returns (2.297) and Friday returns (2.121). Since, Kurtosis values are less than 3, thus, it is inferred that the level of risk associated with the Wednesday and Friday returns of the NSE FMCG sector was low, which means investors may obtain either low level of profit or loss. The other day's returns were found leptokurtic. Since, Kurtosis values are greater than 3, thus, it is inferred that the level of risk associated with the other day's returns of the NSE FMCG index was high, which means investors may obtain either high level of profit or loss.

As the calculated P value of the Shapiro-Wilk test is less than 0.01, it is clearly proved that the data are not normally distributed. Hence, there exists anomaly in the NSE FMCG index returns.

The following table illustrates the determinants of Day of the week effect of NSE FMCG Index.

Table 4.52: Determinants of Day of the Week Effect – NSE Fast Moving Consumer Goods Index

	Coefficient	*Std. Error*	*t-ratio*	*p-value*
Constant	0.0627798	0.058492	1.0733	0.28362
Monday	-0.0146102	0.0387712	-0.3768	0.70645
Tuesday	-0.010757	0.0419787	-0.2562	0.79786
Wednesday	0.0223168	0.045203	0.4937	0.62172
Thursday	-0.0391134	0.0442299	-0.8843	0.37692
R-squared	0.02346	Adjusted R-squared		-0.05141
F(4, 533)	0.313392	P-value(F)		0.869056
Source – Database collected from NSE web portal and computed.				

The result of OLS regression analysis disclose that the select independent variables collectively contribute to 2.34 per cent variation in Friday returns.

4.3.27. NSE IT Index

The following table tries to ascertain, whether Day of the week effect prevails in NSE IT Index.

Table 4.53: Day of the Week Effect – NSE IT Index

	MONDAY	TUESDAY	WEDNESDAY	THURSDAY	FRIDAY
Mean	.0419	.0894	.1447	.0830	.0504
Median	.0927	.0621	.0793	.1160	.0352
Std. Deviation	1.97215	1.77484	1.61716	1.64388	1.89774
Variance	3.889	3.150	2.615	2.702	3.601
Skewness	.139	.657	-.112	-.057	-.460
Kurtosis	8.760	7.693	1.798	1.630	5.813
Shapiro-Wilk	.000	.000	.000	.000	.000
Source – Database collected from NSE web portal and computed.					

High mean returns were noticed during Wednesday (.1447) and low mean returns were found during Monday (.0419). While comparing to variance, high level of volatility was noticed on Monday (3.889) and low level of volatility was noticed on Wednesday (2.615).

Result of the Skewness test disclosed that positive value and it was noticed during Monday returns (.139) and Tuesday returns (.657), which implies that most of the Monday and Tuesday returns were more than the average returns. The other day's returns were found negative skewness, which implies that most of the other day's returns were less than the average returns. The Kurtosis result of the NSE IT Index returns were found platykurtic on Wednesday returns (1.798) and Thursday returns (1.630). Since, Kurtosis values are less than 3, thus, it is inferred that the level of risk associated with the Wednesday and Thursday returns of the NSE IT sector was low, which means investors may obtain either low level of profit or loss. The other day's returns were found leptokurtic. Since, Kurtosis values are greater than 3, thus, it is inferred that the level of risk associated with the other day's returns of the NSE IT index was high, which means investors may obtain either high level of profit or loss.

As the calculated P value of the Shapiro-Wilk test is less than 0.01, it is clearly proved that the data are not normally distributed. Hence, there exists anomaly in the NSE IT index returns.

The following table illustrates the determinants of Day of the week effect of NSE IT Index.

Table 4.54: Determinants of Day of the Week Effect – NSE IT Indcx

	Coefficient	*Std. Error*	*t-ratio*	*p-value*
Constant	0.0640935	0.0823946	0.7779	0.43698
Monday	0.0564348	0.0412882	1.3669	0.17225
Tuesday	-0.0276182	0.0459332	-0.6013	0.54792
Wednesday	-0.0586169	0.0507657	-1.1547	0.24875
Thursday	-0.0521737	0.0500489	-1.0425	0.29767
R-squared	0.09128	Adjusted R-squared		0.01678
F (4, 532)	1.225215	P-value(F)		0.299029
Source – Database collected from NSE web portal and computed.				

The result of OLS regression analysis disclose that the select independent variables collectively contribute to 9.12 per cent variation in Friday returns.

4.3.28. NSE Media Index

The following table tries to ascertain, whether Day of the week effect prevails in NSE Media Index.

Table 4.55: Day of the Week Effect – NSE Media Index

	MONDAY	TUESDAY	WEDNESDAY	THURSDAY	FRIDAY
Mean	.0745	-.0339	.1371	-.0011	.0825
Median	.0472	.0483	.0568	.0159	.1530
Std. Deviation	1.90883	1.79493	1.88833	1.76084	1.74811
Variance	3.644	3.222	3.566	3.101	3.056
Skewness	.014	-.606	.786	-.129	-.133
Kurtosis	7.993	3.215	5.079	5.106	1.633
Shapiro-Wilk	.000	.000	.000	.000	.000
Source – Database collected from NSE web portal and computed.					

High mean returns were noticed during Wednesday (.1371) and low mean returns were found during Tuesday (-.0339). While comparing to variance, high level of volatility was noticed on Monday (3.644) and low level of volatility was noticed on Friday (3.056).

Result of the Skewness test disclosed that positive value and it was noticed during Monday returns (.014) and Wednesday returns (.786), which implies that most of the Monday and Wednesday returns were more than the average returns. The other day's returns were found negative skewness, which implies that most of the other day's returns were less than the average returns. The Kurtosis result of the NSE Media Index returns were found platykurtic on Friday returns (1.633). Since, Kurtosis values are less than 3, thus, it is inferred that the level of risk associated with the Friday returns of the NSE Media sector was low, which means investors may obtain either low level of profit or loss. The other day's returns were found leptokurtic. Since, Kurtosis values are greater than 3, thus, it is inferred that the level of risk associated with the other day's returns of the NSE Media index was high, which means investors may obtain either high level of profit or loss.

As the calculated P value of the Shapiro-Wilk test is less than 0.01, it is clearly proved that the data are not normally distributed. Hence, there exists anomaly in the NSE Media index returns.

The following table illustrates the determinants of Day of the week effect of NSE Media Index.

Table 4.56: Determinants of Day of the Week Effect – NSE Media Index

	Coefficient	***Std. Error***	***t-ratio***	***p-value***
Constant	0.0655658	0.0822845	0.7968	0.42598
Monday	0.0509526	0.0428552	1.1889	0.23509
Tuesday	-0.0655827	0.0453579	-1.4459	0.14891
Wednesday	0.0777175	0.0432501	1.7969	0.07302
Thursday	-0.0766398	0.0467126	-1.6407	0.10157
R-squared	0.19719	Adjusted R-squared		0.10927
F(4, 446)	2.242891	P-value(F)		0.063586
Source – Database collected from NSE web portal and computed.				

The result of OLS regression analysis disclose that the select independent variables collectively contribute to 19.71 per cent variation in Friday returns.

4.3.29. NSE Metal Index

The following table tries to ascertain, whether Day of the week effect prevails in NSE Metal Index.

Table 4.57: Day of the Week Effect – NSE Metal Index

	MONDAY	TUESDAY	WEDNESDAY	THURSDAY	FRIDAY
Mean	.0714	.0703	-.0406	.0917	.1626
Median	.1906	.0290	-.0012	.1073	.0692
Std. Deviation	2.60608	2.55452	2.29088	2.14083	2.37133
Variance	6.792	6.526	5.248	4.583	5.623
Skewness	-.350	3.572	-.182	-.323	-.105
Kurtosis	7.599	42.822	1.897	3.309	3.840
Shapiro-Wilk	.000	.000	.000	.000	.000
Source – Database collected from NSE web portal and computed.					

High mean returns were noticed during Friday (.1626) and low mean returns were found during Wednesday (-.0406). While comparing to variance, high level of volatility was noticed on Monday (6.792) and low level of volatility was noticed on Thursday (4.583).

Result of the Skewness test disclosed that positive value and it was noticed during Tuesday returns (3.572), which implies that most of the Tuesday returns were more than the average returns. The other day's returns were found negative skewness, which implies that most of the other day's returns were less than the average returns. The Kurtosis result of the NSE Metal Index returns were found platykurtic on Wednesday returns (1.897). Since, Kurtosis values are less than 3, thus, it is inferred that the level of risk associated with the Wednesday returns of the NSE Metal sector was low, which means investors may obtain either low level of profit or loss. The other day's returns were found leptokurtic. Since, Kurtosis values are greater than 3, thus, it is inferred that the level of risk associated with the other day's returns of the NSE Metal index was high, which means investors may obtain either high level of profit or loss.

As the calculated P value of the Shapiro-Wilk test is less than 0.01, it is clearly proved that the data are not normally distributed. Hence, there exists anomaly in the NSE Metal index returns.

The following table illustrates the determinants of Day of the week effect of NSE Metal Index.

Table 4.58: Determinants of Day of the Week Effect – NSE Metal Index

	Coefficient	*Std. Error*	*t-ratio*	*p-value*	
Constant	0.15238	0.102165	1.4915	0.13642	
Monday	0.053236	0.0392022	1.3580	0.17504	
Tuesday	0.0813859	0.0401036	2.0294	0.04291	*
Wednesday	0.012705	0.0446114	0.2848	0.77591	
Thursday	0.00153724	0.0480436	0.0320	0.97449	
R-squared	0.12500	Adjusted R-squared		0.05089	
F(4, 533)	1.686747	P-value(F)		0.0151609	
Source – Database collected from NSE web portal and computed.					

The result of OLS disclose that Tuesday return is found to be significant at 5 per cent level.

Tuesday

The regression coefficient indicates that Tuesday returns positively influences Friday returns. The value of the regression coefficient indicates that a unit of increase in Tuesday return shall increase Friday return by 0.081 units. Higher rate of return on Tuesday leads to a higher rate of return on Friday.

The value of R^2 is found to be significant at five per cent level. This shows that the regression equation framed is a good fit. Around 12.50 per cent of variation in Friday return is due to the select variable.

4.3.30. NSE Pharma Index

The following table tries to ascertain, whether Day of the week effect prevails in NSE Pharma Index.

Table 4.59: Day of the Week Effect – NSE Pharma Index

	MONDAY	TUESDAY	WEDNESDAY	THURSDAY	FRIDAY
Mean	.0760	.0572	.0848	.0831	.1058
Median	.1067	.0682	.1204	.1116	.1243
Std. Deviation	1.36732	1.30593	1.17750	1.18449	1.18248
Variance	1.870	1.705	1.387	1.403	1.398
Skewness	-.115	-.680	-.264	-.544	-.094
Kurtosis	15.773	6.370	1.133	2.407	2.630
Shapiro-Wilk	.000	.000	.000	.000	.000

Source – Database collected from NSE web portal and computed.

High mean returns were noticed during Friday (.1058) and low mean returns were found during Tuesday (.0572). While comparing to variance, high level of volatility was noticed on Monday (1.870) and low level of volatility was noticed on Wednesday (1.387).

Result of the Skewness test disclosed that negative value and it was noticed all the days of the week, which implies that all the days of the week returns were less than the average returns. The Kurtosis result of the NSE Pharma Index returns were found leptokurtic on Monday returns (15.773) and Tuesday returns (6.370). Since, Kurtosis values are greater than 3, thus, it is inferred that the level of risk associated with the Monday and Tuesday returns of the NSE Pharmaceutical sector was high, which means investors may obtain either high level of profit or loss. The other day's returns were found platykurtic. Since, Kurtosis values are less than 3, thus, it is inferred that the level of risk associated with the other day's returns of the NSE Pharma index was low, which means investors may obtain either low level of profit or loss.

As the calculated P value of the Shapiro-Wilk test is less than 0.01, it is clearly proved that the data are not normally distributed. Hence, there exists anomaly in the NSE Pharma index returns.

The following table illustrates the determinants of Day of the week effect of NSE Pharma Index.

Table 4.60: Determinants of Day of the Week Effect – NSE Pharma Index

	Coefficient	*Std. Error*	*t-ratio*	*p-value*
Constant	0.104506	0.0512276	2.0400	0.04184
Monday	-0.0244473	0.0374752	-0.6524	0.51445
Tuesday	-0.0604692	0.0392415	-1.5410	0.12392
Wednesday	0.0760497	0.0433656	1.7537	0.08006
Thursday	-0.00186582	0.0431662	-0.0432	0.96554
R-squared	0.11035	Adjusted R-squared		0.03613
F(4, 533)	1.486864	P-value(F)		0.204774
Source – Database collected from NSE web portal and computed.				

The result of OLS regression analysis disclose that the select independent variables collectively contribute to11.03 per cent variation in Friday returns.

4.3.31. NSE Private Banks Index

The following table tries to ascertain, whether Day of the week effect prevails in NSE Private Bank Index.

Table 4.61: Day of the Week Effect – NSE Private Banks Index

	MONDAY	TUESDAY	WEDNESDAY	THURSDAY	FRIDAY
Mean	.1378	.0750	.1351	.0651	.1497
Median	.2442	.0781	.0078	.1331	.1084
Std. Deviation	2.38536	2.02355	1.91139	2.00761	2.21535
Variance	5.690	4.095	3.653	4.030	4.908
Skewness	.821	-.003	.447	.043	-.437
Kurtosis	10.052	2.845	2.865	2.937	4.930
Shapiro-Wilk	.000	.000	.000	.000	.000
Source – Database collected from NSE web portal and computed.					

High mean returns were noticed during Friday (.1497) and low mean returns were found during Thursday (.0651). While comparing to variance, high level of volatility was noticed on Monday (5.690) and low level of volatility was noticed on Wednesday (3.653).

Result of the Skewness test disclosed that negative value and it was noticed during Tuesday returns (-0.003) and Friday returns (-0.437), which implies that most of the Tuesday and Friday returns were less than the average returns. The other day's returns were found positive skewness, which implies that most of the other day's returns were more than the average returns. The Kurtosis result of the NSE Private Bank Index returns were found leptokurtic on Monday returns (10.052) and Friday returns (4.930). Since, Kurtosis values are greater than 3, thus, it is inferred that the level of risk associated with the Monday and Friday returns of the NSE Private Banking sector was high, which means investors may obtain either high level of profit or loss. The other day's returns were found platykurtic. Since, Kurtosis values are less than 3, thus, it is inferred that the level of risk associated with the other day's returns of the NSE Private Bank index was low, which means investors may obtain either low level of profit or loss.

As the calculated P value of the Shapiro-Wilk test is less than 0.01, it is clearly proved that the data are not normally distributed. Hence, there exists anomaly in the NSE Private Bank index returns.

The following table illustrates the determinants of Day of the week effect of NSE Private Bank Index.

Table 4.62: Determinants of Day of the Week Effect – NSE Private Banks Index

	Coefficient	*Std. Error*	*t-ratio*	*p-value*	
Constant	0.121153	0.10043	1.2063	0.22828	
Monday	0.0513075	0.0419893	1.2219	0.22233	
Tuesday	0.0367552	0.0491765	0.7474	0.45518	
Wednesday	0.121246	0.0523035	2.3181	0.02086	*
Thursday	0.0268901	0.049895	0.5389	0.59018	
R-squared	0.14936	Adjusted R-squared		0.06795	
F(4, 484)	1.834653	P-value(F)		0.0120928	

Source – Database collected from NSE web portal and computed.

The result of OLS disclose that Wednesday return is found to be significant at 5 per cent level.

Wednesday

The regression coefficient indicates that Wednesday returns positively influences Friday returns. The value of the regression coefficient indicates that a unit of increase in Wednesday return shall increase Friday return by 0.121 units. Higher rate of return on Wednesday leads to a higher rate of return on Friday.

The value of R2 is found to be significant at five per cent level. This shows that the regression equation framed is a good fit. Around 14.93 per cent of variation in Friday return is due to the select variable.

4.3.32. NSE Public Sector Unit Banks Index

The following table tries to ascertain, whether Day of the week effect prevails in NSE Public Sector Bank Index.

Table 4.63: Day of the Week Effect – NSE PSU Banks Index

	MONDAY	TUESDAY	WEDNESDAY	THURSDAY	FRIDAY
Mean	.1184	-.0017	.0515	.0253	.1571
Median	.2524	.0763	-.0513	.1329	.1115
Std. Deviation	2.47097	2.21962	2.15627	2.09511	2.23728
Variance	6.106	4.927	4.649	4.389	5.005
Skewness	.058	.127	.383	-.068	-.435
Kurtosis	7.790	3.083	2.206	1.452	5.223
Shapiro-Wilk	.000	.000	.000	.000	.000
Source – Database collected from NSE web portal and computed.					

High mean returns were noticed during Friday (.1571) and low mean returns were found during Tuesday (-.0017). While comparing to variance, high level of volatility was noticed on Monday (6.106) and low level of volatility was noticed on Thursday (4.389).

Result of the Skewness test disclosed that negative value and it was noticed during Thursday returns (-0.068) and Friday returns (-0.435), which implies that most of the Thursday and Friday returns were less than the average returns. The other day's returns were found positive skewness, which implies that most of the other day's returns were more than the average returns. The Kurtosis result of the NSE PSU Bank Index returns were found platykurtic on Wednesday returns (2.206) and Thursday returns (1.452). Since, Kurtosis values are less than 3, thus, it is inferred that the level of risk associated with the Wednesday returns and Thursday of the NSE PSU Bank sector was low, which means investors may obtain either low level of profit or loss. The other day's returns were found leptokurtic. Since, Kurtosis values are greater than 3, thus, it is inferred that the level of risk associated with the other day's returns of the NSE PSU Bank index was high, which means investors may obtain either high level of profit or loss.

As the calculated P value of the Shapiro-Wilk test is less than 0.01, it is clearly proved that the data are not normally distributed. Hence, there exists anomaly in the NSE PSU Bank index returns.

The following table illustrates the determinants of Day of the week effect of NSE PSU Bank Index.

Table 4.64: Determinants of Day of the Week Effect – NSE PSU Banks Index

	Coefficient	*Std. Error*	*t-ratio*	*p-value*	
Constant	0.149691	0.0961027	1.5576	0.11992	
Monday	0.080047	0.0390189	2.0515	0.04071	*
Tuesday	0.068281	0.0434028	1.5732	0.11627	
Wednesday	0.0890647	0.0445373	1.9998	0.04603	*
Thursday	0.0443802	0.0460319	0.9641	0.33543	
R-squared	0.22468	Adjusted R-squared		0.15104	
F(4, 531)	3.051202	P-value(F)		0.016699	

Source – Database collected from NSE web portal and computed.

The result of OLS disclose that Monday and Wednesday return is found to be significant at 5 per cent level.

Monday

The regression coefficient indicates that Monday returns positively influences Friday returns. The value of the regression coefficient indicates that a unit of increase in Monday return shall increase Friday return by 0.80 units. Higher rate of return on Monday leads to a higher rate of return on Friday.

Wednesday

The regression coefficient indicates that Wednesday returns positively influences Friday returns. The value of the regression coefficient indicates that a unit of increase in Wednesday return shall increase Friday return by 0.089 units. Higher rate of return on Wednesday leads to a higher rate of return on Friday.

The value of R^2 is found to be significant at five per cent level. This shows that the regression equation framed is a good fit. Around 22.46 per cent of variation in Friday return is due to the select variables.

4.3.33. NSE Realty Index

The following table tries to ascertain, whether Day of the week effect prevails in NSE Realty Index.

Table 4.65: Day of the Week Effect – NSE Realty Index

	MONDAY	TUESDAY	WEDNESDAY	THURSDAY	FRIDAY
Mean	-.0284	-.0176	-.0153	-.1120	.0555
Median	.1243	.1297	.0268	-.0154	-.0288
Std. Deviation	3.40397	3.08994	3.09889	2.72876	2.91600
Variance	11.587	9.548	9.603	7.446	8.503
Skewness	-.275	.192	.338	-.756	.084
Kurtosis	11.880	2.110	2.038	4.534	2.151
Shapiro-Wilk	.000	.000	.000	.000	.000
Source – Database collected from NSE web portal and computed.					

High mean returns were noticed during Friday (.0555) and low mean returns were found during Thursday (-.1120). While comparing to variance, high level of volatility was noticed on Monday (11.587) and low level of volatility was noticed on Thursday (7.446).

Result of the Skewness test disclosed that negative value and it was noticed during Monday returns (-0.275) and Thursday returns (-0.756), which implies that most of the Monday and Thursday returns were less than the average returns. The other day's returns were found positive skewness, which implies that most of the other day's returns were more than the average returns, which implies that most of the other day's returns were more than the average returns. The Kurtosis result of the NSE Realty Index returns were found leptokurtic on Monday returns (11.880) and Thursday returns (4.534). Since, Kurtosis values are greater than 3, thus, it is inferred that the level of risk associated with the Monday and Thursday returns of the NSE Real estate sector was high, which means investors may obtain either high level of profit or loss. The other day's returns were found platykurtic. Since, Kurtosis values are less than 3, thus, it is inferred that the level of risk associated with the other day's returns of the NSE Realty index was low, which means investors may obtain either low level of profit or loss.

As the calculated P value of the Shapiro-Wilk test is less than 0.01, it is clearly proved that the data are not normally distributed. Hence, there exists anomaly in the NSE Realty index returns.

The following table illustrates the determinants of Day of the week effect of NSE Realty sector.

Table 4.66: Determinants of Day of the Week Effect – NSE Realty Index

	Coefficient	*Std. Error*	*t-ratio*	*p-value*	
Constant	0.0548232	0.145332	0.3772	0.70621	
Monday	0.00182806	0.0423961	0.0431	0.96563	
Tuesday	0.0194437	0.046667	0.4166	0.67716	
Wednesday	0.113303	0.0466869	2.4269	0.01568	*
Thursday	0.0132975	0.053459	0.2487	0.80369	
R-squared	0.15518	Adjusted R-squared		0.05574	
F (4, 396)	1.560504	P-value(F)		0.0184079	

Source – Database collected from NSE web portal and computed.

The result of OLS disclose that Wednesday return is found to be significant at 5 per cent level.

Wednesday

The regression coefficient indicates that Wednesday returns positively influences Friday returns. The value of the regression coefficient indicates that a unit of increase in Wednesday return shall increase Friday return by 0.113 units. Higher rate of return on Wednesday leads to a higher rate of return on Friday.

The value of R^2 is found to be significant at five per cent level. This shows that the regression equation framed is a good fit. Around 15.51 per cent of variation in Friday return is due to the select variable.

4.4. Conclusion

From the analysis, it is inferred that the day of the week effect exist in all BSE Sensex, 19 BSE sectoral indices, NSE Nifty and 12 NSE sectoral indices. As far as Day of the week effect is concerned, High level of return is noticed on Wednesday and low level of return noticed on Thursday for BSE Sensex Index. Thus, investors are advised to buy BSE Sensex shares on Thursday and to sell shares on Wednesday. High level of return is noticed on Friday and low level of return noticed on Wednesday for NSE Nifty Index. Hence, investors are advised to buy NSE Nifty shares on Wednesday and to sell on Friday. The next chapter discuss about semi month effect.

CHAPTER V

SEMI MONTH EFFECT IN INDIAN STOCK MARKET

5.1. Introduction

Semi-month Effect, the mean return of the First Half Month has been compared to the rest of the day of the month. The return of the first 15 days has been compared to rest of the day's return of the month. The purpose of studying Semi-Month Effect is to find appropriate investment time during fortnight month.

5.2. Tools for Analysis

The collected data have been analyzed by making use of Returns, Descriptive statistics such as Mean, Standard Deviation, Variance, Skewness, Kurtosis, Shapiro-Wilk test and paired 't' test.

5.2.1. Paired 't' Test

To find whether mean returns differs between first and second half of the month returns in both BSE indices and NSE indices, Paired 't' test is employed.

5.3. Semi Month Effect

The following subsections discuss about the semi month effect of BSE Sensex, 19 BSE sectoral indices, followed by NSE Nifty and 12 NSE sectoral indices.

5.3.1. BSE Sensex Index

The following table exhibits whether semi month effect prevails in BSE Sensex index.

Table 5.1: Semi Month Effect–BSE Sensex Index

	Mean	Median	Std. Deviation	Variance	Skewness	Kurtosis	Shapiro-Wilk
First half	0.06210	0.06986	0.460207	0.212	-0.046	4.636	0.000
Second half	0.07819	0.11587	0.44364	0.197	0.116	2.855	0.000

Source – Database collected from BSE web portal and computed.

High mean returns were noticed during the second half of the month (0.07819) and low mean returns were found during the first half of the month (0.06210). While comparing the variance, high level of volatility was noticed on the first half of the month (0.212) and low level of volatility was noticed in the second half of the month (0.197). Result of the Skewness test disclosed that negative value were noticed during the first half of the month (-.046) returns, which implies that most of the first half of the month returns were less than the average returns. The second half of the month (.116) returns was noticed positive Skewness, which implies that most of the second half of the month returns were more than the average returns. The Kurtosis results of the BSE Sensex index returns were found leptokurtic on First half of the month (4.636). Since, Kurtosis values are greater than 3, thus, it is inferred that the level of risk associated with the BSE Sensex was high, which means investors may obtain either high level of profit or loss. The second half of the month returns were found platykurtic (2.855). Since, Kurtosis values are less than 3, thus, it is inferred that the level of risk associated with the second half of the month BSE Sensex was low, which means investors may obtain either low level of profit or loss.

As the calculated P value of the Shapiro-Wilk test is less than 0.01, it is clearly proved that the data are not normally distributed. Hence, anomaly exists in the BSE Sensex index returns.

The following table depicts, whether first half and second half returns differ in BSE Sensex.

Table 5.2: Semi Month Effect-BSE Sensex Index

	Mean	N	Std. Deviation	Paired t value	P value
First half	.06210	132	.460207	-0.323	0.747
Second half	.07819	132	.443640		
Source – Database collected from BSE web portal and computed.					

As the calculated P value is greater than 0.05, it is inferred that BSE Sensex index returns does not differ between the first half and the second half of the month.

5.3.2. BSE Auto Index

The following table exhibits whether semi month effect prevails in BSE Auto index.

Table 5.3: Semi Month Effect–BSE Auto Index

	Mean	Median	Std. Deviation	Variance	Skewness	Kurtosis	Shapiro-Wilk
First half	0.10062	0.13176	0.472082	0.223	0.012	1.676	0.008
Second half	0.07913	0.1025	0.510781	0.261	0.051	3.061	0.000
Source – Database collected from BSE web portal and computed.							

High mean returns were noticed during the first half of the month (0.10062) and low mean return were found during the second half of the month (0.07913). While comparing the variance, high level of volatility was noticed on the second half of the month (0.261) and low level of volatility was noticed in the first half of the month (0.223).

Result of the Skewness test disclosed that positive value were noticed during both the first half of the month (0.012) and the second half of the month (0.051) returns, which implies that most of the first and second half of the month returns were more than the average returns. The

Kurtosis results of the BSE Auto index returns were found platykurtic on First half of the month (1.676). Since, Kurtosis values are less than 3, thus, it is inferred that the level of risk associated with the BSE Automobile sector was low, which means investors may obtain either low level of profit or loss. The second half of the month returns were found leptokurtic (3.061). Since, Kurtosis values are greater than 3, thus, it is inferred that the level of risk associated with the second half of the month BSE Automobile sector was high, which means investors may obtain either high level of profit or loss.

As the calculated P value of the Shapiro-Wilk test is less than 0.01, it is clearly proved that the data are not normally distributed. Hence, anomaly exists in the BSE AUTO index returns.

The following table depicts, whether first half and second half returns differ in BSE Auto index.

Table 5.4: Semi Month Effect-BSE Auto Index

	Mean	N	Std. Deviation	Paired t value	P value
First half	.10062	132	.472082	0.421	0.675
Second half	.07913	132	.510781		
Source - Database collected from BSE web portal and computed.					

As the calculated P value is greater than 0.05, it is inferred that BSE Auto index returns does not differ between the first half and the second half of the month.

5.3.3. BSE Bank Index

The following table exhibits whether semi month effect prevails in BSE Bank index.

Table 5.5: Semi Month Effect–BSE Bank Index

	Mean	Median	Std. Deviation	Variance	Skewness	Kurtosis	Shapiro-Wilk
First half	0.11885	0.18482	0.62972	0.397	0.154	4.059	0.008
Second half	0.07134	0.09528	0.666488	0.444	0.145	1.929	0.000
Source - Database collected from BSE web portal and computed.							

High mean returns were noticed during the first half of the month (0.11885) and low mean return were found during the second half of the month (0.07134). While comparing the variance, high level of volatility was noticed on the second half of the month (0.444) and low level of volatility was noticed in the first half of the month (0.397).

Result of the Skewness test disclosed that positive value were noticed during both the first half of the month (0.154) and the second half of the month (0.145) returns, which implies that most of the first and second half of the month returns were more than the average returns. The

Kurtosis results of the BSE Bank index returns were found leptokurtic on First half of the month (4.059). Since, Kurtosis values are greater than 3, thus, it is inferred that the level of risk associated with the BSE Banking sector was high, which means investors may obtain either high level of profit or loss. The second half of the month returns were found platykurtic (1.929). Since, Kurtosis values are less than 3, thus, it is inferred that the level of risk associated with the second half of the month BSE Bank index was low, which means investors may obtain either low level of profit or loss.

As the calculated P value of the Shapiro-Wilk test is less than 0.01, it is clearly proved that the data are not normally distributed. Hence, anomaly exists in the BSE Bank index returns.

The following table depicts, whether first half and second half returns differ in BSE Bank index.

Table 5.6: Semi Month Effect-BSE Bank Index

	Mean	N	Std. Deviation	Paired t value	P value
First half	.11885	132	.629722	0.674	0.502
Second half	.07134	132	.666488		
Source – Database collected from BSE web portal and computed.					

As the calculated P value is greater than 0.05, it is inferred that BSE Bank index returns does not differ between the first half and the second half of the month.

5.3.4. BSE Basic Materials Index

The following table exhibits whether semi month effect prevails in BSE Basic Materials index.

Table 5.7: Semi Month Effect–BSE Basic Materials Index

	Mean	Median	Std. Deviation	Variance	Skewness	Kurtosis	Shapiro-Wilk
First half	0.0906	0.1189	0.63483	0.403	-0.390	0.95	0.000
Second half	0.0122	0.034	0.74631	0.557	-1.004	4.383	0.000
Source – Database collected from BSE web portal and computed.							

High mean returns were noticed during the first half of the month (0.0906) and low mean return were found during the second half of the month (0.0122). While comparing the variance, high level of volatility was noticed on the second half of the month (0.557) and low level of volatility was noticed in the first half of the month (0.403).

Result of the Skewness test disclosed that negative value were noticed during both the first half of the month (-0.390) and the second half of the month (-1.004) returns, which implies that most of the first and second half of the month returns were less than the average returns.

The Kurtosis results of the BSE Basic Materials index returns were found platykurtic on First half of the month (0.950). Since, Kurtosis values are less than 3, thus, it is inferred that the level of risk associated with the BSE Basic Materials sector was low, which means investors may obtain either low level of profit or loss. The second half of the month returns were found leptokurtic (4.383). Since, Kurtosis values are greater than 3, thus, it is inferred that the level of risk associated with the second half of the month BSE Basic Materials sector was high, which means investors may obtain either high level of profit or loss.

As the calculated P value of the Shapiro-Wilk test is less than 0.01, it is clearly proved that the data are not normally distributed. Hence, anomaly exists in the BSE Basic Materials index returns.

The following table depicts, whether first half and second half returns differ in BSE Basic Materials index.

Table 5.8: Semi Month Effect-BSE Basic Materials Index

	Mean	N	Std. Deviation	Paired t value	P value
First half	.0906	114	.63483	.865	0.389
Second half	.0122	114	.74631		
Source – Database collected from BSE web portal and computed.					

As the calculated P value is greater than 0.05, it is inferred that BSE Basic Materials index returns does not differ between the first half and the second half of the month.

5.3.5. *BSE Consumer Durables Index*

The following table exhibits whether semi month effect prevails in BSE Consumer Durables index.

Table 5.9: Semi Month Effect–BSE Consumer Durables Index

	Mean	Median	Std. Deviation	Variance	Skewness	Kurtosis	Shapiro-Wilk
First half	0.11693	0.16842	0.698438	0.488	-0.735	4.504	0.000
Second half	0.09147	0.06527	0.6125	0.375	0.733	5.542	0.000
Source – Database collected from BSE web portal and computed.							

High mean returns were noticed during the first half of the month (0.11693) and low mean return were found during the second half of the month (0.09147). While comparing the variance, high level of volatility was noticed on the first half of the month (0.488) and low level of volatility was noticed in the second half of the month (0.375).

Result of the Skewness test disclosed that negative value were noticed during the first half of the month (-.735) returns, which implies that most of the first half of the month returns were less than the average returns. The second half of the month (.733) returns was noticed positive Skewness, which implies that most of the second half of the month returns were more than the average returns. The Kurtosis results of the BSE Consumer Durables index returns were found leptokurtic on both the First half of the month (4.504) and the second half of the month (5.542). Since, Kurtosis values are greater than 3, thus, it is inferred that the level of risk associated with the BSE Consumer Durables sector was high, which means investors may obtain either high level of profit or loss.

As the calculated P value of the Shapiro-Wilk test is less than 0.01, it is clearly proved that the data are not normally distributed. Hence, anomaly exists in the BSE Consumer Durables index returns.

The following table depicts, whether first half and second half returns differ in BSE Consumer Durables index.

Table 5.10: Semi Month Effect-BSE Consumer Durables Index

	Mean	N	Std. Deviation	Paired t value	P value
First half	.11693	132	.698438	0.348	0.728
Second half	.09147	132	.612500		
Source – Database collected from BSE web portal and computed.					

As the calculated P value is greater than 0.05, it is inferred that BSE Consumer Durables index returns does not differ between the first half and the second half of the month.

5.3.6. BSE Consumer Goods Index

The following table exhibits whether semi month effect prevails in BSE Consumer Goods index.

Table 5.11: Semi Month Effect–BSE Consumer Goods Index

	Mean	Median	Std. Deviation	Variance	Skewness	Kurtosis	Shapiro-Wilk
First half	0.11304	0.15248	0.6546	0.428	-0.065	5.894	0.000
Second half	0.07637	0.13973	0.67578	0.457	0.698	3.803	0.000
Source – Database collected from BSE web portal and computed.							

High mean returns were noticed during the first half of the month (0.11304) and low mean return were found during the second half of the month (0.07637). While comparing the variance, high level of volatility was noticed on the second half of the month (0.457) and low level of volatility was noticed in the first half of the month (0.428).

Result of the Skewness test disclosed that negative value were noticed during the first half of the month (-.065) returns, which implies that most of the first half of the month returns were less than the average returns. The second half of the month (.698) returns was noticed positive Skewness, which implies that most of the second half of the month returns were more than the average returns. The Kurtosis results of the BSE Consumer Goods index returns were found leptokurtic on both the First half of the month (5.894) and the second half of the month (3.803). Since, Kurtosis values are greater than 3, thus, it is inferred that the level of risk associated with the BSE Consumer Goods sector was high, which means investors may obtain either high level of profit or loss.

As the calculated P value of the Shapiro-Wilk test is less than 0.01, it is clearly proved that the data are not normally distributed. Hence, anomaly exists in the BSE Consumer Goods index returns.

The following table depicts, whether first half and second half returns differ in BSE Consumer Goods index.

Table 5.12: Semi Month Effect-BSE Consumer Goods Index

	Mean	N	Std. Deviation	Paired t value	P value
First half	.11304	132	.654595	0.509	0.611
Second half	.07637	132	.675777		

Source - Database collected from BSE web portal and computed.

As the calculated P value is greater than 0.05, it is inferred that BSE Consumer Goods index returns does not differ between the first half and the second half of the month.

5.3.7. BSE Energy Index

The following table exhibits whether semi month effect prevails in BSE Energy index.

Table 5.13: Semi Month Effect–BSE Energy Index

	Mean	Median	Std. Deviation	Variance	Skewness	Kurtosis	Shapiro-Wilk
First half	0.0816	0.0907	0.49790	0.248	0.021	0.642	0.000
Second half	0.0318	0.0388	0.64459	0.415	-0.700	4.200	0.000

Source - Database collected from BSE web portal and computed.

High mean returns were noticed during the first half of the month (0.0816) and low mean return were found during the second half of the month (0.0318). While comparing the variance, high level of volatility was noticed on the second half of the month (0.415) and low level of volatility was noticed in the first half of the month (0.248).

Result of the Skewness test disclosed that negative value were noticed during the second half of the month (-.700) returns, which implies that most of the second half of the month returns were less than the average returns. The first half of the month (.021) returns was noticed positive Skewness, which implies that most of the second half of the month returns were more than the average returns. The Kurtosis results of the BSE Energy index returns were found platykurtic on First half of the month (0.642). Since, Kurtosis values are less than 3, thus, it is inferred that the level of risk associated with the BSE Energy sector was low, which means investors may obtain either low level of profit or loss. The second half of the month returns were found leptokurtic (4.200). Since, Kurtosis values are greater than 3, thus, it is inferred that the level of risk associated with the second half of the month BSE Energy sector was high, which means investors may obtain either high level of profit or loss.

As the calculated P value of the Shapiro-Wilk test is less than 0.01, it is clearly proved that the data are not normally distributed. Hence, anomaly exists in the BSE Energy index returns.

The following table depicts, whether first half and second half returns differ in BSE Energy index.

Table 5.14: Semi Month Effect-BSE Energy Index

	Mean	**N**	**Std. Deviation**	**Paired t value**	**P value**
First half	.0816	114	.49790	0.656	0.513
Second half	.0318	114	.64459		
Source – Database collected from BSE web portal and computed.					

As the calculated P value is greater than 0.05, it is inferred that BSE Energy index returns does not differ between the first half and the second half of the month.

5.3.8. BSE Finance Index

The following table exhibits whether semi month effect prevails in BSE Finance index.

Table 5.15: Semi Month Effect–BSE Finance Index

	Mean	**Median**	**Std. Deviation**	**Variance**	**Skewness**	**Kurtosis**	**Shapiro-Wilk**
First half	0.1124	0.1815	0.64429	0.415	-0.529	1.343	0.004
Second half	0.0471	0.1453	0.71768	0.515	-0.098	2.181	0.000
Source – Database collected from BSE web portal and computed.							

High mean returns were noticed during the first half of the month (0.1124) and low mean return were found during the second half of the month (0.0471). While comparing the variance, high level of volatility was noticed on the second half of the month (0.515) and low level of volatility was noticed in the first half of the month (0.415).

Result of the Skewness test disclosed that negative value were noticed during both the first half of the month (-0.529) and the second half of the month (-0.098) returns, which implies that most of the first and second half of the month returns were less than the average returns.

The Kurtosis results of the BSE Finance index returns were found platykurtic on both the First half of the month (1.343) and the second half of the month (2.181). Since, Kurtosis values are less than 3, thus, it is inferred that the level of risk associated with the BSE Finance sector was high, which means investors may obtain either low level of profit or loss.

As the calculated P value of the Shapiro-Wilk test is less than 0.01, it is clearly proved that the data are not normally distributed. Hence, anomaly exists in the BSE Finance index returns.

The following table depicts, whether first half and second half returns differ in BSE Finance index.

Table 5.16: Semi Month Effect-BSE Finance Index

	Mean	N	Std. Deviation	Paired t value	P value
First half	.1124	114	.64429	0.734	0.465
Second half	.0471	114	.71768		
Source – Database collected from BSE web portal and computed.					

As the calculated P value is greater than 0.05, it is inferred that BSE Finance index returns does not differ between the first half and the second half of the month.

5.3.9. *BSE Fast Moving Consumer Goods Index*

The following table exhibits whether semi month effect prevails in BSE FMCG index.

Table 5.17: Semi Month Effect – BSE Fast Moving Consumer Goods Index

	Mean	Median	Std. Deviation	Variance	Skewness	Kurtosis	Shapiro-Wilk
First half	0.1177	0.1702	0.41856	0.175	-0.70	2.210	0.000
Second half	0.0311	0.0718	0.41238	0.170	-0.332	1.325	0.000
Source – Database collected from BSE web portal and computed.							

High mean returns were noticed during the first half of the month (0.1177) and low mean return were found during the second half of the month (0.0311). While comparing the variance, high level of volatility was noticed on the first half of the month (0.175) and low level of volatility was noticed in the second half of the month (0.170).

Result of the Skewness test disclosed that negative value were noticed during both the first half of the month (-0.70) and the second half of the month (-0.332) returns, which implies that most of the first and second half of the month returns were less than the average returns. The Kurtosis results of the BSE FMCG index returns were found platykurtic on both the First half of the month (2.210) and the second half of the month (1.325). Since, Kurtosis values are less than 3, thus, it is inferred that the level of risk associated with the BSE FMCG sector was low, which means investors may obtain either low level of profit or loss.

As the calculated P value of the Shapiro-Wilk test is less than 0.01, it is clearly proved that the data are not normally distributed. Hence, anomaly exists in the BSE FMCG index returns.

The following table depicts, whether first half and second half returns differ in BSE FMCG index.

Table 5.18: Semi Month Effect - BSE Fast Moving Consumer Goods Index

	Mean	N	Std. Deviation	Paired t value	P value
First half	.1177	114	.41856	0.734	0.465
Second half	.0311	114	.41238		
Source – Database collected from BSE web portal and computed.					

As the calculated P value is greater than 0.05, it is inferred that BSE FMCG index returns does not differ between the first half and the second half of the month.

5.3.10. BSE Health Care Index

The following table exhibits whether semi month effect prevails in BSE Health Care index.

Table 5.19: Semi Month Effect – BSE Health Care Index

	Mean	Median	Std. Deviation	Variance	Skewness	Kurtosis	Shapiro-Wilk
First half	0.1398	0.1693	0.40302	0.162	-0.717	1.749	0.000
Second half	0.0267	0.0431	0.42371	0.180	-0.853	2.205	0.000
Source – Database collected from BSE web portal and computed.							

High mean returns were noticed during the first half of the month (0.1398) and low mean return were found during the second half of the month (0.0267). While comparing the variance, high level of volatility was noticed on the second half of the month (0.180) and low level of volatility was noticed in the first half of the month (0.162).

Result of the Skewness test disclosed that negative value were noticed during both the first half of the month (-0.717) and the second half of the month (-0.853) returns, which implies that most of the first and second half of the month returns were less than the average returns. The Kurtosis results of the BSE Health care index returns were found platykurtic on both the First half of the month (1.749) and the second half of the month (2.205). Since, Kurtosis values are less than 3, thus, it is inferred that the level of risk associated with the BSE Health care sector was low, which means investors may obtain either low level of profit or loss. As the calculated P value of the Shapiro-Wilk test is less than 0.01, it is clearly proved that the data are not normally distributed. Hence, anomaly exists in the BSE Health care index returns.

The following table depicts, whether first half and second half returns differ in BSE Health care index.

Table 5.20: Semi Month Effect - BSE Health Care Index

	Mean	N	Std. Deviation	Paired t value	P value
First half	.1398	114	.40302	2.101	0.038
Second half	.0267	114	.42371		
Source – Database collected from BSE web portal and computed.					

As the calculated P value is less than 0.05, it is inferred that BSE Health care index returns differs between the first half and the second half of the month.

5.3.11. BSE Industrial Index

The following table exhibits whether semi month effect prevails in BSE Industrial index.

Table 5.21: Semi Month Effect – BSE Industrial Index

	Mean	Median	Std. Deviation	Variance	Skewness	Kurtosis	Shapiro-Wilk
First half	0.1037	0.137	0.61475	0.378	-0.267	0.931	0.000
Second half	0.0344	0.1077	0.75427	0.569	-0.684	4.029	0.000
Source – Database collected from BSE web portal and computed.							

High mean returns were noticed during the first half of the month (0.1037) and low mean return were found during the second half of the month (0.0344). While comparing the variance, high level of volatility was noticed on the second half of the month (0.569) and low level of volatility was noticed in the first half of the month (0.378).

Result of the Skewness test disclosed that negative value were noticed during both the first half of the month (-0.267) and the second half of the month (-0.684) returns, which implies that most of the first and second half of the month returns were less than the average returns. The Kurtosis results of the BSE Industrial index returns were found platykurtic on First half of the month (0.931). Since, Kurtosis values are less than 3, thus, it is inferred that the level of risk associated with the BSE Industrial sector was low, which means investors may obtain either low level of profit or loss. The second half of the month returns were found leptokurtic (4.029). Since, Kurtosis values are greater than 3, thus, it is inferred that the level of risk associated with the second half of the month BSE Industrial sector was high, which means investors may obtain either high level of profit or loss.

As the calculated P value of the Shapiro-Wilk test is less than 0.01, it is clearly proved that the data are not normally distributed. Hence, anomaly exists in the BSE Industrial index returns.

The following table depicts, whether first half and second half returns differ in BSE Industrial index.

Table 5.22: Semi Month Effect - BSE Industrial Index

	Mean	N	Std. Deviation	Paired t value	P value
First half	.1037	114	.61475	.781	0.437
Second half	.0344	114	.75427		
Source – Database collected from BSE web portal and computed.					

As the calculated P value is greater than 0.05, it is inferred that BSE Industrial index returns does not differ between the first half and the second half of the month.

5.3.12. BSE IT Index

The following table exhibits whether semi month effect prevails in BSE IT index.

Table 5.23: Semi Month Effect – BSE IT Index

	Mean	Median	Std. Deviation	Variance	Skewness	Kurtosis	Shapiro-Wilk
First half	0.1494	0.1276	0.43415	0.188	0.151	0.631	0.000
Second half	-0.0136	0.0059	0.5908	0.349	-0.535	1.088	0.000
Source – Database collected from BSE web portal and computed.							

High mean returns were noticed during the first half of the month (0.1494) and low mean return were found during the second half of the month (-0.0136). While comparing the variance, high level of volatility was noticed on the second half of the month (0.349) and low level of volatility was noticed in the first half of the month (0.188).

Result of the Skewness test disclosed that positive value were noticed during the first half of the month (0.151) returns, which implies that most of the first half of the month returns were more than the average returns. The second half of the month (-.535) returns was noticed negative Skewness, which implies that most of the second half of the month returns were less than the average returns. The Kurtosis results of the BSE IT index returns were found platykurtic on both the First half of the month (0.631) and the second half of the month (1.088). Since, Kurtosis values are less than 3, thus, it is inferred that the level of risk associated with the BSE IT sector was high, which means investors may obtain either low level of profit or loss.

As the calculated P value of the Shapiro-Wilk test is less than 0.01, it is clearly proved that the data are not normally distributed. Hence, anomaly exists in the BSE IT index returns. The following table depicts, whether first half and second half returns differ in BSE IT index.

Table 5.24: Semi Month Effect - BSE IT Index

	Mean	N	Std. Deviation	Paired t value	P value
First half	.1494	114	.43415	2.487	0.014
Second half	-.0136	114	.59080		
Source – Database collected from BSE web portal and computed.					

As the calculated P value is less than 0.05, it is inferred that BSE IT index returns differs between the first half and the second half of the month.

5.3.13. BSE Metal Index

The following table exhibits whether semi month effect prevails in BSE Metal index.

Table 5.25: Semi Month Effect – BSE Metal Index

	Mean	Median	Std. Deviation	Variance	Skewness	Kurtosis	Shapiro-Wilk
First half	0.09917	0.1056	0.466307	0.217	-0.097	1.361	0.000
Second half	0.08638	0.10718	0.50408	0.254	0.157	2.661	0.000
Source – Database collected from BSE web portal and computed.							

High mean returns were noticed during the first half of the month (0.09917) and low mean return were found during the second half of the month (0.08638). While comparing the variance, high level of volatility was noticed on the second half of the month (0.254) and low level of volatility was noticed in the first half of the month (0.217).

Result of the Skewness test disclosed that positive value were noticed during the second half of the month (0.157) returns, which implies that most of the second half of the month returns were more than the average returns. The first half of the month (-.097) returns was noticed negative Skewness, which implies that most of the first half of the month returns were less than the average returns. The Kurtosis results of the BSE Metal index returns were found platykurtic on both the First half of the month (1.361) and the second half of the month (2.661). Since, Kurtosis values are less than 3, thus, it is inferred that the level of risk associated with the BSE Metal sector was low, which means investors may obtain either low level of profit or loss.

As the calculated P value of the Shapiro-Wilk test is less than 0.01, it is clearly proved that the data are not normally distributed. Hence, anomaly exists in the BSE Metal index returns. The following table depicts, whether first half and second half returns differ in BSE Metal index.

Table 5.26: Semi Month Effect-BSE Metal Index

	Mean	N	Std. Deviation	Paired t value	P value
First half	.09917	132	.466307	.254	0.800
Second half	.08638	132	.504080		
Source – Database collected from BSE web portal and computed.					

As the calculated P value is greater than 0.05, it is inferred that BSE Metal index returns does not differ between the first half and the second half of the month.

5.3.14. BSE Oil and Gas Index

The following table exhibits whether semi month effect prevails in BSE Oil and Gas index.

Table 5.27: Semi Month Effect – BSE Oil and Gas Index

	Mean	Median	Std. Deviation	Variance	Skewness	Kurtosis	Shapiro-Wilk
First half	0.07842	0.09719	0.555262	0.308	-0.275	4.728	0.000
Second half	0.03552	0.05284	0.538535	0.290	0.234	2.652	0.000
Source – Database collected from BSE web portal and computed.							

High mean returns were noticed during the first half of the month (0.07842) and low mean return were found during the second half of the month (0.03552). While comparing the variance, high level of volatility was noticed on the first half of the month (0.308) and low level of volatility was noticed in the second half of the month (0.290).

Result of the Skewness test disclosed that positive value were noticed during the second half of the month (0.234) returns, which implies that most of the second half of the month returns were more than the average returns. The first half of the month (-.275) returns was noticed negative Skewness, which implies that most of the first half of the month returns were less than the average returns. The Kurtosis results of the BSE Oil and Gas index returns were found leptokurtic on First half of the month (4.728). Since, Kurtosis values are greater than 3, thus, it is inferred that the level of risk associated with the BSE Oil and Gas sector was high, which means investors may obtain either high level of profit or loss. The second half of the month returns were found platykurtic (2.652). Since, Kurtosis values are less than 3, thus, it is inferred that the level of risk associated with the second half of the month BSE Oil and Gas sector was low, which means investors may obtain either low level of profit or loss.

As the calculated P value of the Shapiro-Wilk test is less than 0.01, it is clearly proved that the data are not normally distributed. Hence, anomaly exists in the BSE Oil and Gas index returns.

The following table depicts, whether first half and second half returns differ in BSE Oil and Gas index.

Table 5.28: Semi Month Effect - BSE Oil and Gas Index

	Mean	N	Std. Deviation	Paired t value	P value
First half	.07842	132	.555262	.680	0.498
Second half	.03552	132	.538535		
Source – Database collected from BSE web portal and computed.					

As the calculated P value is greater than 0.05, it is inferred that BSE Oil and Gas index returns does not differ between the first half and the second half of the month.

5.3.15. BSE Power Index

The following table exhibits whether semi month effect prevails in BSE Power index.

Table 5.29: Semi Month Effect – BSE Power Index

	Mean	Median	Std. Deviation	Variance	Skewness	Kurtosis	Shapiro-Wilk
First half	0.0603	0.0377	0.60349	0.364	0.809	2.835	0.000
Second half	0.0370	0.0779	0.60191	0.362	0.458	3.280	0.000
Source – Database collected from BSE web portal and computed.							

High mean returns were noticed during the first half of the month (0.0603) and low mean return were found during the second half of the month (0.0370). While comparing the variance, high level of volatility was noticed on the first half of the month (0.364) and low level of volatility was noticed in the second half of the month (0.362).

Result of the Skewness test disclosed that positive value were noticed during both the first half of the month (0.809) and the second half of the month (0.458) returns, which implies that most of the first and second half of the month returns were more than the average returns. The Kurtosis results of the BSE Power index returns were found platykurtic on First half of the month (2.835). Since, Kurtosis values are less than 3, thus, it is inferred that the level of risk associated with the BSE Power sector was low, which means investors may obtain either low level of profit or loss. The second half of the month returns were found leptokurtic (3.280). Since, Kurtosis values are greater than 3, thus, it is inferred that the level of risk associated with the second half of the month BSE Power sector was high, which means investors may obtain either high level of profit or loss.

As the calculated P value of the Shapiro-Wilk test is less than 0.01, it is clearly proved that the data are not normally distributed. Hence, anomaly exists in the BSE Power index returns.

The following table depicts, whether first half and second half returns differ in BSE Power index.

Table 5.30: Semi Month Effect - BSE Power Index

	Mean	N	Std. Deviation	Paired t value	P value
First half	.0603	123	.60349	.359	0.720
Second half	.0370	123	.60191		
Source – Database collected from BSE web portal and computed.					

As the calculated P value is greater than 0.05, it is inferred that BSE Power index returns does not differ between the first half and the second half of the month.

5.3.16. BSE Public Sector Unit Index

The following table exhibits whether semi month effect prevails in BSE PSU index.

Table 5.31: Semi Month Effect – BSE Public Sector Unit Index

	Mean	Median	Std. Deviation	Variance	Skewness	Kurtosis	Shapiro-Wilk
First half	0.06287	0.06979	0.529612	0.280	-0.09	3.704	0.000
Second half	0.01971	0.08462	0.584868	0.342	1.055	9.355	0.000
Source – Database collected from BSE web portal and computed.							

High mean returns were noticed during the first half of the month (0.06287) and low mean return were found during the second half of the month (0.01971). While comparing the variance, high level of volatility was noticed on the second half of the month (0.342) and low level of volatility was noticed in the first half of the month (0.280).

Result of the Skewness test disclosed that positive value were noticed during the second half of the month (1.055) returns, which implies that most of the second half of the month returns were more than the average returns. The first half of the month (-0.090) returns was noticed negative Skewness, which implies that most of the first half of the month returns were less than the average returns. The Kurtosis results of the BSE PSU index returns were found leptokurtic on both the First half of the month (3.704) and the second half of the month (9.355). Since, Kurtosis values are greater than 3, thus, it is inferred that the level of risk associated with the BSE PSU sector was high, which means investors may obtain either high level of profit or loss.

As the calculated P value of the Shapiro-Wilk test is less than 0.01, it is clearly proved that the data are not normally distributed. Hence, anomaly exists in the BSE PSU index returns.

The following table depicts, whether first half and second half returns differ in BSE PSU index.

Table 5.32: Semi Month Effect - BSE Public Sector Unit Index

	Mean	N	Std. Deviation	Paired t value	P value
First half	.06287	132	.529612	.711	0.478
Second half	.01971	132	.584868		
Source – Database collected from BSE web portal and computed.					

As the calculated P value is greater than 0.05, it is inferred that BSE PSU index returns does not differ between the first half and the second half of the month.

5.3.17. BSE Realty Index

The following table exhibits whether semi month effect prevails in BSE Realty index.

Table 5.33: Semi Month Effect – BSE Realty Index

	Mean	Median	Std. Deviation	Variance	Skewness	Kurtosis	Shapiro-Wilk
First half	0.1908	0.204	1.2579	1.582	0.652	5.410	0.000
Second half	-0.075	-0.1314	1.11811	1.250	1.067	3.755	0.000
Source – Database collected from BSE web portal and computed.							

High mean returns were noticed during the first half of the month (0.1908) and low mean return were found during the second half of the month (-0.075). While comparing the variance, high level of volatility was noticed on the first half of the month (1.582) and low level of volatility was noticed in the second half of the month (1.250).

Result of the Skewness test disclosed that positive value were noticed during both the first half of the month (0.652) and the second half of the month (1.067) returns, which implies that most of the first and second half of the month returns were more than the average returns. The Kurtosis results of the BSE Realty index returns were found leptokurtic on both the First half of the month (5.410) and the second half of the month (3.755). Since, Kurtosis values are greater than 3, thus, it is inferred that the level of risk associated with the BSE Real estate sector was high, which means investors may obtain either high level of profit or loss.

As the calculated P value of the Shapiro-Wilk test is less than 0.01, it is clearly proved that the data are not normally distributed. Hence, anomaly exists in the BSE Realty index returns.

The following table depicts, whether first half and second half returns differ in BSE Realty index.

Table 5.34: Semi Month Effect - BSE Realty Index

	Mean	N	Std. Deviation	Paired t value	P value
First half	0.1908	111	1.2579	2.012	0.044
Second half	-0.075	111	1.11811		
Source - Database collected from BSE web portal and computed.					

As the calculated P value is less than 0.05, it is inferred that BSE Realty index returns differs between the first half and the second half of the month.

5.3.18. BSE Teck Index

The following table exhibits whether semi month effect prevails in BSE TECK index.

Table 5.35: Semi Month Effect – BSE TECK Index

	Mean	Median	Std. Deviation	Variance	Skewness	Kurtosis	Shapiro-Wilk
First half	0.03522	0.06997	0.521657	0.272	-0.379	0.360	0.000
Second half	0.10834	0.11109	0.38365	0.147	-0.688	2.780	0.000
Source – Database collected from BSE web portal and computed.							

High mean returns were noticed during the second half of the month (0.10834) and low mean return were found during the first half of the month (0.03522). While comparing the variance, high level of volatility was noticed on the first half of the month (0.272) and low level of volatility was noticed in the second half of the month (0.147).

Result of the Skewness test disclosed that negative value were noticed during both the first half of the month (-0.379) and the second half of the month (-0.688) returns, which implies that most of the first and second half of the month returns were less than the average returns. The Kurtosis results of the BSE TECK index returns were found platykurtic on both the First half of the month (0.360) and the second half of the month (2.780). Since, Kurtosis values are less than 3, thus, it is inferred that the level of risk associated with the BSE TECK sector was low, which means investors may obtain either low level of profit or loss.

As the calculated P value of the Shapiro-Wilk test is less than 0.01, it is clearly proved that the data are not normally distributed. Hence, anomaly exists in the BSE TECK index returns.

The following table depicts, whether first half and second half returns differ in BSE TECK index.

Table 5.36: Semi Month Effect - BSE TECK Index

	Mean	N	Std. Deviation	Paired t value	P value
First half	.03522	132	.521657	-1.342	0.182
Second half	.10834	132	.383650		
Source – Database collected from BSE web portal and computed.					

As the calculated P value is greater than 0.05, it is inferred that BSE TECK index returns does not differ between the first half and the second half of the month.

5.3.19. BSE Telecom Index

The following table exhibits whether semi month effect prevails in BSE Telecom index.

Table 5.37: Semi Month Effect – BSE Telecom Index

	Mean	Median	Std. Deviation	Variance	Skewness	Kurtosis	Shapiro-Wilk
First Half	0.1024	0.1433	0.55749	0.311	-0.368	1.411	0.000
Second Half	-0.0162	0.0226	0.63915	0.409	-0.200	1.151	0.000
Source – Database collected from BSE web portal and computed.							

High mean returns were noticed during the first half of the month (0.1024) and low mean return were found during the second half of the month (-0.0162). While comparing the variance, high level of volatility was noticed on the second half of the month (0.409) and low level of volatility was noticed in the first half of the month (0.311).

Result of the Skewness test disclosed that negative value were noticed during both the first half of the month (-0.368) and the second half of the month (-0.200) returns, which implies that most of the first and second half of the month returns were less than the average returns.

The Kurtosis results of the BSE Telecom index returns were found platykurtic on both the First half of the month (1.411) and the second half of the month (1.151). Since, Kurtosis values are less than 3, thus, it is inferred that the level of risk associated with the BSE Telecom sector was low, which means investors may obtain either low level of profit or loss.

As the calculated P value of the Shapiro-Wilk test is less than 0.01, it is clearly proved that the data are not normally distributed. Hence, anomaly exists in the BSE Telecom index returns.

The following table depicts, whether first half and second half returns differ in BSE Telecom index.

Table 5.38: Semi Month Effect - BSE Telecom Index

	Mean	N	Std. Deviation	Paired t value	P value
First half	.1024	114	.55749	1.550	0.141
Second half	-.0162	114	.63915		

Source – Database collected from BSE web portal and computed.

As the calculated P value is greater than 0.05, it is inferred that BSE Telecom index returns does not differ between the first half and the second half of the month.

5.3.20. BSE Utilities Index

The following table exhibits whether semi month effect prevails in BSE Utilities index.

Table 5.39: Semi Month Effect – BSE Utilities Index

	Mean	Median	Std. Deviation	Variance	Skewness	Kurtosis	Shapiro-Wilk
First half	0.1063	0.1139	0.63558	0.404	0.297	3.255	0.000
Second half	-0.024	0.0139	0.63082	0.398	-0.578	2.664	0.000

Source – Database collected from BSE web portal and computed.

High mean returns were noticed during the first half of the month (0.1063) and low mean return were found during the second half of the month (-0.0024). While comparing the variance, high level of volatility was noticed on the first half of the month (0.404) and low level of volatility was noticed in the second half of the month (0.398).

Result of the Skewness test disclosed that positive value were noticed during the first half of the month (0.297) returns, which implies that most of the first half of the month returns were more than the average returns. The second half of the month (-.578) returns was noticed negative Skewness, which implies that most of the second half of the month returns were less than the average returns. The Kurtosis results of the BSE Utilities index returns were found leptokurtic on First half of the month (3.255). Since, Kurtosis values are greater than 3, thus, it is inferred that the level of risk associated with the BSE Utilities sector was high, which means investors may obtain either high level of profit or loss. The second half of the month returns were found platykurtic (2.664). Since, Kurtosis values are less than 3, thus, it is inferred that the level of risk associated with the second half of the month BSE Utilities sector was low, which means investors may obtain either low level of profit or loss.

As the calculated P value of the Shapiro-Wilk test is less than 0.01, it is clearly proved that the data are not normally distributed. Hence, anomaly exists in the BSE Utilities index returns.

The following table depicts, whether first half and second half returns differ in BSE Utilities index.

Table 5.40: Semi Month Effect - BSE Utilities Index

	Mean	N	Std. Deviation	Paired t value	P value
First half	.1063	114	.63558	1.512	0.133
Second half	-.0240	114	.63082		

Source – Database collected from BSE web portal and computed.

As the calculated P value is greater than 0.05, it is inferred that BSE Telecom index returns does not differ between the first half and the second half of the month.

5.3.21. NSE Nifty Index

The following table exhibits whether semi month effect prevails in NSE Nifty index.

Table 5.41: Semi Month Effect – NSE Nifty Index

	Mean	Median	Std. Deviation	Variance	Skewness	Kurtosis	Shapiro-Wilk
First half	0.0653	0.0829	0.46728	0.218	0.081	3.592	0.000
Second half	0.0752	0.1283	0.46353	0.215	-0.087	3.089	0.000

Source – Database collected from NSE web portal and computed.

High mean returns were noticed during the second half of the month (0.0752) and low mean return were found during the first half of the month (0.0653). While comparing the variance, high level of volatility was noticed on the first half of the month (0.218) and low level of volatility was noticed in the second half of the month (0.215).

Result of the Skewness test disclosed that positive value were noticed during the first half of the month (0.081) returns, which implies that most of the first half of the month returns were more than the average returns. The second half of the month (-.087) returns was noticed negative Skewness, which implies that most of the second half of the month returns were less than the average returns. The Kurtosis results of the NSE Nifty index returns were found leptokurtic on both the First half of the month (3.592) and the second half of the month (3.089). Since, Kurtosis values are more than 3, thus, it is inferred that the level of risk associated with the NSE Nifty index was high, which means investors may obtain either high level of profit or loss.

As the calculated P value of the Shapiro-Wilk test is less than 0.01, it is clearly proved that the data are not normally distributed. Hence, anomaly exists in the NSE Nifty index returns.

The following table depicts, whether first half and second half returns differ in NSE Nifty index.

Table 5.42: Semi Month Effect - NSE Nifty Index

	Mean	N	Std. Deviation	Paired t value	P value
First half	.0653	132	.46728	-0.192	0.848
Second half	.0752	132	.46353		

Source – Database collected from NSE web portal and computed.

As the calculated P value is greater than 0.05, it is inferred that NSE Nifty index returns does not differ between the first half and the second half of the month.

5.3.22. NSE Auto Index

The following table exhibits whether semi month effect prevails in NSE Auto index.

Table 5.43: Semi Month Effect – NSE Auto Index

	Mean	Median	Std. Deviation	Variance	Skewness	Kurtosis	Shapiro-Wilk
First half	0.0992	0.1056	0.46631	0.217	-0.097	1.361	0.000
Second half	0.0864	0.1072	0.50408	0.254	0.157	2.661	0.000

Source – Database collected from NSE web portal and computed.

High mean returns were noticed during the first half of the month (0.0992) and low mean return were found during the second half of the month (0.0864). While comparing the variance, high level of volatility was noticed on the second half of the month (0.254) and low level of volatility was noticed in the second half of the month (0.217). Result of the Skewness test disclosed that positive value were noticed during the second half of the month (0.157) returns, which implies that most of the second half of the month returns were more than the average returns. The first half of the month (-.097) returns was noticed negative Skewness, which implies that most of the first half of the month returns were less than the average returns. The Kurtosis results of the NSE Auto index returns were found platykurtic on both the First half of the month (1.361) and the second half of the month (2.661). Since, Kurtosis values are less than 3, thus, it is inferred that the level of risk associated with the NSE Auto index was low, which means investors may obtain either low level of profit or loss.

As the calculated P value of the Shapiro-Wilk test is less than 0.01, it is clearly proved that the data are not normally distributed. Hence, anomaly exists in the NSE Auto index returns.

The following table depicts, whether first half and second half returns differ in NSE Auto index.

Table 5.44: Semi Month Effect - NSE Auto Index

	Mean	N	Std. Deviation	Paired t value	P value
First half	.0992	132	.46631	0.254	0.800
Second half	.0864	132	.50408		
Source – Database collected from NSE web portal and computed.					

As the calculated P value is greater than 0.05, it is inferred that NSE Auto index returns does not differ between the first half and the second half of the month.

5.3.23. NSE Bank Index

The following table exhibits whether semi month effect prevails in NSE Bank index.

Table 5.45: Semi Month Effect – NSE Bank Index

	Mean	Median	Std. Deviation	Variance	Skewness	Kurtosis	Shapiro-Wilk
First half	0.1097	0.1802	0.63587	0.404	-0.056	3.724	0.000
Second half	0.0764	0.0951	0.67448	0.455	0.197	1.841	0.000
Source – Database collected from NSE web portal and computed.							

High mean returns were noticed during the first half of the month (0.1097) and low mean return were found during the second half of the month (0.0764). While comparing the variance, high level of volatility was noticed on the second half of the month (0.455) and low level of volatility was noticed in the second half of the month (0.404).

Result of the Skewness test disclosed that positive value were noticed during the second half of the month (0.197) returns, which implies that most of the second half of the month returns were more than the average returns. The first half of the month (-.056) returns was noticed negative Skewness, which implies that most of the first half of the month returns were less than the average returns. The Kurtosis results of the NSE Bank index returns were found leptokurtic on First half of the month (3.724). Since, Kurtosis values are greater than 3, thus, it is inferred that the level of risk associated with the NSE Banking sector was high, which means investors may obtain either high level of profit or loss. The second half of the month returns were found platykurtic (1.841). Since, Kurtosis values are less than 3, thus, it is inferred that the level of risk associated with the second half of the month NSE Banking sector was low, which means investors may obtain either low level of profit or loss.

As the calculated P value of the Shapiro-Wilk test is less than 0.01, it is clearly proved that the data are not normally distributed. Hence, anomaly exists in the NSE Bank index returns.

The following table depicts, whether first half and second half returns differ in NSE Bank index.

Table 5.46: Semi Month Effect - NSE Bank Index

	Mean	N	Std. Deviation	Paired t value	P value
First half	0.1097	132	0.63587	0.466	0.642
Second half	0.0764	132	0.67448		
Source - Database collected from NSE web portal and computed.					

As the calculated P value is greater than 0.05, it is inferred that NSE Bank index returns does not differ between the first half and the second half of the month.

5.3.24. NSE Energy Index

The following table exhibits whether semi month effect prevails in NSE Energy index

Table 5.47: Semi Month Effect – NSE Energy Index

	Mean	Median	Std. Deviation	Variance	Skewness	Kurtosis	Shapiro-Wilk
First half	0.0629	0.0458	0.50185	0.252	-0.155	3.841	0.000
Second half	0.0278	0.0631	0.51523	0.265	0.003	3.906	0.000
Source – Database collected from NSE web portal and computed.							

High mean returns were noticed during the first half of the month (0.0629) and low mean return were found during the second half of the month (0.0278). While comparing the variance, high level of volatility was noticed on the second half of the month (0.265) and low level of volatility was noticed in the second half of the month (0.252).

Result of the Skewness test disclosed that positive value were noticed during the second half of the month (0.003) returns, which implies that most of the second half of the month returns were more than the average returns. The first half of the month (-.155) returns was noticed negative Skewness, which implies that most of the first half of the month returns were less than the average returns. The Kurtosis results of the NSE Energy index returns were found leptokurtic on both the First half of the month (3.841) and the second half of the month (3.906). Since, Kurtosis values are greater than 3, thus, it is inferred that the level of risk associated with the NSE Energy index was high, which means investors may obtain either high level of profit or loss.

As the calculated P value of the Shapiro-Wilk test is less than 0.01, it is clearly proved that the data are not normally distributed. Hence, anomaly exists in the NSE Energy index returns.

The following table depicts, whether first half and second half returns differ in NSE Energy index.

Table 5.48: Semi Month Effect - NSE Energy Index

	Mean	N	Std. Deviation	Paired t value	P value
First half	.0629	132	.50185	0.607	0.545
Second half	.0278	132	.51523		
Source – Database collected from NSE web portal and computed.					

As the calculated P value is greater than 0.05, it is inferred that NSE Energy index returns does not differ between the first half and the second half of the month.

5.3.25. NSE Finance Index

The following table exhibits whether semi month effect prevails in NSE Finance index

Table 5.49: Semi Month Effect – NSE Finance Index

	Mean	Median	Std. Deviation	Variance	Skewness	Kurtosis	Shapiro-Wilk
First half	0.0993	0.114	0.60263	0.363	0.030	4.324	0.000
Second half	0.0977	0.0871	0.55489	0.308	0.158	2.144	0.000
Source – Database collected from NSE web portal and computed.							

High mean returns were noticed during the first half of the month (0.0993) and low mean return were found during the second half of the month (0.0977). While comparing the variance, high level of volatility was noticed on the first half of the month (0.363) and low level of volatility was noticed in the second half of the month (0.308).

Result of the Skewness test disclosed that positive value were noticed during both the first half of the month (0.030) and the second half of the month (0.158) returns, which implies that most of the first and second half of the month returns were more than the average returns. The Kurtosis results of the NSE Finance index returns were found leptokurtic on First half of the month (4.324). Since, Kurtosis values are greater than 3, thus, it is inferred that the level of risk associated with the NSE Finance sector was high, which means investors may obtain either high level of profit or loss. The second half of the month returns were found platykurtic (2.144). Since, Kurtosis values are less than 3, thus, it is inferred that the level of risk associated with the second half of the month NSE Finance sector was low, which means investors may obtain either low level of profit or loss.

As the calculated P value of the Shapiro-Wilk test is less than 0.01, it is clearly proved that the data are not normally distributed. Hence, anomaly exists in the NSE Finance index returns.

The following table depicts, whether first half and second half returns differ in NSE Finance index.

Table 5.50: Semi Month Effect - NSE Finance Index

	Mean	N	Std. Deviation	Paired t value	P value
First half	.0993	132	.60263	0.025	0.980
Second half	.0977	132	.55489		
Source – Database collected from NSE web portal and computed.					

As the calculated P value is greater than 0.05, it is inferred that NSE Finance index returns does not differ between the first half and the second half of the month.

5.3.26. NSE Fast Moving Consumer Goods Index

The following table exhibits whether semi month effect prevails in NSE FMCG index.

Table 5.51: Semi Month Effect – NSE Fast Moving Consumer Goods Index

	Mean	Median	Std. Deviation	Variance	Skewness	Kurtosis	Shapiro-Wilk
First half	0.0409	0.0581	0.40215	0.162	-0.552	1.448	0.000
Second half	0.1238	0.1487	0.36783	0.135	0.018	1.123	0.000
Source – Database collected from NSE web portal and computed.							

High mean returns were noticed during the second half of the month (0.1238) and low mean return were found during the first half of the month (0.0409). While comparing the variance, high level of volatility was noticed on the first half of the month (0.162) and low level of volatility was noticed in the second half of the month (0.135).

Result of the Skewness test disclosed that positive value were noticed during the second half of the month (0.018) returns, which implies that most of the second half of the month returns were more than the average returns. The first half of the month (-0.552) returns was noticed negative Skewness, which implies that most of the first half of the month returns were less than the average returns. The Kurtosis results of the NSE FMCG index returns were found platykurtic on both the First half of the month (1.448) and the second half of the month (1.123). Since, Kurtosis values are less than 3, thus, it is inferred that the level of risk associated with the NSE FMCG index was low, which means investors may obtain either low level of profit or loss.

As the calculated P value of the Shapiro-Wilk test is less than 0.01, it is clearly proved that the data are not normally distributed. Hence, anomaly exists in the NSE FMCG index returns.

The following table depicts, whether first half and second half returns differ in NSE FMCG index.

Table 5.52: Semi Month Effect - NSE Fast Moving Consumer Goods Index

	Mean	N	Std. Deviation	Paired t value	P value
First half	.0409	132	.40215	-1.821	0.071
Second half	.1238	132	.36783		
Source – Database collected from NSE web portal and computed.					

As the calculated P value is greater than 0.05, it is inferred that NSE FMCG index returns does not differ between the first half and the second half of the month.

5.3.27. NSE IT Index

The following table exhibits whether semi month effect prevails in NSE IT index.

Table 5.53: Semi Month Effect – NSE IT Index

	Mean	Median	Std. Deviation	Variance	Skewness	Kurtosis	Shapiro-Wilk
First half	0.0053	0.0885	0.60433	0.365	-0.683	0.522	0.000
Second half	0.0904	0.0504	0.42523	0.181	-0.659	2.745	0.000
Source – Database collected from NSE web portal and computed.							

High mean returns were noticed during the second half of the month (0.0904) and low mean return were found during the first half of the month (0.0053). While comparing the variance, high level of volatility was noticed on the first half of the month (0.365) and low level of volatility was noticed in the second half of the month (0:181).

Result of the Skewness test disclosed that negative value were noticed during both the first half of the month (-0.683) and the second half of the month (-0.659) returns, which implies that most of the first and second half of the month returns were less than the average returns. The Kurtosis results of the NSE IT index returns were found platykurtic on both the First half of the month (0.522) and the second half of the month (2.745). Since, Kurtosis values are less than 3, thus, it is inferred that the level of risk associated with the NSE IT index was low, which means investors may obtain either low level of profit or loss.

As the calculated P value of the Shapiro-Wilk test is less than 0.01, it is clearly proved that the data are not normally distributed. Hence, anomaly exists in the NSE IT index returns.

The following table depicts, whether first half and second half returns differ in NSE IT index.

Table 5.54: Semi Month Effect – NSE IT Index

	Mean	N	Std. Deviation	Paired t value	P value
First half	.0053	132	.60433	-1.386	0.168
Second half	.0904	132	.42523		
Source – Database collected from NSE web portal and computed.					

As the calculated P value is greater than 0.05, it is inferred that NSE IT index returns does not differ between the first half and the second half of the month.

5.3.28. NSE Media Index

The following table exhibits whether semi month effect prevails in NSE Media index.

Table 5.55: Semi Month Effect – NSE Media Index

	Mean	Median	Std. Deviation	Variance	Skewness	Kurtosis	Shapiro-Wilk
First half	0.0493	0.0696	0.65226	0.425	0.299	5.418	0.000
Second half	0.0519	0.0898	0.62254	0.388	0.468	2.843	0.000

Source – Database collected from NSE web portal and computed.

High mean returns were noticed during the second half of the month (0.0519) and low mean return were found during the first half of the month (0.0493). While comparing the variance, high level of volatility was noticed on the first half of the month (0.425) and low level of volatility was noticed in the second half of the month (0.388).

Result of the Skewness test disclosed that positive value were noticed during both the first half of the month (0.299) and the second half of the month (0.468) returns, which implies that most of the first and second half of the month returns were more than the average returns. The Kurtosis results of the NSE Media index returns were found leptokurtic on First half of the month (5.418). Since, Kurtosis values are greater than 3, thus, it is inferred that the level of risk associated with the NSE Media sector was high, which means investors may obtain either high level of profit or loss. The second half of the month returns were found platykurtic (2.843). Since, Kurtosis values are less than 3, thus, it is inferred that the level of risk associated with the second half of the month NSE Media sector was low, which means investors may obtain either low level of profit or loss.

As the calculated P value of the Shapiro-Wilk test is less than 0.01, it is clearly proved that the data are not normally distributed. Hence, anomaly exists in the NSE Media index returns.

The following table depicts, whether first half and second half returns differ in NSE Media index.

Table 5.56: Semi Month Effect - NSE Media Index

	Mean	N	Std. Deviation	Paired t value	P value
First half	.0493	111	.65226	-1.821	0.071
Second half	.0519	111	.62254		

Source – Database collected from NSE web portal and computed.

As the calculated P value is greater than 0.05, it is inferred that NSE Media index returns does not differ between the first half and the second half of the month.

5.3.29. NSE Metal Index

The following table exhibits whether semi month effect prevails in NSE Metal index.

Table 5.57: Semi Month Effect – NSE Metal Index

	Mean	Median	Std. Deviation	Variance	Skewness	Kurtosis	Shapiro-Wilk
First half	0.0740	0.0729	0.79079	0.625	-0.257	3.30	0.000
Second half	0.0677	0.0319	0.74755	0.559	0.876	2.38	0.000
Source – Database collected from NSE web portal and computed.							

High mean returns were noticed during the first half of the month (0.0740) and low mean return were found during the second half of the month (0.0677). While comparing the variance, high level of volatility was noticed on the first half of the month (0.625) and low level of volatility was noticed in the second half of the month (0.559).

Result of the Skewness test disclosed that positive value were noticed during the second half of the month (0.876) returns, which implies that most of the second half of the month returns were more than the average returns. The first half of the month (-0.257) returns was noticed negative Skewness, which implies that most of the first half of the month returns were less than the average returns. The Kurtosis results of the NSE Metal index returns were found leptokurtic on First half of the month (3.30). Since, Kurtosis values are greater than 3, thus, it is inferred that the level of risk associated with the NSE Metal sector was high, which means investors may obtain either high level of profit or loss. The second half of the month returns were found platykurtic (2.38). Since, Kurtosis values are less than 3, thus, it is inferred that the level of risk associated with the second half of the month NSE Metal sector was low, which means investors may obtain either low level of profit or loss.

As the calculated P value of the Shapiro-Wilk test is less than 0.01, it is clearly proved that the data are not normally distributed. Hence, anomaly exists in the NSE Metal index returns.

The following table depicts, whether first half and second half returns differ in NSE Metal index.

Table 5.58: Semi Month Effect - NSE Metal Index

	Mean	N	Std. Deviation	Paired t value	P value
First half	.0740	132	.79079	0.75	0.940
Second half	.0677	132	.74755		
Source – Database collected from NSE web portal and computed.					

As the calculated P value is greater than 0.05, it is inferred that NSE Metal index returns does not differ between the first half and the second half of the month.

5.3.30. NSE Pharma Index

The following table exhibits whether semi month effect prevails in NSE Pharma index.

Table 5.59: Semi Month Effect – NSE Pharma Index

	Mean	Median	Std. Deviation	Variance	Skewness	Kurtosis	Shapiro-Wilk
First half	0.1007	0.0939	0.39557	0.156	-0.453	2.341	0.000
Second half	0.0688	0.0749	0.42264	0.179	-0.868	2.500	0.000
Source – Database collected from NSE web portal and computed.							

High mean returns were noticed during the first half of the month (0.1007) and low mean return were found during the second half of the month (0.0688). While comparing the variance, high level of volatility was noticed on the second half of the month (0.179) and low level of volatility was noticed in the first half of the month (0.156).

Result of the Skewness test disclosed that negative value were noticed during both the first half of the month (-0.453) and the second half of the month (-0.868) returns, which implies that most of the first and second half of the month returns were less than the average returns. The Kurtosis results of the NSE Pharma index returns were found platykurtic on both the First half of the month (2.341) and the second half of the month (2.500). Since, Kurtosis values are less than 3, thus, it is inferred that the level of risk associated with the NSE Pharma index was low, which means investors may obtain either low level of profit or loss.

As the calculated P value of the Shapiro-Wilk test is less than 0.01, it is clearly proved that the data are not normally distributed. Hence, anomaly exists in the NSE Pharma index returns.

The following table depicts, whether first half and second half returns differ in NSE Pharma index.

Table 5.60: Semi Month Effect - NSE Pharma Index

	Mean	N	Std. Deviation	Paired t value	P value
First half	.1007	132	.39557	0.75	0.940
Second half	.0688	132	.42264		
Source – Database collected from NSE web portal and computed.					

As the calculated P value is greater than 0.05, it is inferred that NSE Pharma index returns does not differ between the first half and the second half of the month.

5.3.31. NSE Private Banks Index

The following table exhibits whether semi month effect prevails in NSE Private Bank index.

Table 5.61: Semi Month Effect – NSE Private Banks Index

	Mean	Median	Std. Deviation	Variance	Skewness	Kurtosis	Shapiro-Wilk
First half	0.1468	0.191	0.66311	0.440	0.642	5.212	0.000
Second half	0.0849	0.1587	0.67375	0.454	-0.066	1.465	0.000
Source – Database collected from NSE web portal and computed.							

High mean returns were noticed during the first half of the month (0.1468) and low mean return were found during the second half of the month (0.0849). While comparing the variance, high level of volatility was noticed on the second half of the month (0.454) and low level of volatility was noticed in the first half of the month (0.440).

Result of the Skewness test disclosed that positive value were noticed during the first half of the month (0.642) returns, which implies that most of the first half of the month returns were more than the average returns. The second half of the month (-0.066) returns was noticed negative Skewness, which implies that most of the second half of the month returns were less than the average returns. The Kurtosis results of the NSE Private Bank index returns were found leptokurtic on First half of the month (5.212). Since, Kurtosis values are greater than 3, thus, it is inferred that the level of risk associated with the NSE Private Bank sector was high, which means investors may obtain either high level of profit or loss. The second half of the month returns were found platykurtic (1.465). Since, Kurtosis values are less than 3, thus, it is inferred that the level of risk associated with the second half of the month NSE Private Bank sector was low, which means investors may obtain either low level of profit or loss.

As the calculated P value of the Shapiro-Wilk test is less than 0.01, it is clearly proved that the data are not normally distributed. Hence, anomaly exists in the NSE Private Bank index returns.

The following table depicts, whether first half and second half returns differ in NSE Private Bank index.

Table 5.62: Semi Month Effect - NSE Private Banks Index

	Mean	N	Std. Deviation	Paired t value	P value
First half	.1468	120	.66311	0.75	0.940
Second half	.0849	120	.67375		
Source – Database collected from NSE web portal and computed.					

As the calculated P value is greater than 0.05, it is inferred that NSE Private Bank index returns does not differ between the first half and the second half of the month.

5.3.32. NSE Public Sector Unit Banks Index

The following table exhibits whether semi month effect prevails in NSE Public Sector Unit Banks index.

Table 5.63: Semi Month Effect – NSE PSU Banks Index

	Mean	Median	Std. Deviation	Variance	Skewness	Kurtosis	Shapiro-Wilk
First half	0.1023	0.1696	0.69507	0.483	-0.276	2.388	0.000
Second half	0.0423	0.0115	0.7578	0.574	0.370	1.634	0.000
Source – Database collected from NSE web portal and computed.							

High mean returns were noticed during the first half of the month (0.1023) and low mean return were found during the second half of the month (0.0423). While comparing the variance, high level of volatility was noticed on the second half of the month (0.574) and low level of volatility was noticed in the first half of the month (0.483).

Result of the Skewness test disclosed that positive value were noticed during the second half of the month (0.370) returns, which implies that most of the second half of the month returns were more than the average returns. The first half of the month (-0.276) returns was noticed negative Skewness, which implies that most of the first half of the month returns were less than the average returns. The Kurtosis results of the NSE PSU Banks index returns were found platykurtic on both the First half of the month (2.388) and the second half of the month (1.634). Since, Kurtosis values are less than 3, thus, it is inferred that the level of risk associated with the NSE PSU Banks index was low, which means investors may obtain either low level of profit or loss.

As the calculated P value of the Shapiro-Wilk test is less than 0.01, it is clearly proved that the data are not normally distributed. Hence, anomaly exists in the NSE PSU Banks index returns.

The following table depicts, whether first half and second half returns differ in NSE PSU Banks index.

Table 5.64: Semi Month Effect - NSE PSU Banks Index

	Mean	N	Std. Deviation	Paired t value	P value
First half	.1023	132	.69507	0.742	.460
Second half	.0423	132	.75780		
Source – Database collected from NSE web portal and computed.					

As the calculated P value is greater than 0.05, it is inferred that NSE PSU index returns does not differ between the first half and the second half of the month.

5.3.33. NSE Realty Index

The following table exhibits whether semi month effect prevails in NSE Realty index

Table 5.65: Semi Month Effect – NSE Realty Index

	Mean	Median	Std. Deviation	Variance	Skewness	Kurtosis	Shapiro-Wilk
First half	0.0386	0.0138	0.64108	0.411	0.637	6.293	0.000
Second half	-0.1795	-0.201	1.07174	1.149	1.018	4.909	0.000
Source – Database collected from NSE web portal and computed.							

High mean returns were noticed during the first half of the month (0.0386) and low mean return were found during the second half of the month (-0.1795). While comparing the variance, high level of volatility was noticed on the second half of the month (1.149) and low level of volatility was noticed in the first half of the month (0.411).

Result of the Skewness test disclosed that positive value were noticed during both the first half of the month (0.637) and the second half of the month (1.018) returns, which implies that most of the first and second half of the month returns were more than the average returns. The Kurtosis results of the NSE Realty index returns were found leptokurtic on both the First half of the month (6.293) and the second half of the month (4.909). Since, Kurtosis values are more than 3, thus, it is inferred that the level of risk associated with the NSE Realty index was high, which means investors may obtain either high level of profit or loss.

As the calculated P value of the Shapiro-Wilk test is less than 0.01, it is clearly proved that the data are not normally distributed. Hence, anomaly exists in the NSE Realty index returns.

The following table depicts, whether first half and second half returns differ in NSE Realty index.

Table 5.66: Semi Month Effect - NSE Realty Index

	Mean	N	Std. Deviation	Paired t value	P value
First half	.0386	99	.64108	2.021	.041
Second half	-.1795	99	1.07174		

Source – Database collected from NSE web portal and computed.

As the calculated P value is less than 0.05, it is inferred that NSE Realty index returns differs between the first half and the second half of the month.

5.4. Conclusion

From the analysis, it is inferred that the semi month effect exists in all BSE Sensex, 19 BSE sectoral indices, NSE Nifty and 12 NSE sectoral indices. As far as semi month effect is concerned, High level return is noticed on second half of the month and low level of return noticed on first half of the month for BSE Sensex and NSE Nifty Index. Hence, investors are advised to buy BSE Sensex and NSE Nifty shares on First half of the month and to sell during second half of the month. The next chapter discuss about Turn of the month effect.

CHAPTER VI

TURN OF THE MONTH EFFECT IN INDIAN STOCK MARKET

6.1. Introduction

The trend of stock prices to increase during the last two days and the first three days of each month, is called Turn of the Month Effect. For the purpose of this study, the average return on the last two trading days of the preceding month, and the first three days of the subsequent month were computed and compared with the mean return for the rest of the days in the subsequent month.

Some analysts credit the turn of the month effect to distributions from pension funds and other retirement accounts that the pensioners immediately reinvest in the stock market.

6.2. Tools for Analysis

The collected data have been analysed by making use of Returns, Descriptive statistics such as Mean, Standard Deviation, Variance, Skewness, Kurtosis, Shapiro-Wilk test and paired 't' test.

6.3. Turn of the Month Effect

The following subsections discuss about the Turn of the month effect of BSE Sensex, 19 BSE sectoral indices, followed by NSE Nifty and 12 NSE sectoral indices.

6.3.1. BSE Sensex Index

The following table exhibits whether Turn of the month effect prevails in BSE Sensex index.

Table 6.1: Turn of the Month Effect – BSE Sensex Index

	Mean	Std. Deviation	Variance	Skewness	Kurtosis	Shapiro-Wilk
First Half	0.1982	0.68205	0.465	-0.774	2.048	0.000
Rest of the Month	-0.0012	0.42159	0.178	-0.793	5.091	0.000
Source – Database collected from BSE web portal and computed.						

High mean returns were noticed during the First half of the month (0.1982) and low mean returns were found during the rest of the month (-0.0012). While comparing the variance, high level of volatility was noticed on the First half of the month (0.465) and low level of volatility was noticed in rest of the month (0.178). Result of the Skewness test disclosed that negative returns were noticed in the First half of the month and rest of the month returns, which implies that most of the First and rest of the month returns were less than the average returns. The

Kurtosis results of the BSE Sensex return were found platykurtic in the first half of the month (2.048). Since, Kurtosis values are less than 3, thus, it is inferred that the level of risk associated with the first half of the month returns of the BSE Sensex was low, which means investors may obtain either low level of profit or loss. The rest of the month return were found leptokurtic (5.091). Since, Kurtosis values are greater than 3, thus, it is inferred that the level of risk associated with the rest of the month returns of the BSE Sensex index was low, which means investors may obtain either low level of profit or loss.

As the calculated P value of the Shapiro-Wilk test is less than 0.01, it is clearly proved that the data are not normally distributed. Hence, anomaly exists in the BSE Sensex returns.

The following table depicts, whether first half and rest of the month returns differ in BSE Sensex.

Table 6.2: Turn of the Month Effect – BSE Sensex Index

	Mean	N	Std. Deviation	Paired t value	P value
First Half	.1982	132	.68205	2.891	.004
Rest of the Month	-.0012	132	.42159		

Source – Database collected from BSE web portal and computed.

6.3.2. *BSE Auto Index*

The following table exhibits whether Turn of the month effect prevails in BSE Auto index.

Table 6.3: Turn of the Month Effect – BSE Auto Index

	Mean	Std. Deviation	Variance	Skewness	Kurtosis	Shapiro-Wilk
First Half	0.2651	0.79374	0.630	-1.041	2.262	0.000
Rest of the Month	0.0001	0.46714	0.218	-1.122	6.974	0.000

Source – Database collected from BSE web portal and computed.

High mean returns were noticed during the First half of the month (0.2651) and low mean returns were found during the rest of the month (0.0001). While comparing the variance, high level of volatility was noticed on the First half of the month (0.630) and low level of volatility was noticed in rest of the month (0.218).

Result of the Skewness test disclosed that negative returns were noticed in the First half of the month and rest of the month returns, which implies that most of the First half of the month and rest of the month returns were less than the average returns. The Kurtosis results of the BSE Auto index returns were found platykurtic in the first half of the month (2.262). Since, Kurtosis values are less than 3, thus, it is inferred that the level of risk associated with the first half of the month returns of the BSE Automobile sector was low, which means investors may obtain either low level of profit or loss. The rest of the month return were found leptokurtic (6.974). Since, Kurtosis values are greater than 3, thus, it is inferred that the level of risk associated with the rest of the month returns of the BSE Automobile sector was high, which means investors may obtain either high level of profit or loss.

As the calculated P value of the Shapiro-Wilk test is less than 0.01, it is clearly proved that the data are not normally distributed. Hence, anomaly exists in the BSE Auto index returns.

The following table depicts, whether first half and rest of the month returns differ in BSE Auto index.

Table 6.4: Turn of the Month Effect – BSE Auto Index

	Mean	N	Std. Deviation	Paired t value	P value
First Half	0.2651	132	0.79374	3.279	0.001
Rest of the Month	0.0001	132	0.46714		
Source – Database collected from BSE web portal and computed.					

As the calculated P value is less than 0.01, it is inferred that BSE Auto index returns differs between the first half and rest of the month.

6.3.3. BSE Bank Index

The following table exhibits whether Turn of the month effect prevails in BSE Bank index

Table 6.5: Turn of the Month Effect – BSE Bank Index

	Mean	Std. Deviation	Variance	Skewness	Kurtosis	Shapiro-Wilk
First Half	0.2426	0.95272	0.908	-0.375	1.859	0.000
Rest of the Month	-0.01	0.61157	0.374	-0.277	1.004	0.000
Source – Database collected from BSE web portal and computed.						

High mean returns were noticed during the First half of the month (0.2426) and low mean returns were found during the rest of the month (-0.0100). While comparing the variance, high level of volatility was noticed on the First half of the month (0.908) and low level of volatility was noticed in rest of the month (0.374).

Result of the Skewness test disclosed that negative returns were noticed in the First half of the month and rest of the month returns, which implies that most of the First half of the month and rest of the month returns were less than the average returns. The Kurtosis results of the BSE Bank index returns were found platykurtic in both the First half of the month (1.859) and the rest of the month (1.004). Since, Kurtosis values are less than 3, thus, it is inferred that the level of risk associated with the first half of the month and rest of the month returns of the BSE Bank index was low, which means investors may obtain either low level of profit or loss.

As the calculated P value of the Shapiro-Wilk test is less than 0.01, it is clearly proved that the data are not normally distributed. Hence, anomaly exists in the BSE Bank index returns.

The following table depicts, whether first half and rest of the month returns differ in BSE Bank Index.

Table 6.6: Turn of the Month Effect – BSE Bank Index

	Mean	N	Std. Deviation	Paired t value	P value
First Half	.2426	132	.95272	2.448	0.016
Rest of the Month	-.0100	132	.61157		

Source – Database collected from BSE web portal and computed.

As the calculated P value is less than 0.05, it is inferred that BSE Bank index returns differs between the first half and rest of the month.

6.3.4. BSE Basic Materials Index

The following table exhibits whether Turn of the month effect prevails in BSE Basic Materials index.

Table 6.7: Turn of the Month Effect – BSE Basic Materials Index

	Mean	Std. Deviation	Variance	Skewness	Kurtosis	Shapiro-Wilk
First Half	-0.0072	1.02817	1.057	-0.055	4.838	0.000
Rest of the Month	0.0708	0.58574	0.343	-1.054	8.308	0.000

Source – Database collected from BSE web portal and computed.

High mean returns were noticed during the Rest of the month (0.0708) and low mean returns were found during the First half of the month (-0.0072). While comparing the variance, high level of volatility was noticed on the First half of the month (1.057) and low level of volatility was noticed in rest of the month (0.343).

Result of the Skewness test disclosed that negative returns were noticed in the First half of the month and rest of the month returns, which implies that most of the First half of the month and rest of the month returns were less than the average returns. The Kurtosis results of the BSE Basic Materials index returns were found leptokurtic in both the First half of the month (4.838) and rest of the month (8.308). Since, Kurtosis values are greater than 3, thus, it is inferred that the level of risk associated with the first half of the month and rest of the returns of the BSE Basic Materials index was high, which means investors may obtain either high level of profit or loss.

As the calculated P value of the Shapiro-Wilk test is less than 0.01, it is clearly proved that the data are not normally distributed. Hence, anomaly exists in the BSE Basic Materials index returns.

The following table depicts, whether first half and rest of the month returns differ in BSE Basic Materials Index.

Table 6.8: Turn of the Month Effect – BSE Basic Materials Index

	Mean	**N**	**Std. Deviation**	**Paired t value**	**P value**
First Half	-.0072	114	1.02817	-.718	0.474
Rest of the Month	.0708	114	0.58574		
Source – Database collected from BSE web portal and computed.					

As the calculated P value is greater than 0.05, it is inferred that BSE Basic Materials index returns does not differ between the first half and the rest of the month.

6.3.5. BSE Consumer Durables Index

The following table exhibits whether Turn of the month effect prevails in BSE Consumer Durables index.

Table 6.9: Turn of the Month Effect – BSE Consumer Durables Index

	Mean	**Std. Deviation**	**Variance**	**Skewness**	**Kurtosis**	**Shapiro-Wilk**
First Half	0.3164	0.95482	0.912	-0.397	2.844	0.000
Rest of the Month	-0.0113	0.54577	0.298	-0.326	2.042	0.000
Source – Database collected from BSE web portal and computed.						

High mean returns were noticed during the First half of the month (0.3164) and low mean returns were found during the rest of the month (-0.0113). While comparing the variance, high level of volatility was noticed on the First half of the month (0.912) and low level of volatility was noticed in rest of the month (0.298).

Result of the Skewness test disclosed that negative returns were noticed in the First half of the month and rest of the month returns, which implies that most of the First half of the month and rest of the month returns were less than the average returns. The Kurtosis results of the BSE Consumer Durables index returns were found platykurtic in both the First half of the month (2.844) and rest of the month (2.042). Since, Kurtosis values are less than 3, thus, it is inferred that the level of risk associated with the first half of the month and rest of the month returns of the BSE Consumer Durables sector was low, which means investors may obtain either low level of profit or loss.

As the calculated P value of the Shapiro-Wilk test is less than 0.01, it is clearly proved that the data are not normally distributed. Hence, anomaly exists in the BSE Consumer Durables index returns.

The following table depicts, whether first half and rest of the month returns differ in BSE Consumer Durables Index.

Table 6.10: Turn of the Month Effect – BSE Consumer Durables Index

	Mean	N	Std. Deviation	Paired t value	P value
First Half	.3164	132	.95482	3.666	0.000
Rest of the Month	-.0113	132	.54577		
Source – Database collected from BSE web portal and computed.					

As the calculated P value is less than 0.01, it is inferred that BSE Consumer Durables index returns differs between the first half and rest of the month.

6.3.6. BSE Consumer Goods Index

The following table exhibits whether Turn of the month effect prevails in BSE Consumer Goods index.

Table 6.11: Turn of the Month Effect – BSE Consumer Goods Index

	Mean	Std. Deviation	Variance	Skewness	Kurtosis	Shapiro-Wilk
First Half	0.2363	0.85578	0.732	-0.761	1.247	0.000
Rest of the Month	-0.0012	0.58387	0.341	-0.006	1.69	0.000
Source – Database collected from BSE web portal and computed.						

High mean returns were noticed during the First half of the month (0.2363) and low mean returns were found during the rest of the month (-0.0012). While comparing the variance, high level of volatility was noticed on the First half of the month (0.732) and low level of volatility was noticed in rest of the month (0.341).

Result of the Skewness test disclosed that negative returns were noticed in the First half of the month and rest of the month returns, which implies that most of the First half of the month and rest of the month returns were less than the average returns. The Kurtosis results of the BSE Consumer Goods index returns were found platykurtic in both the First half of the month (1.247) and rest of the month (1.690). Since, Kurtosis values are less than 3, thus, it is inferred that the level of risk associated with the first half of the month returns and rest of the month of the BSE Consumer Goods sector was low, which means investors may obtain either low level of profit or loss.

As the calculated P value of the Shapiro-Wilk test is less than 0.01, it is clearly proved that the data are not normally distributed. Hence, anomaly exists in the BSE Consumer Goods index returns.

The following table depicts, whether first half and rest of the month returns differ in BSE Consumer Goods Index.

Table 6.12: Turn of the Month Effect – BSE Consumer Goods Index

	Mean	N	Std. Deviation	Paired t value	P value
First Half	.2363	132	.85578	2.701	.008
Rest of the Month	-.0012	132	.58387		
Source – Database collected from BSE web portal and computed.					

As the calculated P value is less than 0.01, it is inferred that BSE Consumer Goods index returns differs between the first half and rest of the month.

6.3.7. *BSE Energy Index*

The following table exhibits whether Turn of the month effect prevails in BSE Energy index.

Table 6.13: Turn of the Month Effect – BSE Energy Index

	Mean	Std. Deviation	Variance	Skewness	Kurtosis	Shapiro-Wilk
First Half	-0.0685	0.94327	0.89	-1.077	7.717	0.000
Rest of the Month	0.0494	0.4858	0.236	-0.495	4.221	0.000
Source – Database collected from BSE web portal and computed.						

High mean returns were noticed during the rest of the month (0.0494) and low mean returns were found during the first half of the month (-0.0685). While comparing the variance, high level of volatility was noticed on the First half of the month (0.890) and low level of volatility was noticed in rest of the month (0.236).

Result of the Skewness test disclosed that negative returns were noticed in the First half of the month and rest of the month returns, which implies that most of the First half of the month and rest of the month returns were less than the average returns. The Kurtosis results of the BSE Energy index returns were found leptokurtic in both the First half of the month (7.717) and the rest of the month (4.221). Since, Kurtosis values are greater than 3, thus, it is inferred that the level of risk associated with the first half of the month and rest of the month returns of the BSE Energy sector was high, which means investors may obtain either high level of profit or loss.

As the calculated P value of the Shapiro-Wilk test is less than 0.01, it is clearly proved that the data are not normally distributed. Hence, anomaly exists in the BSE Energy index returns.

The following table depicts, whether first half and rest of the month returns differ in BSE Energy Index.

Table 6.14: Turn of the Month Effect – BSE Energy Index

	Mean	N	Std. Deviation	Paired t value	P value
First Half	-.0685	114	.94327	-1.199	0.233
Rest of the Month	.0494	114	.48580		
Source – Database collected from BSE web portal and computed.					

As the calculated P value is greater than 0.05, it is inferred that BSE Energy index returns does not differ between the first half and the rest of the month.

6.3.8. BSE Finance Index

The following table exhibits whether Turn of the month effect prevails in BSE Finance index.

Table 6.15: Turn of the Month Effect – BSE Finance Index

	Mean	Std. Deviation	Variance	Skewness	Kurtosis	Shapiro-Wilk
First Half	-0.0845	1.02041	1.041	-1.132	3.485	0.000
Rest of the Month	0.0416	0.77135	0.595	-3.323	22.62	0.000
Source – Database collected from BSE web portal and computed.						

High mean returns were noticed during the rest of the month (0.0416) and low mean returns were found during the first half of the month (-0.0845). While comparing the variance, high level of volatility was noticed on the First half of the month (1.041) and low level of volatility was noticed in rest of the month (0.595).

Result of the Skewness test disclosed that negative returns were noticed in the First half of the month and rest of the month returns, which implies that most of the First half of the month and rest of the month returns were less than the average returns. The Kurtosis results of the BSE Finance index returns were found leptokurtic in both the First half of the month (3.485) and the rest of the month (22.620). Since, Kurtosis values are greater than 3, thus, it is inferred that the level of risk associated with the first half of the month and rest of the month returns of the BSE Finance sector was high, which means investors may obtain either high level of profit or loss.

As the calculated P value of the Shapiro-Wilk test is less than 0.01, it is clearly proved that the data are not normally distributed. Hence, anomaly exists in the BSE Finance index returns.

The following table depicts, whether first half and rest of the month returns differ in BSE Finance Index.

Table 6.16: Turn of the Month Effect – BSE Finance Index

	Mean	N	Std. Deviation	Paired t value	P value
First Half	-.0845	114	1.02041	-1.024	0.308
Rest of the Month	.0416	114	.77135		
Source – Database collected from BSE web portal and computed.					

As the calculated P value is greater than 0.05, it is inferred that BSE Finance index returns does not differ between the first half and the rest of the month.

6.3.9. *BSE Fast Moving Consumer Goods Index*

The following table exhibits whether Turn of the month effect prevails in BSE FMCG index.

Table 6.17: Turn of the Month Effect – BSE Fast Moving Consumer Goods Index

	Mean	Std. Deviation	Variance	Skewness	Kurtosis	Shapiro-Wilk
First Half	0.0697	0.62008	0.384	-1.407	6.675	0.000
Rest of the Month	0.0488	0.3322	0.11	-0.609	0.896	0.000
Source – Database collected from BSE web portal and computed.						

High mean returns were noticed during the First half of the month (0.0697) and low mean returns were found during the rest of the month (0.0488). While comparing the variance, high level of volatility was noticed on the First half of the month (0.384) and low level of volatility was noticed in rest of the month (0.110).

Result of the Skewness test disclosed that negative returns were noticed in the First half of the month and rest of the month returns, which implies that most of the First half of the month and rest of the month returns were less than the average returns. The Kurtosis results of the BSE FMCG index returns were found leptokurtic in the First half of the month (6.675). Since, Kurtosis values are greater than 3, thus, it is inferred that the level of risk associated with the First half of the month returns of the BSE FMCG sector was high, which means investors may obtain either high level of profit or loss. The rest of the month return were found platykurtic (0.896). Since, Kurtosis values are less than 3, thus, it is inferred that the level of risk associated with the rest of the month returns of the BSE FMCG sector was low, which means investors may obtain either low level of profit or loss.

As the calculated P value of the Shapiro-Wilk test is less than 0.01, it is clearly proved that the data are not normally distributed. Hence, anomaly exists in the BSE FMCG index returns.

The following table depicts, whether first half and rest of the month returns differ in BSE FMCG Index.

Table 6.18: Turn of the Month Effect - BSE Fast Moving Consumer Goods Index

	Mean	N	Std. Deviation	Paired t value	P value
First Half	.0697	114	.62008	0.328	0.774
Rest of the Month	.0488	114	.33220		

Source - Database collected from BSE web portal and computed.

As the calculated P value is greater than 0.05, it is inferred that BSE FMCG index returns does not differ between the first half and the rest of the month.

6.3.10. BSE Health Care Index

The following table exhibits whether Turn of the month effect prevails in BSE Health Care index.

Table 6.19: Turn of the Month Effect - BSE Healthcare Index

	Mean	Std. Deviation	Variance	Skewness	Kurtosis	Shapiro-Wilk
First Half	0.093	0.64815	0.42	-1.63	8.253	0.000
Rest of the Month	0.0598	0.34093	0.116	-0.405	3.538	0.000

Source - Database collected from BSE web portal and computed.

High mean returns were noticed during the First half of the month (0.0930) and low mean returns were found during the rest of the month (0.0598). While comparing the variance, high level of volatility was noticed on the First half of the month (0.420) and low level of volatility was noticed in rest of the month (0.116).

Result of the Skewness test disclosed that negative returns were noticed in the First half of the month and rest of the month returns, which implies that most of the First half of the month and rest of the month returns were less than the average returns. The Kurtosis results of the BSE Health Care index returns were found leptokurtic in both the First half of the month (8.253) and the rest of the month (3.538). Since, Kurtosis values are greater than 3, thus, it is inferred that the level of risk associated with the first half of the month and rest of the month returns of the BSE Health Care sector was high, which means investors may obtain either high level of profit or loss.

As the calculated P value of the Shapiro-Wilk test is less than 0.01, it is clearly proved that the data are not normally distributed. Hence, anomaly exists BSE Health Care index returns.

The following table depicts, whether first half and rest of the month returns differ in BSE Health Care Index.

Table 6.20: Turn of the Month Effect – BSE Healthcare Index

	Mean	N	Std. Deviation	Paired t value	P value
First Half	.0930	114	.64815	0.493	0.623
Rest of the Month	.0598	114	.34093		

Source – Database collected from BSE web portal and computed.

As the calculated P value is greater than 0.05, it is inferred that BSE Health Care index returns does not differ between the first half and the rest of the month.

6.3.11. BSE IT Index

The following table exhibits whether Turn of the month effect prevails in BSE IT index.

Table 6.21: Turn of the Month Effect – BSE IT Index

	Mean	Std. Deviation	Variance	Skewness	Kurtosis	Shapiro-Wilk
First Half	0.0589	0.55713	0.31	-0.333	1.647	0.000
Rest of the Month	0.0283	0.4574	0.209	-0.913	2.208	0.000

Source – Database collected from BSE web portal and computed.

High mean returns were noticed during the First half of the month (0.0589) and low mean returns were found during the rest of the month (0.0283). While comparing the variance, high level of volatility was noticed on the First half of the month (0.310) and low level of volatility was noticed in rest of the month (0.209).

Result of the Skewness test disclosed that negative returns were noticed in the First half of the month and rest of the month returns, which implies that most of the First half of the month and rest of the month returns were less than the average returns. The Kurtosis results of the BSE IT index returns were found platykurtic in both the First half of the month (1.647) and the rest of the month (2.208). Since, Kurtosis values are less than 3, thus, it is inferred that the level of risk associated with the first half of the month and rest of the month returns of the BSE IT sector was low, which means investors may obtain either low level of profit or loss.

As the calculated P value of the Shapiro-Wilk test is less than 0.01, it is clearly proved that the data are not normally distributed. Hence, anomaly exists in the BSE IT index returns.

The following table depicts, whether first half and rest of the month returns differ in BSE IT Index.

Table 6.22: Turn of the Month Effect – BSE IT Index

	Mean	N	Std. Deviation	Paired t value	P value
First Half	.0589	114	.55713	0.464	0.644
Rest of the Month	.0283	114	.45740		

Source – Database collected from BSE web portal and computed.

As the calculated P value is greater than 0.05, it is inferred that BSE IT index returns does not differ between the first half and the rest of the month.

6.3.12. BSE Industrial Index

The following table exhibits whether Turn of the month effect prevails in BSE Industrial index.

Table 6.23: Turn of the Month Effect – BSE Industrial Index

	Mean	Std. Deviation	Variance	Skewness	Kurtosis	Shapiro-Wilk
First Half	-0.039	1.05922	1.122	-1.518	7.526	0.000
Rest of the Month	0.0379	0.70193	0.493	-1.215	4.804	0.000

Source – Database collected from BSE web portal and computed.

High mean returns were noticed during the rest of the month (0.0379) and low mean returns were found during the first half of the month (-0.0390). While comparing the variance, high level of volatility was noticed on the First half of the month (1. 122) and low level of volatility was noticed in rest of the month (0.493).

Result of the Skewness test disclosed that negative returns were noticed in the First half of the month and rest of the month returns, which implies that most of the first half of the month and rest of the month returns were less than the average returns. The Kurtosis results of the BSE Industrial index returns were found leptokurtic in both the First half of the month (7.526) and the rest of the month (4.804). Since, Kurtosis values are greater than 3, thus, it is inferred that the level of risk associated with the first of the month and rest of the month returns of the BSE Industrial sector was high, which means investors may obtain either high level of profit or loss.

As the calculated P value of the Shapiro-Wilk test is less than 0.01, it is clearly proved that the data are not normally distributed. Hence, anomaly exists in the BSE Industrial index returns. The following table depicts, whether first half and rest of the month returns differ in BSE Industrial Index.

Table 6.24: Turn of the Month Effect – BSE Industrial Index

	Mean	N	Std. Deviation	Paired t value	P value
First Half	-.0390	114	1.05922	-0.630	0.530
Rest of the Month	.0379	114	.70193		
Source – Database collected from BSE web portal and computed.					

As the calculated P value is greater than 0.05, it is inferred that BSE Industrial index returns does not differ between the first half and the rest of the month.

6.3.13. BSE Metal Index

The following table exhibits whether Turn of the month effect prevails in BSE Metal index.

Table 6.25: Turn of the Month Effect – BSE Metal Index

	Mean	Std. Deviation	Variance	Skewness	Kurtosis	Shapiro-Wilk
First Half	0.2495	1.06839	1.141	-0.712	3.365	0.000
Rest of the Month	-0.0733	0.72833	0.53	-0.783	4.367	0.000
Source – Database collected from BSE web portal and computed.						

High mean returns were noticed during the First half of the month (0.2495) and low mean returns were found during the rest of the month (-0.0733). While comparing the variance, high level of volatility was noticed on the First half of the month (1.141) and low level of volatility was noticed in rest of the month (0.530).

Result of the Skewness test disclosed that negative returns were noticed in the First half of the month and rest of the month returns, which implies that most of the First half of the month and rest of the month returns were less than the average returns. The Kurtosis results of the BSE Metal index returns were found leptokurtic in both the First half of the month (3.365) and the rest of the month (4.367). Since, Kurtosis values are greater than 3, thus, it is inferred that the level of risk associated with the first half of the month and rest of the month returns of the BSE Metal sector was high, which means investors may obtain either high level of profit or loss.

As the calculated P value of the Shapiro-Wilk test is less than 0.01, it is clearly proved that the data are not normally distributed. Hence, anomaly exists in the BSE Metal index returns.

The following table depicts, whether first half and rest of the month returns differ in BSE Metal Index.

Table 6.26: Turn of the Month Effect – BSE Metal Index

	Mean	N	Std. Deviation	Paired t value	P value
First Half	.2495	132	1.06839	3.038	0.003
Rest of the Month	-.0733	132	.72833		
Source – Database collected from BSE web portal and computed.					

As the calculated P value is less than 0.01, it is inferred that BSE Metal index returns differs between the first half and rest of the month.

6.3.14. BSE Oil and Gas Index

The following table exhibits whether Turn of the month effect prevails in BSE Oil and Gas index.

Table 6.27: Turn of the Month Effect – BSE Oil and Gas Index

	Mean	Std. Deviation	Variance	Skewness	Kurtosis	Shapiro-Wilk
First Half	0.2049	0.73638	0.542	-0.763	2.312	0.000
Rest of the Month	-0.0361	0.52428	0.275	-1.16	8.27	0.000
Source – Database collected from BSE web portal and computed.						

High mean returns were noticed during the First half of the month (0.2049) and low mean returns were found during the rest of the month (-0.0361). While comparing the variance, high level of volatility was noticed on the First half of the month (0.542) and low level of volatility was noticed in rest of the month (0.275).

Result of the Skewness test disclosed that negative returns were noticed in the First half of the month and rest of the month returns, which implies that most of the First half of the month and rest of the month returns were less than the average returns. The Kurtosis results of the BSE Oil and Gas index returns were found platykurtic in the First half of the month (2.312). Since, Kurtosis values are less than 3, thus, it is inferred that the level of risk associated with the first half of the month returns of the BSE Oil and Gas sector was low, which means investors may obtain either low level of profit or loss. The rest of the month return were found leptokurtic (8.270). Since, Kurtosis values are greater than 3, thus, it is inferred that the level of risk associated with the rest of the month returns of the BSE Oil and Gas sector was high, which means investors may obtain either high level of profit or loss.

As the calculated P value of the Shapiro-Wilk test is less than 0.01, it is clearly proved that the data are not normally distributed. Hence, anomaly exists in the BSE Oil and Gas index returns.

The following table depicts, whether first half and rest of the month returns differ in BSE Oil and Gas Index.

Table 6.28: Turn of the Month Effect – BSE Oil and Gas Index

	Mean	N	Std. Deviation	Paired t value	P value
First Half	.2049	132	.73638	3.151	0.002
Rest of the Month	-.0361	132	.52428		
Source – Database collected from BSE web portal and computed.					

As the calculated P value is less than 0.01, it is inferred that BSE Oil and Gas index returns differs between the first half and rest of the month.

6.3.15. BSE Power Index

The following table exhibits whether Turn of the month effect prevails in BSE Power index.

Table 6.29: Turn of the Month Effect – BSE Power Index

	Mean	Std. Deviation	Variance	Skewness	Kurtosis	Shapiro-Wilk
First Half	0.2042	1.06051	1.125	0.096	2.691	0.000
Rest of the Month	-0.0126	0.67904	0.461	-0.559	7.861	0.000
Source – Database collected from BSE web portal and computed.						

High mean returns were noticed during the First half of the month (0.2042) and low mean returns were found during the rest of the month (-0.0126). While comparing the variance, high level of volatility was noticed on the First half of the month (1.125) and low level of volatility was noticed in rest of the month (0.461).

Result of the Skewness test disclosed that positive returns were noticed in the first half of the month returns, which implies that most of the first half of the month returns were more than the average returns. The rest of the month returns found negative Skewness, which implies that rest of the month returns were less than the average returns. The Kurtosis results of the BSE Power index returns were found leptokurtic in the rest of the month (7.861). Since, Kurtosis values are greater than 3, thus, it is inferred that the level of risk associated with the rest of the month returns of the BSE Power sector was high, which means investors may obtain either high level of profit or loss. The first half of the month return were found platykurtic (2.691). Since, Kurtosis values are less than 3, thus, it is inferred that the level of risk associated with the first half of the month returns of the BSE Power sector was low, which means investors may obtain either low level of profit or loss.

As the calculated P value of the Shapiro-Wilk test is less than 0.01, it is clearly proved that the data are not normally distributed. Hence, anomaly exists in the BSE Power index returns.

The following table depicts, whether first half and rest of the month returns differ in BSE Power Index.

Table 6.30: Turn of the Month Effect – BSE Power Index

	Mean	N	Std. Deviation	Paired t value	P value
First Half	.2042	123	1.06051	2.003	0.047
Rest of the Month	-.0126	123	.67904		
Source – Database collected from BSE web portal and computed.					

As the calculated P value is less than 0.05, it is inferred that BSE Power index returns differs between the first half and rest of the month.

6.3.16. BSE Public Sector Unit Index

The following table exhibits whether Turn of the month effect prevails in BSE PSU index.

Table 6.31: Turn of the Month Effect – BSE PSU Index

	Mean	**Std. Deviation**	**Variance**	**Skewness**	**Kurtosis**	**Shapiro-Wilk**
First Half	0.2394	0.72143	0.52	-0.635	1.269	0.000
Rest of the Month	-0.0572	0.515	0.265	-0.412	4.075	0.000
Source – Database collected from BSE web portal and computed.						

High mean returns were noticed during the First half of the month (0.2394) and low mean returns were found during the rest of the month (-0.0572). While comparing the variance, high level of volatility was noticed on the First half of the month (0.520) and low level of volatility was noticed in rest of the month (0.265).

Result of the Skewness test disclosed that negative returns were noticed in the First half of the month and rest of the month returns, which implies that most of the First half of the month and rest of the month returns were less than the average returns. The Kurtosis results of the BSE PSU index returns were found platykurtic in the First half of the month (1.269). Since, Kurtosis values are less than 3, thus, it is inferred that the level of risk associated with the first half of the month returns of the BSE PSU sector was low, which means investors may obtain either low level of profit or loss. The rest of the month return were found leptokurtic (4.075). Since, Kurtosis values are greater than 3, thus, it is inferred that the level of risk associated with the rest of the month returns of the BSE PSU sector was high, which means investors may obtain either high level of profit or loss.

As the calculated P value of the Shapiro-Wilk test is less than 0.01, it is clearly proved that the data are not normally distributed. Hence, anomaly exists in the BSE PSU index returns.

The following table depicts, whether first half and rest of the month returns differ in BSE PSU Index.

Table 6.32: Turn of the Month Effect – BSE PSU Index

	Mean	N	Std. Deviation	Paired t value	P value
First Half	.2394	132	.85578	3.803	.000
Rest of the Month	-.0572	132	.58387		
Source – Database collected from BSE web portal and computed.					

As the calculated P value is less than 0.01, it is inferred that BSE PSU index returns differs between the first half and rest of the month.

6.3.17. BSE Realty Index

The following table exhibits whether Turn of the month effect prevails in BSE Realty index.

Table 6.33: Turn of the Month Effect – BSE Realty Index

	Mean	Std. Deviation	Variance	Skewness	Kurtosis	Shapiro-Wilk
First Half	0.2743	1.36699	1.869	-0.857	1.256	0.000
Rest of the Month	-0.1608	0.9806	0.962	0.001	0.967	0.000
Source – Database collected from BSE web portal and computed.						

High mean returns were noticed during the First half of the month (0.2743) and low mean returns were found during the rest of the month (-0.1608). While comparing the variance, high level of volatility was noticed on the First half of the month (1.869) and low level of volatility was noticed in rest of the month (0.962).

Result of the Skewness test disclosed that negative returns were noticed in the first half of the month returns, which implies that most of the first half of the month returns were less than the average returns and the rest of the month returns found positive Skewness, which implies that rest of the month returns were more than the average returns. The Kurtosis results of the BSE Realty index returns were found platykurtic in both the First half of the month (1.256) and the rest of the month (0.967). Since, Kurtosis values are less than 3, thus, it is inferred that the level of risk associated with the first half of the month and rest of the month returns of the BSE Realty sector was low, which means investors may obtain either low level of profit or loss.

As the calculated P value of the Shapiro-Wilk test is less than 0.01, it is clearly proved that the data are not normally distributed. Hence, anomaly exists in the BSE Realty index returns.

The following table depicts, whether first half and rest of the month returns differ in BSE Realty Index.

Table 6.34: Turn of the Month Effect – BSE Realty Index

	Mean	N	Std. Deviation	Paired t value	P value
First Half	.2743	108	1.36699	2.666	0.009
Rest of the Month	-.1608	108	.98060		
Source – Database collected from BSE web portal and computed.					

As the calculated P value is less than 0.01, it is inferred that BSE Realty index returns differs between the first half and rest of the month.

6.3.18. BSE Teck Index

The following table exhibits whether Turn of the month effect prevails in BSE Teck index.

Table 6.35: Turn of the Month Effect – BSE Teck Index

	Mean	Std. Deviation	Variance	Skewness	Kurtosis	Shapiro-Wilk
First Half	0.2127	0.61805	0.382	-0.954	1.826	0.000
Rest of the Month	-0.0056	0.38327	0.147	-0.668	1.082	0.000
Source – Database collected from BSE web portal and computed.						

High mean returns were noticed during the First half of the month (0.2127) and low mean returns were found during the rest of the month (-0.0056). While comparing the variance, high level of volatility was noticed on the First half of the month (0.382) and low level of volatility was noticed in rest of the month (0.147).

Result of the Skewness test disclosed that negative returns were noticed in the First half of the month and rest of the month returns, which implies that most of the First half of the month and rest of the month returns were less than the average returns. The Kurtosis results of the BSE TECK index returns were found platykurtic in both the First half of the month (1.826) and the rest of the month (1.082). Since, Kurtosis values are less than 3, thus, it is inferred that the level of risk associated with the first half of the month and rest of the month returns of the BSE Teck sector was low, which means investors may obtain either low level of profit or loss.

As the calculated P value of the Shapiro-Wilk test is less than 0.01, it is clearly proved that the data are not normally distributed. Hence, anomaly exists in the BSE Teck index returns.

The following table depicts, whether first half and rest of the month returns differ in BSE Teck Index.

Table 6.36: Turn of the Month Effect – BSE Teck Index

	Mean	N	Std. Deviation	Paired t value	P value
First Half	.2127	132	.61805	3.571	.000
Rest of the Month	-.0056	132	.38327		
Source – Database collected from BSE web portal and computed.					

As the calculated P value is less than 0.01, it is inferred that BSE Teck index returns differs between the first half and rest of the month.

6.3.19. BSE Telecom Index

The following table exhibits whether Turn of the month effect prevails in BSE Telecom index.

Table 6.37: Turn of the Month Effect – BSE Telecom Index

	Mean	Std. Deviation	Variance	Skewness	Kurtosis	Shapiro-Wilk
First Half	-0.0256	0.94045	0.884	-0.595	2.194	0.000
Rest of the Month	0.0332	0.6257	0.392	-0.167	3.75	0.000
Source – Database collected from BSE web portal and computed.						

High mean returns were noticed during the rest of the month (0.0332) and low mean returns were found during the first half of the month (-0.0256). While comparing the variance, high level of volatility was noticed on the First half of the month (0.884) and low level of volatility was noticed in rest of the month (0.392).

Result of the Skewness test disclosed that negative returns were noticed in the First half of the month and rest of the month returns, which implies that most of the First half of the month and rest of the month returns were less than the average returns. The Kurtosis results of the BSE Telecom index returns were found leptokurtic in the rest of the month (3.750). Since, Kurtosis values are greater than 3, thus, it is inferred that the level of risk associated with the rest of the month returns of the BSE Telecom sector was high, which means investors may obtain either high level of profit or loss. The first half of the month return were found platykurtic (2.194). Since, Kurtosis values are less than 3, thus, it is inferred that the level of risk associated with the first half of the month returns of the BSE Telecom sector was low, which means investors may obtain either low level of profit or loss.

As the calculated P value of the Shapiro-Wilk test is less than 0.01, it is clearly proved that the data are not normally distributed. Hence, anomaly exists in the BSE Telecom index returns.

The following table depicts, whether first half and rest of the month returns differ in BSE Telecom Index.

Table 6.38: Turn of the Month Effect – BSE Telecom Index

	Mean	N	Std. Deviation	Paired t value	P value
First Half	-.0256	114	.94045	-0.508	0.613
Rest of the Month	.0332	114	.62570		

Source – Database collected from BSE web portal and computed.

As the calculated P value is greater than 0.05, it is inferred that BSE Telecom index returns does not differ between the first half and the rest of the month.

6.3.20. BSE Utilities Index

The following table exhibits whether Turn of the month effect prevails in BSE Utilities index.

Table 6.39: Turn of the Month Effect – BSE Utilities Index

	Mean	Std. Deviation	Variance	Skewness	Kurtosis	Shapiro-Wilk
First Half	0.0102	0.90512	0.819	0.405	6.228	0.000
Rest of the Month	0.0494	0.48236	0.233	0.004	3.464	0.000

Source – Database collected from BSE web portal and computed.

High mean returns were noticed during the Rest of the month (0.0494) and low mean returns were found during the First half of the month (0.0102). While comparing the variance, high level of volatility was noticed on the First half of the month (0.819) and low level of volatility was noticed in rest of the month (0.233).

Result of the Skewness test disclosed that positive returns were noticed in the First half of the month and rest of the month returns, which implies that most of the first half of the month and rest of the month returns were more than the average returns. The Kurtosis results of the BSE Utilities index returns were found leptokurtic in both the First half of the month (6.228) and rest of the month (3.464). Since, Kurtosis values are greater than 3, thus, it is inferred that the level of risk associated with the first half of the month and rest of the month returns of the BSE Utilities Index was high, which means investors may obtain either high level of profit or loss.

As the calculated P value of the Shapiro-Wilk test is less than 0.01, it is clearly proved that the data are not normally distributed. Hence, anomaly exists in the BSE Utilities index returns.

The following table depicts, whether first half and rest of the month returns differ in BSE Utilities Index.

Table 6.40: Turn of the Month Effect – BSE Utilities Index

	Mean	N	Std. Deviation	Paired t value	P value
First Half	.0102	114	.90512	-.416	0.678
Rest of the Month	.0494	114	.48236		
Source – Database collected from BSE web portal and computed.					

As the calculated P value is greater than 0.05, it is inferred that BSE Utilities index returns does not differ between the first half and the rest of the month.

6.3.21. NSE Nifty Index

The following table exhibits whether Turn of the month effect prevails in NSE Nifty index.

Table 6.41: Turn of the Month Effect – NSE Nifty Index

	Mean	Std. Deviation	Variance	Skewness	Kurtosis	Shapiro-Wilk
First Half	0.1993	0.67677	0.458	-0.837	1.905	0.000
Rest of the Month	-0.0052	0.42751	0.183	-0.911	3.947	0.000
Source – Database collected from NSE web portal and computed.						

High mean returns were noticed during the First half of the month (0.1993) and low mean returns were found during the rest of the month (-0.0052). While comparing the variance, high level of volatility was noticed on the First half of the month (0.458) and low level of volatility was noticed in rest of the month (0.183).

Result of the Skewness test disclosed that negative returns were noticed in the First half of the month and rest of the month returns, which implies that most of the first half of the month and rest of the month returns were less than the average returns. The Kurtosis results of the NSE Nifty index returns were found leptokurtic in the rest of the month (3.947). Since, Kurtosis values are greater than 3, thus, it is inferred that the level of risk associated with the rest of the month returns of the NSE Nifty Index was high, which means investors may obtain either high level of profit or loss. The first half of the month return were found platykurtic (1.905). Since, Kurtosis values are less than 3, thus, it is inferred that the level of risk associated with the first half of the month returns of the NSE Nifty index was low, which means investors may obtain either low level of profit or loss.

As the calculated P value of the Shapiro-Wilk test is less than 0.01, it is clearly proved that the data are not normally distributed. Hence, anomaly exists in the NSE Nifty index returns.

The following table depicts, whether first half and rest of the month returns differ in NSE Nifty Index.

Table 6.42: Turn of the Month Effect – NSE Nifty Index

	Mean	N	Std. Deviation	Paired t value	P value
First Half	.1993	132	.676770	2.949	0.004
Rest of the Month	-.0052	132	.427507		

Source – Database collected from NSE web portal and computed.

As the calculated P value is less than 0.01, it is inferred that NSE Nifty index returns differs between the first half and rest of the month.

6.3.22. NSE Auto Index

The following table exhibits whether Turn of the month effect prevails in NSE Auto index.

Table 6.43: Turn of the Month Effect – NSE Auto Index

	Mean	Std. Deviation	Variance	Skewness	Kurtosis	Shapiro-Wilk
First Half	0.2649	0.78432	0.615	-1.048	2.177	0.000
Rest of the Month	0.0033	0.46036	0.212	-0.843	4.217	0.000

Source – Database collected from NSE web portal and computed.

High mean returns were noticed during the First half of the month (0.2649) and low mean returns were found during the rest of the month (0.0033). While comparing the variance, high level of volatility was noticed on the First half of the month (0.615) and low level of volatility was noticed in rest of the month (0.212).

Result of the Skewness test disclosed that negative returns were noticed in the First half of the month and rest of the month returns, which implies that most of the first half of the month and rest of the month returns were less than the average returns. The Kurtosis results of the NSE Auto index return were found platykurtic in the first half of the month (2.177). Since, Kurtosis values are less than 3, thus, it is inferred that the level of risk associated with the rest of the month returns of the NSE Auto sector was low, which means investors may obtain either low level of profit or loss. The rest of the month return were found leptokurtic (4.217). Since, Kurtosis values are greater than 3, thus, it is inferred that the level of risk associated with the rest of the month returns of the NSE Auto sector was high, which means investors may obtain either high level of profit or loss.

As the calculated P value of the Shapiro-Wilk test is less than 0.01, it is clearly proved that the data are not normally distributed. Hence, anomaly exists in the NSE Auto index returns.

The following table depicts, whether first half and rest of the month returns differ in NSE Auto Index.

Table 6.44: Turn of the Month Effect – NSE Auto Index

	Mean	N	Std. Deviation	Paired t value	P value
First Half	.2649	132	.784315	3.276	0.001
Rest of the Month	.00331	132	.460355		
Source – Database collected from NSE web portal and computed.					

As the calculated P value is less than 0.01, it is inferred that NSE Auto index returns differs between the first half and rest of the month.

6.3.23. NSE Bank Index

The following table exhibits whether Turn of the month effect prevails in NSE Bank index.

Table 6.45: Turn of the Month Effect – NSE Bank Index

	Mean	Std. Deviation	Variance	Skewness	Kurtosis	Shapiro-Wilk
First Half	0.2607	0.96337	0.928	-0.373	1.77	0.000
Rest of the Month	-0.0197	0.61216	0.375	-0.177	0.612	0.000
Source – Database collected from NSE web portal and computed.						

High mean returns were noticed during the First half of the month (0.2607) and low mean returns were found during the rest of the month (-0.0197). While comparing the variance, high level of volatility was noticed on the First half of the month (0.928) and low level of volatility was noticed in rest of the month (0.375).

Result of the Skewness test disclosed that negative returns were noticed in the First half of the month and rest of the month returns, which implies that most of the first half of the month and rest of the month returns were less than the average returns. The Kurtosis results of the NSE Bank index returns were found platykurtic in both the First half of the month (1.770) and rest of the month (0.612). Since, Kurtosis values are less than 3, thus, it is inferred that the level of risk associated with the first half of the month and rest of the month returns of the NSE Bank sector was low, which means investors may obtain either low level of profit or loss.

As the calculated P value of the Shapiro-Wilk test is less than 0.01, it is clearly proved that the data are not normally distributed. Hence, anomaly exists in the NSE Bank index returns.

The following table depicts, whether first half and rest of the month returns differ in NSE Bank Index.

Table 6.46: Turn of the Month Effect – NSE Bank Index

	Mean	N	Std. Deviation	Paired t value	P value
First Half	.2607	132	.963369	2.693	0.008
Rest of the Month	-.0197	132	.612155		

Source – Database collected from NSE web portal and computed.

As the calculated P value is less than 0.01, it is inferred that NSE Bank index returns differs between the first half and rest of the month.

6.3.24. NSE Energy Index

The following table exhibits whether Turn of the month effect prevails in NSE Energy index.

Table 6.47: Turn of the Month Effect – NSE Energy Index

	Mean	Std. Deviation	Variance	Skewness	Kurtosis	Shapiro-Wilk
First Half	0.2106	0.68686	0.472	-0.473	1.218	0.000
Rest of the Month	-0.0475	0.4656	0.217	-1.107	5.547	0.000

Source – Database collected from NSE web portal and computed.

High mean returns were noticed during the First half of the month (0.2106) and low mean returns were found during the rest of the month (-0.0475). While comparing the variance, high level of volatility was noticed on the First half of the month (0.472) and low level of volatility was noticed in rest of the month (0.217).

Result of the Skewness test disclosed that negative returns were noticed in the First half of the month and rest of the month returns, which implies that most of the first half of the month and rest of the month returns were less than the average returns. The Kurtosis results of the NSE Energy index return were found platykurtic in the first half of the month (1.218). Since, Kurtosis values are less than 3, thus, it is inferred that the level of risk associated with the first half of the month returns of the NSE Energy sector was low, which means investors may obtain either low level of profit or loss. The rest of the month return were found leptokurtic (5.547). Since, Kurtosis values are greater than 3, thus, it is inferred that the level of risk associated with the rest of the month returns of the NSE ENERGY sector was high, which means investors may obtain either high level of profit or loss.

As the calculated P value of the Shapiro-Wilk test is less than 0.01, it is clearly proved that the data are not normally distributed. Hence, anomaly exists in the NSE Energy index returns.

The following table depicts, whether first half and rest of the month returns differ in NSE Energy Index.

Table 6.48: Turn of the Month Effect – NSE Energy Index

	Mean	N	Std. Deviation	Paired t value	P value
First Half	.2106	132	.686858	3.641	0.001
Rest of the Month	-.0475	132	.465602		
Source – Database collected from NSE web portal and computed.					

As the calculated P value is less than 0.01, it is inferred that NSE Energy index returns differs between the first half and rest of the month.

6.3.25. NSE Finance Index

The following table exhibits whether Turn of the month effect prevails in NSE Finance index.

Table 6.49: Turn of the Month Effect – NSE Finance Index

	Mean	Std. Deviation	Variance	Skewness	Kurtosis	Shapiro-Wilk
First Half	0.2432	0.90398	0.817	-0.569	1.812	0.000
Rest of the Month	-0.0079	0.58689	0.344	-0.32	1.286	0.000
Source – Database collected from NSE web portal and computed.						

High mean returns were noticed during the First half of the month (0.2432) and low mean returns were found during the rest of the month (-0.0079). While comparing the variance, high level of volatility was noticed on the First half of the month (0.817) and low level of volatility was noticed in rest of the month (0.344).

Result of the Skewness test disclosed that negative returns were noticed in the First half of the month and rest of the month returns, which implies that most of the first half of the month and rest of the month returns were less than the average returns. The Kurtosis results of the NSE Finance index returns were found platykurtic in both the First half of the month (1.812) and rest of the month (1.286). Since, Kurtosis values are less than 3, thus, it is inferred that the level of risk associated with the first half of the month and rest of the month returns of the NSE Finance sector was low, which means investors may obtain either low level of profit or loss.

As the calculated P value of the Shapiro-Wilk test is less than 0.01, it is clearly proved that the data are not normally distributed. Hence, anomaly exists in the NSE Finance index returns.

The following table depicts, whether first half and rest of the month returns differ in NSE Finance Index.

Table 6.50: Turn of the Month Effect – NSE Finance Index

	Mean	N	Std. Deviation	Paired t value	P value
First Half	.2432	132	.903977	2.562	0.012
Rest of the Month	-.0079	132	.586888		

Source – Database collected from NSE web portal and computed.

As the calculated P value is less than 0.05, it is inferred that NSE Finance index returns differs between the first half and rest of the month.

6.3.26. NSE Fast Moving Consumer Goods Index

The following table exhibits whether Turn of the month effect prevails in NSE FMCG index.

Table 6.51: Turn of the Month Effect – NSE Fast Moving Consumer Goods Index

	Mean	Std. Deviation	Variance	Skewness	Kurtosis	Shapiro-Wilk
First Half	0.1249	0.62059	0.385	-0.471	1.573	0.000
Rest of the Month	0.048	0.33476	0.112	-0.606	0.866	0.000

Source – Database collected from NSE web portal and computed.

High mean returns were noticed during the First half of the month (0.1249) and low mean returns were found during the rest of the month (0.0480). While comparing the variance, high level of volatility was noticed on the First half of the month (0.385) and low level of volatility was noticed in rest of the month (0.112).

Result of the Skewness test disclosed that negative returns were noticed in the First half of the month and rest of the month returns, which implies that most of the first half of the month and rest of the month returns were less than the average returns. The Kurtosis results of the

NSE FMCG index returns were found platykurtic in both the First half of the month (1.573) and rest of the month (0.866). Since, Kurtosis values are less than 3, thus, it is inferred that the level of risk associated with the first half of the month and rest of the month returns of the NSE FMCG sector was low, which means investors may obtain either low level of profit or loss.

As the calculated P value of the Shapiro-Wilk test is less than 0.01, it is clearly proved that the data are not normally distributed. Hence, anomaly exists in the NSE FMCG index returns.

The following table depicts, whether first half and rest of the month returns differ in NSE FMCG Index.

Table 6.52: Turn of the Month Effect – NSE Fast Moving Consumer Goods Index

	Mean	N	Std. Deviation	Paired t value	P value
First Half	.1249	132	.620590	1.279	0.203
Rest of the Month	.0480	132	.334762		

Source – Database collected from NSE web portal and computed.

As the calculated P value is greater than 0.05, it is inferred that NSE FMCG returns does not differs between the first half and rest of the month.

6.3.27. NSE IT Index

The following table exhibits whether Turn of the month effect prevails in NSE IT index.

Table 6.53: Turn of the Month Effect – NSE IT Index

	Mean	Std. Deviation	Variance	Skewness	Kurtosis	Shapiro-Wilk
First Half	0.2174	0.6532	0.427	-0.649	1.634	0.000
Rest of the Month	-0.0064	0.43881	0.193	-0.774	1.503	0.000

Source – Database collected from NSE web portal and computed.

High mean returns were noticed during the First half of the month (0.2174) and low mean returns were found during the rest of the month (-0.0064). While comparing the variance, high level of volatility was noticed on the First half of the month (0.427) and low level of volatility was noticed in rest of the month (0.193).

Result of the Skewness test disclosed that negative returns were noticed in the First half of the month and rest of the month returns, which implies that most of the first half of the month and rest of the month returns were less than the average returns. The Kurtosis results of the NSE IT index returns were found platykurtic in both the First half of the month (1.634) and rest of the month (1.503). Since, Kurtosis values are less than 3, thus, it is inferred that the level of risk associated with the first half of the month and rest of the month returns of the NSE IT sector was low, which means investors may obtain either low level of profit or loss.

As the calculated P value of the Shapiro-Wilk test is less than 0.01, it is clearly proved that the data are not normally distributed. Hence, anomaly exists in the NSE IT index returns.

The following table depicts, whether first half and rest of the month returns differ in NSE IT Index.

Table 6.54: Turn of the Month Effect – NSE IT Index

	Mean	N	Std. Deviation	Paired t value	P value
First Half	.2174	130	.653197	3.438	0.001
Rest of the Month	-.0064	130	.438808		

Source – Database collected from NSE web portal and computed.

As the calculated P value is less than 0.01, it is inferred that NSE IT index returns differs between the first half and rest of the month.

6.3.28. NSE Media Index

The following table exhibits whether Turn of the month effect prevails in NSE Media index.

Table 6.55: Turn of the Month Effect – NSE Media Index

	Mean	Std. Deviation	Variance	Skewness	Kurtosis	Shapiro-Wilk
First Half	0.3113	0.83003	0.689	-0.935	2.754	0.000
Rest of the Month	-0.0738	0.56708	0.322	-0.555	3.417	0.000

Source – Database collected from NSE web portal and computed.

High mean returns were noticed during the First half of the month (0.3113) and low mean returns were found during the rest of the month (-0.0738). While comparing the variance, high level of volatility was noticed on the First half of the month (0.689) and low level of volatility was noticed in rest of the month (0.322).

Result of the Skewness test disclosed that negative returns were noticed in the First half of the month and rest of the month returns, which implies that most of the first half of the month and rest of the month returns were less than the average returns. The Kurtosis results of the NSE Media index return were found platykurtic in the first half of the month (2.754). Since, Kurtosis values are less than 3, thus, it is inferred that the level of risk associated with the first half of the month returns of the NSE Media sector was low, which means investors may obtain either low level of profit or loss. The rest of the month return were found leptokurtic (3.417). Since, Kurtosis values are greater than 3, thus, it is inferred that the level of risk associated with the rest of the month returns of the NSE Media sector was high, which means investors may obtain either high level of profit or loss.

As the calculated P value of the Shapiro-Wilk test is less than 0.01, it is clearly proved that the data are not normally distributed. Hence, anomaly exists in the NSE Media index returns.

The following table depicts, whether first half and rest of the month returns differ in NSE Media Index.

Table 6.56: Turn of the Month Effect – NSE Media Index

	Mean	N	Std. Deviation	Paired t value	P value
First Half	.3113	111	.83003	4.116	0.000
Rest of the Month	-.0738	111	.56708		
Source – Database collected from NSE web portal and computed.					

As the calculated P value is less than 0.01, it is inferred that NSE Media index returns differs between the first half and rest of the month.

6.3.29. NSE Metal Index

The following table exhibits whether Turn of the month effect prevails in NSE Metal index.

Table 6.57: Turn of the Month Effect – NSE Metal Index

	Mean	Std. Deviation	Variance	Skewness	Kurtosis	Shapiro-Wilk
First Half	0.2243	1.06114	1.126	-0.809	3.206	0.000
Rest of the Month	-0.0553	0.71019	0.504	-0.59	3.271	0.000
Source – Database collected from NSE web portal and computed.						

High mean returns were noticed during the First half of the month (0.2243) and low mean returns were found during the rest of the month (-0.0553). While comparing the variance, high level of volatility was noticed on the First half of the month (1.126) and low level of volatility was noticed in rest of the month (0.504).

Result of the Skewness test disclosed that negative returns were noticed in the First half of the month and rest of the month returns, which implies that most of the first half of the month and rest of the month returns were less than the average returns. The Kurtosis results of the NSE Metal index returns were found leptokurtic in both the First half of the month (3.206) and rest of the month (3.271). Since, Kurtosis values are greater than 3, thus, it is inferred that the level of risk associated with the first half of the month and rest of the month returns of the NSE Metal sector was high, which means investors may obtain either high level of profit or loss.

As the calculated P value of the Shapiro-Wilk test is less than 0.01, it is clearly proved that the data are not normally distributed. Hence, anomaly exists in the NSE Metal index returns.

The following table depicts, whether first half and rest of the month returns differ in NSE Metal Index.

Table 6.58: Turn of the Month Effect – NSE Metal Index

	Mean	N	Std. Deviation	Paired t value	P value
First Half	.2243	132	1.061139	2.677	0.008
Rest of the Month	-.0553	132	.710186		

Source – Database collected from NSE web portal and computed.

As the calculated P value is less than 0.01, it is inferred that NSE Metal index returns differs between the first half and rest of the month.

6.3.30. NSE Pharma Index

The following table exhibits whether Turn of the month effect prevails in NSE Pharma index.

Table 6.59: Turn of the Month Effect – NSE Pharma Index

	Mean	Std. Deviation	Variance	Skewness	Kurtosis	Shapiro-Wilk
First Half	0.2737	0.54923	0.302	-0.581	2.185	0.000
Rest of the Month	-0.0052	0.42751	0.183	-0.911	3.947	0.000

Source – Database collected from NSE web portal and computed.

High mean returns were noticed during the First half of the month (0.2737) and low mean returns were found during the rest of the month (-0.0052). While comparing the variance, high level of volatility was noticed on the First half of the month (0.302) and low level of volatility was noticed in rest of the month (0.183).

Result of the Skewness test disclosed that negative returns were noticed in the First half of the month and rest of the month returns, which implies that most of the first half of the month and rest of the month returns were less than the average returns. The Kurtosis results of the NSE Pharma index return were found platykurtic in the first half of the month (2.185). Since, Kurtosis values are less than 3, thus, it is inferred that the level of risk associated with the first half of the month returns of the NSE Pharma sector was low, which means investors may obtain either low level of profit or loss. The rest of the month return were found leptokurtic (3.947). Since, Kurtosis values are greater than 3, thus, it is inferred that the level of risk associated with the rest of the month returns of the NSE Pharma sector was high, which means investors may obtain either high level of profit or loss.

As the calculated P value of the Shapiro-Wilk test is less than 0.01, it is clearly proved that the data are not normally distributed. Hence, anomaly exists in the NSE Pharma index returns.

The following table depicts, whether first half and rest of the month returns differ in NSE Pharma Index.

Table 6.60: Turn of the Month Effect – NSE Pharma Index

	Mean	N	Std. Deviation	Paired t value	P value
First Half	.2737	132	.549225	4.879	0.000
Rest of the Month	-.0052	132	.427507		

Source – Database collected from NSE web portal and computed.

As the calculated P value is less than 0.01, it is inferred that NSE Pharma index returns differs between the first half and rest of the month.

6.3.31. NSE Private Banks Index

The following table exhibits whether Turn of the month effect prevails in NSE Private Banks index.

Table 6.61: Turn of the Month Effect – NSE Private Banks Index

	Mean	Std. Deviation	Variance	Skewness	Kurtosis	Shapiro-Wilk
First Half	0.2982	1.05452	1.112	-0.165	2.148	0.000
Rest of the Month	0.0637	0.62102	0.386	0.083	1.836	0.000

Source – Database collected from NSE web portal and computed.

High mean returns were noticed during the First half of the month (0.2982) and low mean returns were found during the rest of the month (0.0637). While comparing the variance, high level of volatility was noticed on the First half of the month (1.112) and low level of volatility was noticed in rest of the month (0.386).

Result of the Skewness test disclosed that negative returns were noticed in the first half of the month returns, which implies that most of the first half of the month returns were less than the average returns. The rest of the month returns found positive Skewness, which implies that rest of the month returns were more than the average returns. The Kurtosis results of the NSE Private Banks index returns were found platykurtic in both the First half of the month (2.148) and rest of the month (1.836). Since, Kurtosis values are less than 3, thus, it is inferred that the level of risk associated with the first half of the month and rest of the month returns of the NSE Private Banks sector was low, which means investors may obtain either low level of profit or loss.

As the calculated P value of the Shapiro-Wilk test is less than 0.01, it is clearly proved that the data are not normally distributed. Hence, anomaly exists in the NSE Private Banks index returns.

The following table depicts, whether first half and rest of the month returns differ in NSE Private Banks Index.

Table 6.62: Turn of the Month Effect – NSE Private Banks Index

	Mean	N	Std. Deviation	Paired t value	P value
First Half	.2982	119	1.05452	2.015	0.046
Rest of the Month	.0637	119	.62102		
Source – Database collected from NSE web portal and computed.					

As the calculated P value is less than 0.05, it is inferred that NSE Private Banks index returns differs between the first half and rest of the month.

6.3.32. NSE Public Sector Unit Banks Index

The following table exhibits whether Turn of the month effect prevails in NSE PSU Bank index.

Table 6.63: Turn of the Month Effect – NSE PSU Banks Index

	Mean	Std. Deviation	Variance	Skewness	Kurtosis	Shapiro-Wilk
First Half	0.2605	1.09796	1.206	-0.193	0.594	0.000
Rest of the Month	-0.0222	0.72931	0.532	-0.414	7.468	0.000
Source – Database collected from NSE web portal and computed.						

High mean returns were noticed during the First half of the month (0.2605) and low mean returns were found during the rest of the month (-0.0222). While comparing the variance, high level of volatility was noticed on the First half of the month (1.206) and low level of volatility was noticed in rest of the month (0.532).

Result of the Skewness test disclosed that negative returns were noticed in the First half of the month and rest of the month returns, which implies that most of the first half of the month and rest of the month returns were less than the average returns. The Kurtosis results of the NSE PSU Bank index return were found platykurtic in the first half of the month (0.594). Since, Kurtosis values are less than 3, thus, it is inferred that the level of risk associated with the rest of the month returns of the NSE PSU Bank sector was low, which means investors may obtain either low level of profit or loss. The rest of the month return were found leptokurtic (7.468). Since, Kurtosis values are greater than 3, thus, it is inferred that the level of risk associated with the rest of the month returns of the NSE PSU Bank sector was high, which means investors may obtain either high level of profit or loss. As the calculated P value of the Shapiro-Wilk test is less than 0.01, it is clearly proved that the data are not normally distributed. Hence, anomaly exists in the NSE PSU Bank index returns.

The following table depicts, whether first half and rest of the month returns differ in NSE PSU Bank Index.

Table 6.64: Turn of the Month Effect – NSE PSU Banks Index

	Mean	N	Std. Deviation	Paired t value	P value
First Half	.2605	132	1.097962	2.373	0.019
Rest of the Month	-.0222	132	.729310		
Source – Database collected from NSE web portal and computed.					

As the calculated P value is less than 0.05, it is inferred that NSE PSU Bank index returns differs between the first half and rest of the month.

6.3.33. NSE Realty Index

The following table exhibits whether Turn of the month effect prevails in NSE Realty index.

Table 6.65: Turn of the Month Effect – NSE Realty Index

	Mean	Std. Deviation	Variance	Skewness	Kurtosis	Shapiro-Wilk
First Half	0.1778	0.67671	0.458	-0.668	1.723	0.000
Rest of the Month	-0.0291	0.46271	0.214	-0.714	1.343	0.000
Source – Database collected from NSE web portal and computed.						

High mean returns were noticed during the First half of the month (0.1778) and low mean returns were found during the rest of the month (-0.0291). While comparing the variance, high level of volatility was noticed on the First half of the month (0.458) and low level of volatility was noticed in rest of the month (0.214).

Result of the Skewness test disclosed that negative returns were noticed in the First half of the month and rest of the month returns, which implies that most of the first half of the month and rest of the month returns were less than the average returns. The Kurtosis results of the NSE Realty index returns were found platykurtic in both the First half of the month (1.723) and rest of the month (1.343). Since, Kurtosis values are less than 3, thus, it is inferred that the level of risk associated with the first half of the month and rest of the month returns of the NSE Realty sector was low, which means investors may obtain either low level of profit or loss.

As the calculated P value of the Shapiro-Wilk test is less than 0.01, it is clearly proved that the data are not normally distributed. Hence, anomaly exists in the NSE Realty index returns.

The following table depicts, whether first half and rest of the month returns differ in NSE Realty Index.

Table 6.66: Turn of the Month Effect – NSE Realty Index

	Mean	N	Std. Deviation	Paired t value	P value
First Half	.1778	99	.67671	2.728	0.008
Rest of the Month	-.0291	99	.46271		
Source – Database collected from NSE web portal and computed.					

As the calculated P value is less than 0.01, it is inferred that NSE Realty index returns differs between the first half and rest of the month.

6.4. Conclusion

From the analysis, it is inferred that the turn of the month effect exists in all BSE Sensex, 19 BSE sectoral indices, NSE Nifty and 12 NSE sectoral indices. As far as turn of the month effect is concerned, High level return is noticed on first half of the month and low level of return noticed on rest of the month for BSE Sensex and NSE Nifty Index. Hence, investors are advised to buy BSE Sensex and NSE Nifty shares on rest of the month and to sell during first half of the month. The next chapter discuss about monthly effect.

CHAPTER VII

MONTHLY EFFECT AND APRIL EFFECT IN INDIAN STOCK MARKET

7.1. Introduction

The Monthly Effect is also known as the month of the year effect. The Monthly effect is one of the most important calendar anomalies. The month-of-the-year effect would be present when returns in some months are higher than other months. It is caused normally by a significant low return in March.

7.2. Tools for Analysis

The collected data have been analyzed by making use of Returns, Descriptive statistics such as Mean, Standard Deviation, Variance, Skewness, Kurtosis, Shapiro-Wilk test and paired 't' test.

7.3. Monthly Effect and April Effect

The following subsections discuss about the monthly effect and April effect of BSE Sensex, 19 BSE sectoral indices, NSE Nifty and 12 NSE sectoral indices

7.3.1. BSE Sensex Index

The following table exhibits whether monthly effect prevails in BSE Sensex index.

Table 7.1: Monthly Effect – BSE Sensex Index

	Mean	Std. Deviation	Variance	Skewness	Kurtosis
April	3.5061	6.37865	40.687	1.019	1.084
May	0.3514	12.22974	149.567	1.028	1.786
June	0.784	6.9343	48.085	-2.187	6.024
July	3.1052	3.9968	15.974	-0.155	-1.46
August	0.3576	4.25249	18.084	-0.146	2.233
September	5.1959	7.19176	51.721	-1.4	2.038
October	0.0563	10.48028	109.836	-1.087	1.829
November	1.6502	6.67903	44.609	-0.146	-1.077
December	2.4159	3.91059	15.293	-0.744	-0.576
January	-0.7782	7.32652	53.678	-0.184	-0.491
February	-0.7246	4.17256	17.41	-0.57	-0.901
March	1.7815	6.70518	44.959	-0.499	-0.665
Shapiro-Wilk test :0.000					
Source – Database collected from BSE web portal and computed.					

High mean returns were noticed during the month of September (5.1959) and low mean returns were found during the month of January (-0.7782). While comparing the variance, high level of volatility was noticed on the month of May (149.567) and low level of volatility was noticed in the month of December (15.293).

Result of Skewness test disclosed the positive value and it was noticed during the month of April (1.019) and May (1.028) returns, which implies that most of the April and May month returns were more than the average returns. The other Month's returns were found negative Skewness, which implies that most of the Other Month's returns were less than the average returns. The Kurtosis results of the BSE Sensex index returns were found leptokurtic in the month of June (6.024) returns. Since, Kurtosis values are greater than 3, thus, it is inferred that the level of risk associated with the month of June returns of the BSE Sensex index was high, which means investors may obtain either high level of profit or loss. The other month's returns were found platykurtic. Since, Kurtosis values are less than 3, thus, it is inferred that the level of risk associated with the other month's returns of the BSE Sensex sector was low, which means investors may obtain either low level of profit or loss.

As the calculated P value of the Shapiro-Wilk test is less than 0.01, it is clearly proved that the data are not normally distributed. Hence, there exists anomaly in the BSE Sensex index returns.

The financial houses, whose values have fallen to book losses, may sell their shares to reduce their taxes. Consequently, the stock prices decline. However, as soon as March ends, people start acquiring shares. As a result, the stock prices bounce back. This leads to higher returns in the beginning of the financial year, which is April. This is also called the 'April Effect'.

Our results do confirm the April effect for BSE Sensex index in India. The average return for March is low as compared to the April average return. This evidence is consistent with the 'tax-loss-selling' hypothesis. It appears that investors in India sell shares that have declined in values, and book losses to save taxes. This causes share prices to decline in March that results in lower returns.

7.3.2. BSE Auto Index

The following table exhibits whether monthly effect prevails in BSE Auto index.

Table 7.2: Monthly Effect – BSE Auto Index

	Mean	Std. Deviation	Variance	Skewness	Kurtosis
April	3.475	4.9706	24.707	0.631	1.342
May	-0.5437	13.52196	182.843	1.089	1.959
June	-0.5567	6.87503	47.266	-1.301	2.768
July	3.0053	7.99089	63.854	2.196	5.979
August	2.3247	5.77255	33.322	0.242	-0.81
September	5.7294	6.5541	42.956	-0.881	0.251
October	-0.1136	9.92345	98.475	-1.866	4.863
November	2.4549	8.52879	72.74	-0.4	0.265
December	2.6545	4.20163	17.654	-0.209	-1.219
January	-1.997	8.35499	69.806	0.241	-0.399
February	1.0143	6.71891	45.144	0.076	-1.519
March	2.5294	7.42944	55.197	0.164	-1.473
Shapiro-Wilk test :0.000					
Source – Database collected from BSE web portal and computed.					

High mean returns were noticed during the month of September (5.7294) and low mean returns were found during the month of January (-1.9970). While comparing the variance, high level of volatility was noticed on the month of May (182.843) and low level of volatility was noticed in the month of December (17.654).

Result of Skewness test disclosed the negative value and it was noticed during the month of June (-1.301), September (-0.881), October (-1.866), November (-.400) and December (-.209) returns, which implies that most of the June, September, October, November and December month returns were less than the average returns. The other Month's returns were found positive Skewness, which implies that most of the Other Month's returns were more than the average returns. The Kurtosis results of the BSE Auto index returns were found leptokurtic on the month of July (5.979) and October (4.863) returns. Since, Kurtosis values are greater than 3, thus, it is inferred that the level of risk associated with the month of July and October returns of the BSE Auto index was high, which means investors may obtain either high level of profit or loss. The other month's returns were found platykurtic. Since, Kurtosis values are less than 3, thus, it is inferred that the level of risk associated with the other month's returns of the BSE Automobile sector was low, which means investors may obtain either low level of profit or loss.

As the calculated P value of the Shapiro-Wilk test is less than 0.01, it is clearly proved that the data are not normally distributed. Hence, there exists anomaly in the BSE Auto index returns. Our results do confirm the April effect for BSE Auto index in India. The average return for March is low as compared to the April average return. This evidence is consistent with the 'tax-loss-selling' hypothesis. It appears that investors in India sell shares that have declined in values, and book losses to save taxes. This causes share prices to decline in March that results in lower returns.

7.3.3. *BSE Bank Index*

The following table exhibits whether monthly effect prevails in BSE Bank index.

Table 7.3: Monthly Effect – BSE Bank Index

	Mean	Std. Deviation	Variance	Skewness	Kurtosis
April	5.2851	9.40173	88.393	1.022	1.894
May	1.4074	18.5005	342.269	1.237	2.581
June	-1.0123	9.09395	82.7	-1.623	3.022
July	3.52	8.33954	69.548	-0.288	1.4
August	-0.8895	7.26291	52.75	0.058	-0.713
September	9.0535	9.12024	83.179	-0.65	-0.779
October	1.1902	12.02617	144.629	-0.595	0.295
November	3.4044	9.42779	88.883	-0.318	-0.088
December	3.4958	7.05429	49.763	0.834	0.573
January	-0.3098	10.01761	100.352	1.523	3.199
February	-2.2884	6.9641	48.499	-0.386	-1.142
March	1.1223	11.05769	122.272	-0.79	1.94
Shapiro-Wilk test :0.000					
Source – Database collected from BSE web portal and computed.					

High mean returns were noticed during the month of September (9.0535) and low mean returns were found during the month of February (-2.2884). While comparing the variance, high level of volatility was noticed on the month of May (342.269) and low level of volatility was noticed in the month of February (48.499).

Result of Skewness test disclosed the positive value and it was noticed during the month of April (1.022), May (1.237), August (0.058), December (.834) and January (1.523) returns, which implies that most of the April, May, August, December, and January month returns were more than the average returns. The other Month's returns were found negative Skewness, which implies that most of the Other Month's returns were less than the average returns. The Kurtosis results of the BSE Bank index returns were found leptokurtic on the month of June (3.022) and January (3.199) returns. Since, Kurtosis values are greater than 3, thus, it is inferred that the level of risk associated with the month of June and January returns of the BSE Bank index was high, which means investors may obtain either high level of profit or loss. The other month's returns were found platykurtic. Since, Kurtosis values are less than 3, thus, it is inferred that the level of risk associated with the other month's returns of the BSE Banking sector was low, which means investors may obtain either low level of profit or loss.

As the calculated P value of the Shapiro-Wilk test is less than 0.01, it is clearly proved that the data are not normally distributed. Hence, there exists anomaly in the BSE Bank index returns.

Our results do confirm the April effect for BSE Bank index in India. The average return for March is low as compared to the April average return. This evidence is consistent with the 'tax-loss-selling' hypothesis. It appears that investors in India sell shares that have declined in values, and book losses to save taxes. This causes share prices to decline in March that results in lower returns.

7.3.4. BSE Basic Materials Index

The following table exhibits whether monthly effect prevails in BSE Basic Materials index.

Table 7.4: Monthly Effect – BSE Basic Materials Index

	Mean	Std. Deviation	Variance	Skewness	Kurtosis
April	9.2812	10.44584	109.116	0.435	-1.29
May	0.3966	15.93804	254.021	0.134	-0.15
June	0.7422	9.75206	95.103	0.235	0.067
July	0.018	8.6963	75.626	-0.348	3.116
August	-0.7055	8.09937	65.6	-1.272	0.368
September	5.772	9.85636	97.148	-0.545	1.791
October	-0.8737	14.28117	203.952	-2.450	6.469
November	-2.7151	8.59873	73.938	-1.107	2.426
December	4.3435	7.4202	55.059	0.732	1.187
January	-1.9187	10.28678	105.818	-0.603	1.291
February	-0.1059	7.87284	61.982	1.144	0.924
March	-2.8411	9.82664	96.563	1.104	0.455
Shapiro-Wilk test :0.000					
Source – Database collected from BSE web portal and computed.					

High mean returns were noticed during the month of April (9.2812) and low mean returns were found during the month of March (-2.8411). While comparing the variance, high level of volatility was noticed on the month of May (254.021) and low level of volatility was noticed in the month of December (55.059). Result of Skewness test disclosed the positive value and it was noticed during the month of April (0.435), May (0.134), June (0.235), December (0.732), February (1.144) and March (1.104) returns, which implies that most of the April, May, June, December, February and March month returns were more than the average returns. The other Month's returns were found negative Skewness, which implies that most of the Other Month's returns were less than the average returns. The Kurtosis results of the BSE Basic Materials index returns were found leptokurtic on the month of July (3.116) and October (6.469) returns. Since, Kurtosis values are greater than 3, thus, it is inferred that the level of risk associated with the month of July and October returns of the BSE Basic Materials index was high, which means investors may obtain either high level of profit or loss. The other month's returns were found platykurtic. Since, Kurtosis values are less than 3, thus, it is inferred that the level of risk associated with the other month's returns of the BSE Basic Materials sector was low, which means investors may obtain either low level of profit or loss.

As the calculated P value of the Shapiro-Wilk test is less than 0.01, it is clearly proved that the data are not normally distributed. Hence, there exists anomaly in the BSE Basic Materials index returns.

Our results do confirm the April effect for BSE Basic Materials index in India. The average return for March is low as compared to the April average return. This evidence is consistent with the 'tax-loss-selling' hypothesis. It appears that investors in India sell shares that have declined in values, and book losses to save taxes. This causes share prices to decline in March that results in lower returns.

7.3.5. BSE Consumer Durables Index

The following table exhibits whether monthly effect prevails in BSE Consumer Durables index.

Table 7.5: Monthly Effect – BSE Consumer Durables Index

	Mean	**Std. Deviation**	**Variance**	**Skewness**	**Kurtosis**
April	5.935	4.6749	21.855	1.332	2.33
May	6.4247	20.40098	416.2	1.575	3.248
June	-0.6595	11.32352	128.222	-0.833	-0.222
July	4.2681	5.98789	35.855	0.56	-0.734
August	3.858	7.5366	56.8	-0.686	0.116
September	3.1702	9.82059	96.444	-2.294	6.435
October	-0.3862	10.66642	113.772	-2.199	5.951
November	1.9705	12.04895	145.177	0.368	-0.327
December	5.9224	9.94042	98.812	1.283	2.506
January	-2.3658	10.37681	107.678	-0.985	2.441
February	-1.5879	7.5255	56.633	0.295	-0.9
March	1.4447	7.6025	57.798	-1.452	3.421
Shapiro-Wilk test :0.000					
Source – Database collected from BSE web portal and computed.					

High mean returns were noticed during the month of May (6.4247) and low mean returns were found during the month of January (-2.3658). While comparing the variance, high level of volatility was noticed on the month of May (416.200) and low level of volatility was noticed in the month of April (21.855).

Result of Skewness test disclosed the positive value and it was noticed during the month of April (1.332), May (1.575), July (0.560), November (0.368), December (1.283) and February (0.295) returns, which implies that most of the April, May, July, November, December and February month returns were more than the average returns. The other Month's returns were found negative Skewness, which implies that most of the Other Month's returns were less than the average returns.

The Kurtosis results of the BSE Consumer Durables index returns were found leptokurtic on the month of May (3.248), September (6.435), October (5.951) and March (3.421) returns. Since, Kurtosis values are greater than 3, thus, it is inferred that the level of risk associated with the month of May, September, October and March returns of the BSE Consumer Durables index was high, which means investors may obtain either high level of profit or loss. The other month's returns were found platykurtic.

Since, Kurtosis values are less than 3, thus, it is inferred that the level of risk associated with the other month's returns of the BSE Consumer Durables sector was low, which means investors may obtain either low level of profit or loss.

As the calculated P value of the Shapiro-Wilk test is less than 0.01, it is clearly proved that the data are not normally distributed. Hence, there exists anomaly in the BSE Consumer Durables index returns.

Our results do confirm the April effect for BSE Consumer Durables index in India. The average return for March is low as compared to the April average return. This evidence is consistent with the 'tax-loss-selling' hypothesis. It appears that investors in India sell shares that have declined in values, and book losses to save taxes. This causes share prices to decline in March that results in lower returns.

7.3.6. BSE Consumer Goods Index

The following table exhibits whether monthly effect prevails in BSE Consumer Goods index.

Table 7.6: Monthly Effect – BSE Consumer Goods Index

	Mean	Std. Deviation	Variance	Skewness	Kurtosis
April	4.0347	7.58414	57.519	1.366	2.775
May	3.5774	19.90033	396.023	1.332	2.4
June	3.1225	10.42267	108.632	-1.831	3.825
July	1.1428	8.83211	78.006	0.379	-1.22
August	1.007	6.97897	48.706	-0.888	0.879
September	4.0747	8.99304	80.875	-0.794	-0.481
October	2.2901	17.07742	291.638	-0.206	2.07
November	1.9068	8.87377	78.744	0.506	1.203
December	1.5346	7.6896	59.13	-1.272	2.346
January	0.0237	12.99366	168.835	0.672	-0.648
February	0.5026	8.06899	65.109	-0.13	-1.096
March	2.0877	8.36822	70.027	-0.126	-0.365
Shapiro-Wilk test :0.000					
Source – Database collected from BSE web portal and computed.					

High mean returns were noticed during the month of September (4.0747) and low mean returns were found during the month of January (0.237). While comparing the variance, high level of volatility was noticed on the month of May (396.023) and low level of volatility was noticed in the month of August (48.706).

Result of Skewness test disclosed the positive value and it was noticed during the month of April (1.366), May (1.332), July (0.379), November (0.506) and January (0.672) returns, which implies that most of the April, May, July, November, and January month returns were more than the average returns. The other Month's returns were found negative Skewness, which implies that most of the Other Month's returns were less than the average returns. The Kurtosis results of the BSE Consumer Goods index returns were found leptokurtic in the month of June (3.825) returns. Since, Kurtosis values are greater than 3, thus, it is inferred that the level of risk associated with the month of June returns of the BSE Consumer Goods index was high, which means investors may obtain either high level of profit or loss. The other month's returns were found platykurtic. Since, Kurtosis values are less than 3, thus, it is inferred that the level of risk associated with the other month's returns of the BSE Consumer Goods sector was low, which means investors may obtain either low level of profit or loss.

As the calculated P value of the Shapiro-Wilk test is less than 0.01, it is clearly proved that the data are not normally distributed. Hence, there exists anomaly in the BSE Consumer Goods index returns.

Our results do confirm the April effect for BSE Consumer Goods index in India. The average return for March is low as compared to the April average return. This evidence is consistent with the 'tax-loss-selling' hypothesis. It appears that investors in India sell shares that have declined in values, and book losses to save taxes. This causes share prices to decline in March that results in lower returns.

7.3.7. BSE Energy Index

The following table exhibits whether monthly effect prevails in BSE Energy index.

Table 7.7: Monthly Effect – BSE Energy Index

	Mean	Std. Deviation	Variance	Skewness	Kurtosis
April	6.5432	8.17505	66.831	0.165	-2.151
May	3.0366	12.69892	161.262	1.134	0.849
June	-0.9659	6.97926	48.71	-0.684	-0.68
July	-0.8503	4.9471	24.474	0.797	-0.986
August	0.816	5.72604	32.788	1.251	2.129
September	2.963	6.94836	48.28	0.441	1.193
October	0.4874	14.89699	221.92	-1.1	2.758
November	-2.0886	6.39734	40.926	0.317	-1.068
December	1.5351	5.80684	33.719	-1.076	-0.019
January	-0.4229	10.72888	115.109	-0.47	-0.399
February	-1.8987	3.73124	13.922	-0.088	-0.332
March	2.4384	9.07678	82.388	0.21	-1.446
Shapiro-Wilk test :0.000					
Source – Database collected from BSE web portal and computed.					

High mean returns were noticed during the month of April (6.5432) and low mean returns were found during the month of November (-2.0886). While comparing the variance, high level of volatility was noticed on the month of October (221.920) and low level of volatility was noticed in the month of February (13.922).

Result of Skewness test disclosed the negative value and it was noticed during the month of June (-0.684), October (-1.100), December (-1.076), January (-.470) and February (-0.088) returns, which implies that most of the June, October, December, January and February month returns were less than the average returns. The other Month's returns were found positive Skewness, which implies that most of the Other Month's returns were more than the average returns. The Kurtosis results of the BSE Energy index returns were found platykurtic in all the months. Since, Kurtosis values are less than 3, thus, it is inferred that the level of risk associated with the all the months returns of the BSE Energy index was low, which means investors may obtain either low level of profit or loss.

As the calculated P value of the Shapiro-Wilk test is less than 0.01, it is clearly proved that the data are not normally distributed. Hence, there exists anomaly in the BSE Energy index returns.

Our results do confirm the April effect for BSE Energy index in India. The average return for March is low as compared to the April average return. This evidence is consistent with the 'tax-loss-selling' hypothesis. It appears that investors in India sell shares that have declined in values, and book losses to save taxes. This causes share prices to decline in March that results in lower returns.

7.3.8. BSE Finance Index

The following table exhibits whether monthly effect prevails in BSE Finance index.

Table 7.8: Monthly Effect – BSE Finance Index

	Mean	Std. Deviation	Variance	Skewness	Kurtosis
April	6.4602	8.86713	78.626	1.469	2.031
May	3.9045	17.41719	303.359	1.822	3.596
June	-1.4263	9.89807	97.972	-1.588	2.665
July	1.614	6.56442	43.092	-1.141	2.374
August	-0.2176	7.11692	50.651	-0.133	-0.544
September	7.9015	10.10237	102.058	-0.547	-0.869
October	2.0408	11.70759	137.068	-1.258	2.302
November	0.8827	8.2055	67.33	-0.596	-1.283
December	1.8096	5.89018	34.694	1.188	2.723
January	-1.1299	10.36097	107.35	1.366	1.842
February	-3.1179	6.46729	41.826	-0.436	-1.294
March	1.3098	11.2026	125.498	-1.027	1.68
Shapiro-Wilk test :0.000					
Source – Database collected from BSE web portal and computed.					

High mean returns were noticed during the month of September (7.9015) and low mean returns were found during the month of February (-3.119). While comparing the variance, high level of volatility was noticed on the month of May (303.359) and low level of volatility was noticed in the month of December (34.694).

Result of Skewness test disclosed the positive value and it was noticed during the month of April (1.469), May (1.822), December (1.188) and January (1.366) returns, which implies that most of the April, May, December and January month returns were more than the average returns. The other Month's returns were found negative Skewness, which implies that most of the Other Month's returns were less than the average returns. The Kurtosis results of the BSE Finance index returns were found leptokurtic on the month of May (3.596) returns. Since, Kurtosis values are greater than 3, thus, it is inferred that the level of risk associated with the month of May returns of the BSE Finance index was high, which means investors may obtain either high level of profit or loss. The other month's returns were found platykurtic. Since, Kurtosis values are less than 3, thus, it is inferred that the level of risk associated with the other month's returns of the BSE Finance sector was low, which means investors may obtain either low level of profit or loss.

As the calculated P value of the Shapiro-Wilk test is less than 0.01, it is clearly proved that the data are not normally distributed. Hence, there exists anomaly in the BSE Finance index returns.

Our results do confirm the April effect for BSE Finance index in India. The average return for March is low as compared to the April average return. This evidence is consistent with the 'tax-loss-selling' hypothesis. It appears that investors in India sell shares that have declined in values, and book losses to save taxes. This causes share prices to decline in March that results in lower returns.

7.3.9. BSE Fast Moving Consumer Goods Index

The following table exhibits whether monthly effect prevails in BSE FMCG index.

Table 7.9: Monthly Effect – BSE Fast Moving Consumer Goods Index

	Mean	Std. Deviation	Variance	Skewness	Kurtosis
April	3.9069	3.79562	14.407	-0.196	0.324
May	-0.7368	7.61132	57.932	-1.373	1.877
June	1.0928	7.32233	53.617	-0.817	0.218
July	4.3985	6.40154	40.98	1.856	4.681
August	1.215	4.99831	24.983	-0.564	-0.882
September	4.8408	4.97741	24.775	0.064	-1.396
October	-1.5791	7.24175	52.443	-0.672	1.002
November	3.4805	6.2468	39.023	0.752	-0.177
December	1.1648	3.64509	13.287	0.439	-0.313
January	0.1603	4.92471	24.253	-0.381	-0.481
February	0.3371	5.42433	29.423	1.249	2.29
March	3.1169	5.31736	28.274	0.038	-0.719
Shapiro-Wilk test :0.000					
Source – Database collected from BSE web portal and computed.					

High mean returns were noticed during the month of September (4.8408) and low mean returns were found during the month of October (-1.5791). While comparing the variance, high level of volatility was noticed on the month of May (57.932) and low level of volatility was noticed in the month of December (13.287).

Result of Skewness test disclosed the positive value and it was noticed during the month of July (1.856), September (0.064), November (0.752), December (0.439), February (1.249) and March (0.038) returns, which implies that most of the July, September, November, December, February and March month returns were more than the average returns. The other Month's returns were found negative Skewness, which implies that most of the Other Month's returns were less than the average returns.

The Kurtosis results of the BSE FMCG index returns were found leptokurtic in the month of July (4.681) returns. Since, Kurtosis values are greater than 3, thus, it is inferred that the level of risk associated with the month of July returns of the BSE FMCG index was high, which means investors may obtain either high level of profit or loss. The other month's returns were found platykurtic. Since, Kurtosis values are less than 3, thus, it is inferred that the level of risk associated with the other month's returns of the BSE FMCG sector was low, which means investors may obtain either low level of profit or loss.

As the calculated P value of the Shapiro-Wilk test is less than 0.01, it is clearly proved that the data are not normally distributed. Hence, there exists anomaly in the BSE FMCG index returns.

Our results do confirm the April effect for BSE FMCG index in India. The average return for March is low as compared to the April average return. This evidence is consistent with the 'tax-loss-selling' hypothesis. It appears that investors in India sell shares that have declined in values, and book losses to save taxes. This causes share prices to decline in March that results in lower returns.

7.3.10. BSE Health Care Index

The following table exhibits whether monthly effect prevails in BSE Healthcare index.

Table 7.10: Monthly Effect – BSE Healthcare Index

	Mean	Std. Deviation	Variance	Skewness	Kurtosis
April	4.3404	4.81196	23.155	-0.365	-0.508
May	0.7434	7.75181	60.091	-0.301	-0.14
June	0.6722	5.26394	27.709	0.301	0.316
July	2.5504	3.41826	11.684	-0.12	-0.819
August	2.0344	5.01135	25.114	-0.316	-0.256
September	4.0099	7.84897	61.606	-1.291	2.775
October	-1.8743	8.96651	80.398	-1.902	3.695
November	3.3391	4.25602	18.114	0.477	0.042
December	4.2549	5.56428	30.961	1.036	0.857
January	-2.7739	8.28899	68.707	-0.449	-0.495
February	0.1584	6.16476	38.004	0.124	-1.269
March	3.6986	5.36398	28.772	-0.849	-0.217
Shapiro-Wilk test :0.000					
Source – Database collected from BSE web portal and computed.					

High mean returns were noticed during the month of April (4.3404) and low mean returns were found during the month of January (-2.7739). While comparing the variance, high level of volatility was noticed on the month of October (80.398) and low level of volatility was noticed in the month of July (11.684).

Result of Skewness test disclosed the positive value and it was noticed during the month of June (0.301), November (0.477), December (1.036) and February (0.124) returns, which implies that most of the June, November, December, and February month returns were more than the average returns. The other Month's returns were found negative Skewness, which implies that most of the Other Month's returns were less than the average returns. The Kurtosis results of the BSE Health Care index returns were found leptokurtic in the month of October (3.695) returns. Since, Kurtosis values are greater than 3, thus, it is inferred that the level of risk associated with the month of October returns of the BSE Health Care index was high, which means investors may obtain either high level of profit or loss. The other month's returns were found platykurtic. Since, Kurtosis values are less than 3, thus, it is inferred that the level of risk associated with the other month's returns of the BSE Health Care sector was low, which means investors may obtain either low level of profit or loss.

As the calculated P value of the Shapiro-Wilk test is less than 0.01, it is clearly proved that the data are not normally distributed. Hence, there exists anomaly in the BSE Health Care index returns. Our results do confirm the April effect for BSE Health Care index in India. The average return for March is low as compared to the April average return. This evidence is consistent with the 'tax-loss-selling' hypothesis. It appears that investors in India sell shares that have declined in values, and book losses to save taxes. This causes share prices to decline in March that results in lower returns.

7.3.11. BSE Industrial Index

The following table exhibits whether monthly effect prevails in BSE Industrial index.

Table 7.11: Monthly Effect – BSE Industrial Index

	Mean	Std. Deviation	Variance	Skewness	Kurtosis
April	6.0474	7.71304	59.491	2.045	5.038
May	4.2527	20.60029	424.372	1.84	3.636
June	-0.066	10.50128	110.277	-1.566	2.291
July	-0.1422	6.26456	39.245	0.771	-0.537
August	0.5337	6.47586	41.937	-0.134	-0.035
September	3.6059	9.27923	86.104	-1.015	0.535
October	1.6388	16.80932	282.553	-1.09	2.992
November	-0.4389	7.5577	57.119	-1.029	-0.391
December	1.9243	6.48598	42.068	-0.909	1.428
January	-2.1146	12.65624	160.18	1.172	1.173
February	-1.8135	7.17518	51.483	0.498	-1.307
March	1.2498	8.18509	66.996	-0.516	-0.227
Shapiro-Wilk test :0.000					
Source – Database collected from BSE web portal and computed.					

High mean returns were noticed during the month of April (6.0474) and low mean returns were found during the month of January (-2.1146). While comparing the variance, high level of volatility was noticed on the month of May (424.372) and low level of volatility was noticed in the month of July (39.245).

Result of Skewness test disclosed the positive value and it was noticed during the month of April (2.045), May (1.840), July (0.771) January (1.172), and February (0.498) returns, which implies that most of the April, May, July, January and February month returns were more than the average returns. The other Month's returns were found negative Skewness, which implies that most of the Other Month's returns were less than the average returns. The Kurtosis results of the BSE Industrial index returns were found leptokurtic on the month of April (5.038) and May (3.636) returns. Since, Kurtosis values are greater than 3, thus, it is inferred that the level of risk associated with the month of April and May returns of the BSE Industrial index was high, which means investors may obtain either high level of profit or loss. The other month's returns were found platykurtic. Since, Kurtosis values are less than 3, thus, it is inferred that the level of risk associated with the other month's returns of the BSE Industrial sector was low, which means investors may obtain either low level of profit or loss.

As the calculated P value of the Shapiro-Wilk test is less than 0.01, it is clearly proved that the data are not normally distributed. Hence, there exists anomaly in the BSE Industrial index returns.

Our results do confirm the April effect for BSE Industrial index in India. The average return for March is low as compared to the April average return. This evidence is consistent with the 'tax-loss-selling' hypothesis. It appears that investors in India sell shares that have declined in values, and book losses to save taxes. This causes share prices to decline in March that results in lower returns.

7.3.12. BSE IT Index

The following table exhibits whether monthly effect prevails in BSE IT index.

Table 7.12: Monthly Effect – BSE IT Index

	Mean	Std. Deviation	Variance	Skewness	Kurtosis
April	0.6012	11.28075	127.255	0.274	-0.249
May	1.733	8.13345	66.153	0.665	-0.575
June	2.5789	6.21222	38.592	-1.649	4.747
July	3.4542	9.60009	92.162	0.755	-0.192
August	2.4907	6.8084	46.354	-1.504	1.78
September	2.2365	8.8545	78.402	-2.305	6.357
October	2.043	6.0556	36.67	0.146	-1.267
November	1.5682	7.39167	54.637	-0.459	-0.784
December	2.9305	7.90078	62.422	-0.79	-0.191
January	-0.6199	7.70891	59.427	-0.794	2.387
February	1.4659	5.42165	29.394	-0.807	-0.953
March	0.4052	6.39924	40.95	-0.2	-0.726
Shapiro-Wilk test :0.000					
Source – Database collected from BSE web portal and computed.					

High mean returns were noticed during the month of July (3.4542) and low mean returns were found during the month of January (-0.6199). While comparing the variance, high level of volatility was noticed on the month of April (127.255) and low level of volatility was noticed in the month of February (29.394).

Result of Skewness test disclosed the positive value and it was noticed during the month of April (0.274), May (0.665), July (0.755) and October (0.146) returns, which implies that most of the April, May, July and October month returns were more than the average returns. The other Month's returns were found negative Skewness, which implies that most of the Other Month's returns were less than the average returns. The Kurtosis results of the BSE IT index returns were found leptokurtic in the month of June (4.747) and September (6.357) returns. Since, Kurtosis values are greater than 3, thus, it is inferred that the level of risk associated with the month of June and September returns of the BSE IT index was high, which means investors may obtain either high level of profit or loss. The other month's returns were found platykurtic. Since, Kurtosis values are less than 3, thus, it is inferred that the level of risk associated with the other month's returns of the BSE IT sector was low, which means investors may obtain either low level of profit or loss.

As the calculated P value of the Shapiro-Wilk test is less than 0.01, it is clearly proved that the data are not normally distributed. Hence, there exists anomaly in the BSE IT index returns.

Our results do confirm the April effect for BSE IT index in India. The average return for March is low as compared to the April average return. This evidence is consistent with the 'tax-loss-selling' hypothesis. It appears that investors in India sell shares that have declined in values, and book losses to save taxes. This causes share prices to decline in March that results in lower returns.

7.3.13. BSE Metal Index

The following table exhibits whether monthly effect prevails in BSE Metal index.

Table 7.13: Monthly Effect – BSE Metal Index

	Mean	Std. Deviation	Variance	Skewness	Kurtosis
April	4.539	11.13542	123.998	0.318	-1.179
May	2.3102	22.22648	494.016	1.731	3.582
June	-2.2984	7.97948	63.672	-1.493	3.235
July	2.6599	10.53441	110.974	0.625	-0.231
August	-0.6289	7.64452	58.439	0.249	0.065
September	4.3688	13.69424	187.532	-1.347	1.742
October	-1.1395	17.37744	301.976	-0.882	2.325
November	-0.5961	10.33041	106.717	-0.095	-0.154
December	6.9411	8.43115	71.084	-0.659	-0.014
January	-2.2983	11.92802	142.278	0.676	2.073
February	-0.9334	7.70072	59.301	-0.293	-0.982
March	3.2998	13.28929	176.605	0.323	-1.052
Shapiro-Wilk test :0.000					
Source – Database collected from BSE web portal and computed.					

High mean returns were noticed during the month of December (6.9411) and low mean returns were found during the month of June (-2.2984). While comparing the variance, high level of volatility was noticed on the month of May (494.016) and low level of volatility was noticed in the month of August (58.439).

Result of Skewness test disclosed the positive value and it was noticed during the month of April (0.318), May (1.731), July (0.625), August (0.249), January (.676) and March (0.323) returns, which implies that most of the April, May, July, August, January and March month returns were more than the average returns. The other Month's returns were found negative Skewness, which implies that most of the Other Month's returns were less than the average returns. The Kurtosis results of the BSE Metal index returns were found leptokurtic on the month of May (3.582) and June (3.235) returns. Since, Kurtosis values are greater than 3, thus, it is inferred that the level of risk associated with the month of May and June returns of the BSE Metal index was high, which means investors may obtain either high level of profit or loss. The other month's returns were found platykurtic. Since, Kurtosis values are less than 3, thus, it is inferred that the level of risk associated with the other month's returns of the BSE Metal sector was low, which means investors may obtain either low level of profit or loss.

As the calculated P value of the Shapiro-Wilk test is less than 0.01, it is clearly proved that the data are not normally distributed. Hence, there exists anomaly in the BSE Metal index returns.

Our results do confirm the April effect for BSE Metal index in India. The average return for March is low as compared to the April average return. This evidence is consistent with the 'tax-loss-selling' hypothesis. It appears that investors in India sell shares that have declined in values, and book losses to save taxes. This causes share prices to decline in March that results in lower returns.

7.3.14. BSE Oil and Gas Index

The following table exhibits whether monthly effect prevails in BSE Oil and Gas index.

Table 7.14: Monthly Effect – BSE Oil and Gas Index

	Mean	Std. Deviation	Variance	Skewness	Kurtosis
April	4.7491	7.9153	62.652	0.488	-1.754
May	0.2882	14.28507	204.063	0.144	0.976
June	0.6608	7.32128	53.601	-0.788	-0.06
July	0.7361	5.94389	35.33	0.59	-0.856
August	0.808	4.83734	23.4	1.143	2.188
September	4.1641	6.46974	41.857	0.284	0.772
October	0.0432	13.412	179.882	-1.064	2.826
November	-0.4641	7.00822	49.115	0.256	-0.991
December	2.2934	5.79418	33.572	-1.307	0.775
January	-0.2778	9.42131	88.761	-0.661	0.336
February	-1.5966	3.61656	13.08	0.047	-0.976
March	2.5583	8.69359	75.579	0.204	-1.448
Shapiro-Wilk test :0.000					
Source – Database collected from BSE web portal and computed.					

High mean returns were noticed during the month of April (4.7491) and low mean returns were found during the month of February (-1.5966). While comparing the variance, high level of volatility was noticed on the month of May (204.063) and low level of volatility was noticed in the month of February (13.080).

Result of Skewness test disclosed the negative value and it was noticed during the month of June (-0.788), October (-1.064), December (-1.307) and January (-.661) returns, which implies that most of the June, October, December, and January month returns were less than the average returns. The other Month's returns were found positive Skewness, which implies that most of the Other Month's returns were more than the average returns. The Kurtosis results of the BSE Oil and Gas index returns were found platykurtic in all the months. Since, Kurtosis values are less than 3, thus, it is inferred that the level of risk associated with the all the months returns of the BSE Oil and Gas index was low, which means investors may obtain either low level of profit or loss. As the calculated P value of the Shapiro-Wilk test is less than 0.01, it is clearly proved that the data are not normally distributed. Hence, there exists anomaly in the BSE Oil and Gas index returns.

Our results do confirm the April effect for BSE Oil and Gas index in India. The average return for March is low as compared to the April average return. This evidence is consistent with the 'tax-loss-selling' hypothesis. It appears that investors in India sell shares that have declined in values, and book losses to save taxes. This causes share prices to decline in March that results in lower returns.

7.3.15. BSE Power Index

The following table exhibits whether monthly effect prevails in BSE Power index.

Table 7.15: Monthly Effect – BSE Power Index

	Mean	Median	Std. Deviation	Variance	Skewness	Kurtosis
April	3.1808	2.1619	5.90974	34.925	0.754	-0.312
May	3.127	-2.2045	17.33465	300.49	1.025	0.225
June	-0.0647	2.0639	9.80359	96.11	-1.582	3.088
July	1.0351	0.4564	7.81113	61.014	0.381	-1.147
August	-0.4748	-0.3256	5.73912	32.938	0.229	-0.304
September	3.7286	6.523	8.54507	73.018	-0.762	0.39
October	0.2508	0.0308	16.04579	257.467	0.291	2.452
November	1.1925	1.5763	7.66057	58.684	0.292	1.832
December	2.047	3.3242	5.7515	33.08	-0.021	-0.197
January	-0.4663	-2.0078	10.68988	114.273	0.187	-0.491
February	-1.4351	-2.0717	6.37188	40.601	0.404	-0.346
March	0.8929	2.6586	8.79041	77.271	-0.2	-1.286
Shapiro-Wilk test :0.000						
Source – Database collected from BSE web portal and computed.						

High mean returns were noticed during the month of September (3.7286) and low mean returns were found during the month of February (-1.4351). While comparing the variance, high level of volatility was noticed on the month of May (300.490) and low level of volatility was noticed in the month of August (32.938).

Result of Skewness test disclosed the negative value and it was noticed during the month of June (-1.582), September (-0.762), December (-0.021) and March (-.200) returns, which implies that most of the June, September, December, and March month returns were less than the average returns. The other Month's returns were found positive Skewness, which implies that most of the Other Month's returns were more than the average returns. The Kurtosis results of the BSE Power index returns were found leptokurtic in the month of June (3.088) returns. Since, Kurtosis values are greater than 3, thus, it is inferred that the level of risk associated with the month of June returns of the BSE Power index was high, which means investors may obtain either high level of profit or loss. The other month's returns were found platykurtic. Since, Kurtosis values are less than 3, thus, it is inferred that the level of risk associated with the other month's returns of the BSE Power sector was low, which means investors may obtain either low level of profit or loss.

As the calculated P value of the Shapiro-Wilk test is less than 0.01, it is clearly proved that the data are not normally distributed. Hence, there exists anomaly in the BSE Power index returns.

Our results do confirm the April effect for BSE Power index in India.The average return for March is low as compared to the April average return. This evidence is consistent with the 'tax-loss-selling' hypothesis. It appears that investors in India sell shares that have declined in values, and book losses to save taxes. This causes share prices to decline in March that results in lower returns.

7.3.16. BSE Public Sector Unit Index

The following table exhibits whether monthly effect prevails in BSE PSU index.

Table 7.16: Monthly Effect – BSE PSU Index

	Mean	Std. Deviation	Variance	Skewness	Kurtosis
April	3.2937	5.10631	26.074	0.069	-0.033
May	0.9786	19.60333	384.291	0.945	1.389
June	-1.4281	7.95049	63.21	-1.245	1.935
July	2.1524	8.23898	67.881	0.281	0.512
August	-0.3169	5.09653	25.975	0.086	1.253
September	4.5656	6.65106	44.237	-0.499	-0.031
October	-1.0671	11.3611	129.075	-0.91	2.219
November	1.559	6.50173	42.273	-0.271	-0.377
December	3.735	6.66672	44.445	0.211	-0.413
January	-1.457	9.32389	86.935	-0.504	2.153
February	-1.3892	5.23232	27.377	-0.452	-0.458
March	0.2157	8.17414	66.817	0.339	-0.549
Shapiro-Wilk test :0.000					
Source – Database collected from BSE web portal and computed.					

High mean returns were noticed during the month of September (4.5656) and low mean returns were found during the month of January (-1.4570). While comparing the variance, high level of volatility was noticed on the month of May (384.291) and low level of volatility was noticed in the month of August (25.975).

Result of Skewness test disclosed the negative value and it was noticed during the month of June (-1.245), September (-0.499), October (-0.910), November (-.271), January (-0.504) and

February (-.452) returns, which implies that most of the June, September, October, November, January and February month returns were less than the average returns. The other Month's returns were found positive Skewness, which implies that most of the Other Month's returns were more than the average returns. The Kurtosis results of the BSE PSU index returns were found platykurtic in all the months. Since, Kurtosis values are less than 3, thus, it is inferred that the level of risk associated with the all the months returns of the BSE PSU index was low, which means investors may obtain either low level of profit or loss.

As the calculated P value of the Shapiro-Wilk test is less than 0.01, it is clearly proved that the data are not normally distributed. Hence, there exists anomaly in the BSE PSU index returns.

Our results do confirm the April effect for BSE PSU index in India. The average return for March is low as compared to the April average return. This evidence is consistent with the 'tax-loss-selling' hypothesis. It appears that investors in India sell shares that have declined in values, and book losses to save taxes. This causes share prices to decline in March that results in lower returns.

7.3.17. BSE Realty Index

The following table exhibits whether monthly effect prevails in BSE Realty index.

Table 7.17: Monthly Effect – BSE Realty Index

	Mean	Median	Std. Deviation	Variance	Skewness	Kurtosis
April	12.9636	6.8103	22.2704	495.971	1.518	1.932
May	11.6018	-0.0977	30.87731	953.408	1.463	2.134
June	-7.1806	-7.2604	13.37054	178.771	-0.987	1.623
July	2.4439	1.0674	11.62969	135.25	0.328	-0.952
August	-4.1104	-7.7386	8.37838	70.197	0.983	0.998
September	7.7789	2.1767	21.55993	464.831	-0.002	0.368
October	-1.0649	-1.7612	19.45635	378.55	-1.367	2.202
November	-2.1512	0.9267	14.95659	223.7	0.003	-1.297
December	6.101	5.3362	17.59664	309.642	1.584	2.867
January	-5.6888	-9.2215	18.11925	328.307	0.539	-1.077
February	-6.1258	-7.529	10.60353	112.435	0.542	0.96
March	0.1348	-0.0669	14.35064	205.941	0.256	-0.957
Shapiro-Wilk test :0.000						
Source – Database collected from BSE web portal and computed.						

High mean returns were noticed during the month of April (12.9636) and low mean returns were found during the month of June (-7.1806). While comparing the variance, high level of volatility was noticed on the month of May (953.408) and low level of volatility was noticed in the month of August (70.197). Result of Skewness test disclosed the negative value and it was noticed during the month of June (-0.987), September (-0.002) and October (-1.367) returns, which implies that most of the June, September and October month returns were less than the average returns. The other Month's returns were found positive Skewness, which implies that most of the Other Month's returns were more than the average returns. The Kurtosis results of the BSE Realty index returns were found platykurtic in all the months. Since, Kurtosis values are less than 3, thus, it is inferred that the level of risk associated with the all the months returns of the BSE Realty index was low, which means investors may obtain either low level of profit or loss.

As the calculated P value of the Shapiro-Wilk test is less than 0.01, it is clearly proved that the data are not normally distributed. Hence, there exists anomaly in the BSE Realty index returns.

Our results do confirm the April effect for BSE Realty index in India. The average return for March is low as compared to the April average return. This evidence is consistent with the 'tax-loss-selling' hypothesis. It appears that investors in India sell shares that have declined in values, and book losses to save taxes. This causes share prices to decline in March that results in lower returns.

7.3.18. BSE Teck Index

The following table exhibits whether monthly effect prevails in BSE Teck index.

Table 7.18: Monthly Effect – BSE Teck Index

	Mean	Std. Deviation	Variance	Skewness	Kurtosis
April	1.1745	9.1662	84.019	0.463	-0.471
May	1.1718	8.1363	66.199	0.842	0.329
June	1.7419	6.28539	39.506	-2.414	7.334
July	4.3914	6.44544	41.544	0.548	0.082
August	1.2399	5.6481	31.901	-1.316	2.455
September	2.9419	7.26182	52.734	-2.427	6.854
October	0.3235	8.33956	69.548	-0.786	-0.38
November	2.3291	6.98179	48.745	-0.265	-1.276
December	3.2231	5.33956	28.511	-0.26	-1.577
January	-1.2795	7.75396	60.124	-0.825	1.403
February	0.0277	4.02842	16.228	-0.74	-0.438
March	0.91	5.80187	33.662	0.229	-0.758
Shapiro-Wilk test :0.000					
Source – Database collected from BSE web portal and computed.					

High mean returns were noticed during the month of July (4.3914) and low mean returns were found during the month of January (-1.2795). While comparing the variance, high level of volatility was noticed on the month of April (84.019) and low level of volatility was noticed in the month of February (16.228). Result of Skewness test disclosed the positive value and it was noticed during the month of April (0.463), May (0.842), July (0.548) and March (0.229) returns, which implies that most of the April, May, July and March month returns were more than the average returns. The other Month's returns were found negative Skewness, which implies that most of the Other Month's returns were less than the average returns. The

Kurtosis results of the BSE TECK index returns were found leptokurtic on the month of June (7.334) and September (6.854) returns. Since, Kurtosis values are greater than 3, thus, it is inferred that the level of risk associated with the month of June and September returns of the BSE TECK index was high, which means investors may obtain either high level of profit or loss. The other month's returns were found platykurtic. Since, Kurtosis values are less than 3, thus, it is inferred that the level of risk associated with the other month's returns of the BSE TECK sector was low, which means investors may obtain either low level of profit or loss.

As the calculated P value of the Shapiro-Wilk test is less than 0.01, it is clearly proved that the data are not normally distributed. Hence, there exists anomaly in the BSE TECK index returns.

Our results do confirm the April effect for BSE TECK index in India. The average return for March is low as compared to the April average return. This evidence is consistent with the 'tax-loss-selling' hypothesis. It appears that investors in India sell shares that have declined in values, and book losses to save taxes. This causes share prices to decline in March that results in lower returns.

7.3.19. BSE Telecom Index

The following table exhibits whether monthly effect prevails in BSE Telecom index.

Table 7.19: Monthly Effect – BSE Telecom Index

	Mean	Median	Std. Deviation	Variance	Skewness	Kurtosis
April	5.1432	4.8461	8.86439	78.577	-0.132	-0.797
May	-0.625	-2.9084	9.95423	99.087	0.888	0.861
June	-0.6606	0.482	7.76547	60.302	-1.781	4.916
July	6.4981	6.682	5.88284	34.608	0.392	-0.053
August	-3.6865	-2.8194	7.20296	51.883	-0.037	-0.356
September	4.2367	8.3008	7.21132	52.003	-1.27	0.174
October	-2.7417	-0.1839	15.59527	243.212	-0.915	0.068
November	2.1522	-0.3135	9.61924	92.53	1.385	1.386
December	0.8837	0.4044	7.06922	49.974	-0.084	-0.751
January	-2.0056	-4.0576	11.2043	125.536	-0.042	-1.415
February	-4.3972	-4.1541	2.0347	4.14	-0.399	-0.859
March	3.3784	7.6033	7.43398	55.264	-0.663	-1.469
Shapiro-Wilk test :0.000						
Source – Database collected from BSE web portal and computed.						

High mean returns were noticed during the month of July (6.4981) and low mean returns were found during the month of February (-4.3972). While comparing the variance, high level of volatility was noticed on the month of October (243.212) and low level of volatility was noticed in the month of February (4.140). Result of Skewness test disclosed the positive value and it was noticed during the month of May (0.888), July (0.392) and November (1.385) returns, which implies that most of the May, July and November month returns were more than the average returns. The other Month's returns were found negative Skewness, which implies that most of the Other Month's returns were less than the average returns. The Kurtosis results of the BSE Telecom index returns were found leptokurtic in the month of June (4.916) returns. Since, Kurtosis values are greater than 3, thus, it is inferred that the level of risk associated with the month of June returns of the BSE Telecom index was high, which means investors may obtain either high level of profit or loss. The other month's returns were found platykurtic. Since, Kurtosis values are less than 3, thus, it is inferred that the level of risk associated with the other month's returns of the BSE Telecom sector was low, which means investors may obtain either low level of profit or loss.

As the calculated P value of the Shapiro-Wilk test is less than 0.01, it is clearly proved that the data are not normally distributed. Hence, there exists anomaly in the BSE Telecom index returns.

Our results do confirm the April effect for BSE Telecom index in India.The average return for March is low as compared to the April average return. This evidence is consistent with the 'tax-loss-selling' hypothesis. It appears that investors in India sell shares that have declined in values, and book losses to save taxes. This causes share prices to decline in March that results in lower returns.

7.3.20. BSE Utilities Index

The following table exhibits whether monthly effect prevails in BSE Utilities index.

Table 7.20: Monthly Effect – BSE Utilities Index

	Mean	Std. Deviation	Variance	Skewness	Kurtosis
April	6.3655	7.22694	52.229	.432	.412
May	1.2880	14.61534	213.608	.708	-.265
June	.2310	8.94746	80.057	-.936	-.029
July	1.2792	7.63653	58.317	1.514	3.293
August	-1.9297	7.76945	60.364	.042	-1.579
September	4.7070	8.68945	75.507	.947	1.503
October	.8052	11.86099	140.683	-1.422	3.621
November	-.3426	11.21563	125.790	1.528	2.744
December	2.2824	8.78192	77.122	1.868	3.814
January	-1.0969	9.33208	87.088	-.748	.472
February	-1.0740	6.64988	44.221	.891	1.238
March	-4.2165	7.18016	51.555	.248	.950
Shapiro-Wilk test :0.000					
Source – Database collected from BSE web portal and computed.					

High mean returns were noticed during the month of April (6.3655) and low mean returns were found during the month of March (-4.2165). While comparing the variance, high level of volatility was noticed on the month of May (213.608) and low level of volatility was noticed in the month of February (44.221).

Result of Skewness test disclosed the negative value and it was noticed during the month of June (-0.936), October (-1.422) and January (-.748) returns, which implies that most of the

June, October and January month returns were less than the average returns. The other Month's returns were found positive Skewness, which implies that most of the Other Month's returns were more than the average returns. The Kurtosis results of the BSE Utilities index returns were found leptokurtic on the month of July (3.293), October (3.621) and December (3.814) returns. Since, Kurtosis values are greater than 3, thus, it is inferred that the level of risk associated with the month of July, October and December returns of the BSE Utilities index was high, which means investors may obtain either high level of profit or loss. The other month's returns were found platykurtic. Since, Kurtosis values are less than 3, thus, it is inferred that the level of risk associated with the other month's returns of the BSE Utilities sector was low, which means investors may obtain either low level of profit or loss.

As the calculated P value of the Shapiro-Wilk test is less than 0.01, it is clearly proved that the data are not normally distributed. Hence, there exists anomaly in the BSE Utilities index returns.

Our results do confirm the April effect for BSE Utilities index in India. The average return for March is low as compared to the April average return. This evidence is consistent with the 'tax-loss-selling' hypothesis. It appears that investors in India sell shares that have declined in values, and book losses to save taxes. This causes share prices to decline in March that results in lower returns.

7.3.21. NSE Nifty Index

The following table exhibits whether monthly effect prevails in NSE Nifty index.

Table 7.21: Monthly Effect – NSE Nifty Index

	Mean	Std. Deviation	Variance	Skewness	Kurtosis
April	2.992	5.87878	34.56	0.582	0.658
May	0.1716	12.47756	155.69	0.914	1.531
June	0.5229	6.73785	45.399	-1.931	4.663
July	2.7343	4.02924	16.235	0.185	-1.443
August	0.2004	4.41865	19.524	-0.287	1.709
September	5.1371	6.61151	43.712	-1.292	1.675
October	0.185	11.57337	133.943	-1.047	2.096
November	1.9154	6.52045	42.516	-0.117	-0.865
December	2.7287	4.13237	17.076	-0.59	-0.88
January	-0.9389	8.13534	66.184	-0.324	0.072
February	-0.5498	3.99518	15.961	-0.886	-0.548
March	2.3454	6.66757	44.456	-0.315	-1.132
Shapiro-Wilk test :0.000					
Source – Database collected from NSE web portal and computed.					

High mean returns were noticed during the month of September (5.1371) and low mean returns were found during the month of January (-0.9389). While comparing the variance, high level of volatility was noticed on the month of May (155.690) and low level of volatility was noticed in the month of February (15.961). Result of Skewness test disclosed the positive value and it was noticed during the month of April (0.582), May (0.914) and July (0.185) returns, which implies that most of the April, May and July month returns were more than the average returns. The other Month's returns were found negative Skewness, which implies that most of the Other Month's returns were less than the average returns. The Kurtosis results of the NSE Nifty Index returns were found leptokurtic in the month of June (4.663) returns. Since, Kurtosis values are greater than 3, thus, it is inferred that the level of risk associated with the month of June returns of the NSE Nifty Index was high, which means investors may obtain either high level of profit or loss. The other month's returns were found platykurtic. Since, Kurtosis values are less than 3, thus, it is inferred that the level of risk associated with the other month's returns of the NSE Nifty Index was low, which means investors may obtain either low level of profit or loss.

As the calculated P value of the Shapiro-Wilk test is less than 0.01, it is clearly proved that the data are not normally distributed. Hence, there exists anomaly in the NSE Nifty Index returns.

Our results do confirm the April effect for NSE Nifty index in India. The average return for March is low as compared to the April average return. This evidence is consistent with the 'tax-loss-selling' hypothesis. It appears that investors in India sell shares that have declined in values, and book losses to save taxes. This causes share prices to decline in March that results in lower returns.

7.3.22. NSE Auto Index

The following table exhibits whether monthly effect prevails in NSE Auto index.

Table 7.22: Monthly Effect – NSE Auto Index

	Mean	Std. Deviation	Variance	Skewness	Kurtosis
April	4.219	4.07609	16.614	0.82	0.949
May	-0.9613	13.93728	194.248	1.035	1.48
June	-0.206	7.13384	50.892	-1.199	1.926
July	3.1909	8.45378	71.466	2.004	4.831
August	2.7768	5.23439	27.399	0.554	-0.827
September	6.715	6.31394	39.866	-1.019	1.111
October	-0.4513	9.91682	98.343	-1.601	3.799
November	2.4715	8.97407	80.534	-0.351	-0.236
December	3.2227	4.13476	17.096	-0.602	-0.573
January	-1.4165	8.6306	74.487	-0.022	-0.435
February	2.1174	6.47225	41.89	-0.19	-1.373
March	1.8205	7.48909	56.087	0.359	-1.363
Shapiro-Wilk test :0.000					
Source – Database collected from NSE web portal and computed.					

High mean returns were noticed during the month of September (6.7150) and low mean returns were found during the month of January (-1.4165). While comparing the variance, high level of volatility was noticed in the month of May (194.248) and low level of volatility was noticed in the month of April (16.614). Result of Skewness test disclosed the positive value and it was noticed during the month of April (0.820), May (1.035), July (2.004), August (0.554) and

March (0.359) returns, which implies that most of the April, May, July, August and March month returns were more than the average returns. The other Month's returns were found negative Skewness, which implies that most of the Other Month's returns were less than the average returns. The Kurtosis results of the NSE Auto returns were found leptokurtic in the month of July (4.831) and October (3.799) returns. Since, Kurtosis values are greater than 3, thus, it is inferred that the level of risk associated with the month of July and October returns of the NSE Auto Index was high, which means investors may obtain either high level of profit or loss. The other month's returns were found platykurtic. Since, Kurtosis values are less than 3, thus, it is inferred that the level of risk associated with the other month's returns of the NSE Auto Index was low, which means investors may obtain either low level of profit or loss.

As the calculated P value of the Shapiro-Wilk test is less than 0.01, it is clearly proved that the data are not normally distributed. Hence, there exists anomaly in the NSE Auto Index returns.

Our results do confirm the April effect for NSE Auto index in India. The average return for March is low as compared to the April average return. This evidence is consistent with the 'tax-loss-selling' hypothesis. It appears that investors in India sell shares that have declined in values, and book losses to save taxes. This causes share prices to decline in March that results in lower returns.

7.3.23. NSE Bank Index

The following table exhibits whether monthly effect prevails in NSE Bank index.

Table 7.23: Monthly Effect – NSE Bank Index

	Mean	Std. Deviation	Variance	Skewness	Kurtosis
April	4.9957	9.41549	88.652	0.508	0.708
May	1.2796	18.80943	353.794	1.064	2.045
June	-1.2656	9.2968	86.43	-1.516	2.642
July	3.985	8.92264	79.614	-0.141	0.972
August	-0.851	7.50426	56.314	0.2	-0.463
September	9.3402	8.78821	77.233	-0.489	-1.251
October	0.941	11.74209	137.877	-0.498	0.299
November	3.8453	9.616	92.467	-0.159	0.535
December	3.4763	7.4044	54.825	0.89	0.346
January	-0.9193	10.05513	101.106	1.694	3.772
February	-2.3156	6.92961	48.019	-0.271	-1.191
March	0.9548	11.01837	121.404	-0.726	1.673
Shapiro-Wilk test :0.000					
Source – Database collected from NSE web portal and computed.					

High mean returns were noticed during the month of September (9.3402) and low mean returns were found during the month of February (-2.3156). While comparing the variance, high level of volatility was noticed in the month of May (353.794) and low level of volatility was noticed in the month of February (48.019). Result of Skewness test disclosed the positive value and it was noticed during the month of April (0.508), May (1.064), August (0.200),

December (0.890) and January (1.694) returns, which implies that most of the April, May, August, December and January month returns were more than the average returns. The other Month's returns were found negative Skewness, which implies that most of the Other Month's returns were less than the average returns. The Kurtosis results of the NSE Bank returns were found leptokurtic in the month of January (3.772) returns. Since, Kurtosis values are greater than 3, thus, it is inferred that the level of risk associated with the month of January returns of the NSE Bank Index was high, which means investors may obtain either high level of profit or loss. The other month's returns were found platykurtic. Since, Kurtosis values are less than 3, thus, it is inferred that the level of risk associated with the other month's returns of the NSE Bank Index was low, which means investors may obtain either low level of profit or loss.

As the calculated P value of the Shapiro-Wilk test is less than 0.01, it is clearly proved that the data are not normally distributed. Hence, there exists anomaly in the NSE Bank Index returns.

Our results do confirm the April effect for NSE Bank index in India. The average return for March is low as compared to the April average return. This evidence is consistent with the 'tax-loss-selling' hypothesis. It appears that investors in India sell shares that have declined in values, and book losses to save taxes. This causes share prices to decline in March that results in lower returns.

7.3.24. NSE Energy Index

The following table exhibits whether monthly effect prevails in NSE Energy index.

Table 7.24: Monthly Effect – NSE Energy Index

	Mean	Std. Deviation	Variance	Skewness	Kurtosis
April	2.9433	5.68275	32.294	0.435	-1.36
May	-0.2472	14.67361	215.315	0.045	0.512
June	0.3415	6.16493	38.006	-1.006	0.229
July	1.2213	5.79027	33.527	0.576	-1.031
August	0.6689	4.30382	18.523	0.668	2.153
September	3.9314	6.05219	36.629	0.729	1.879
October	0.3279	13.28599	176.518	-0.5	2.656
November	-0.436	5.84438	34.157	0.53	0.619
December	2.4967	5.82931	33.981	-1.043	0.089
January	-0.9407	9.28322	86.178	-0.679	0.704
February	-1.0828	3.96404	15.714	-0.361	-0.5
March	1.8244	7.5931	57.655	0	-1.888
Shapiro-Wilk test :0.000					
Source – Database collected from NSE web portal and computed.					

High mean returns were noticed during the month of September (3.9314) and low mean returns were found during the month of February (-1.0828). While comparing the variance, high level of volatility was noticed in the month of May (215.315) and low level of volatility was noticed in the month of February (15.714).

Result of Skewness test disclosed the negative value and it was noticed during the month of June (-1.006), October (-0.500), December (-1.043), January (-.679) and February (-.361) returns, which implies that most of the June, October, December, January and February month returns were less than the average returns. The other Month's returns were found positive Skewness, which implies that most of the Other Month's returns were more than the average returns. The Kurtosis results of the NSE Energy index returns were found platykurtic in all the months. Since, Kurtosis values are less than 3, thus, it is inferred that the level of risk associated with the all the months returns of the NSE Energy index was low, which means investors may obtain either low level of profit or loss. As the calculated P value of the Shapiro-Wilk test is less than 0.01, it is clearly proved that the data are not normally distributed. Hence, there exists anomaly in the NSE Energy Index returns.

Our results do confirm the April effect for NSE Energy index in India. The average return for March is low as compared to the April average return. This evidence is consistent with the 'tax-loss-selling' hypothesis. It appears that investors in India sell shares that have declined in values, and book losses to save taxes. This causes share prices to decline in March that results in lower returns.

7.3.25. NSE Finance Index

The following table exhibits whether monthly effect prevails in NSE Finance index.

Table 7.25: Monthly Effect – NSE Finance Index

	Mean	Std. Deviation	Variance	Skewness	Kurtosis
April	4.8662	8.71231	75.904	1.026	1.457
May	1.8584	17.86174	319.042	1.214	2.317
June	-0.3912	9.32502	86.956	-1.755	3.684
July	3.946	7.69721	59.247	-0.464	1.383
August	-0.4644	6.52499	42.575	0.234	0.095
September	8.2543	8.95621	80.214	-0.542	-0.568
October	0.7225	11.61694	134.953	-0.721	0.682
November	3.6757	9.88094	97.633	-0.244	-0.356
December	3.2288	6.21186	38.587	0.922	0.235
January	-0.874	9.3389	87.215	1.276	1.988
February	-1.9252	6.22118	38.703	-0.456	-1.117
March	0.9059	10.22783	104.608	-0.992	1.909
Shapiro-Wilk test :0.000					
Source – Database collected from NSE web portal and computed.					

High mean returns were noticed during the month of September (8.2543) and low mean returns were found during the month of February (-1.9252). While comparing the variance, high level of volatility was noticed in the month of May (319.042) and low level of volatility was noticed in the month of December (38.587).

Result of Skewness test disclosed the positive value and it was noticed during the month of April (1.026), May (1.214), August (0.234), December (0.922) and January (1.276) returns, which implies that most of the April, May, August, December and January month returns were more than the average returns. The other Month's returns were found negative Skewness, which implies that most of the Other Month's returns were less than the average returns. The Kurtosis results of the NSE Finance returns were found leptokurtic in the month of June (3.684) returns. Since, Kurtosis values are greater than 3, thus, it is inferred that the level of risk associated with the month of June returns of the NSE Finance Index was high, which means investors may obtain either high level of profit or loss. The other month's returns were found platykurtic. Since, Kurtosis values are less than 3, thus, it is inferred that the level of risk associated with the other month's returns of the NSE Finance Index was low, which means investors may obtain either low level of profit or loss.

As the calculated P value of the Shapiro-Wilk test is less than 0.01, it is clearly proved that the data are not normally distributed. Hence, there exists anomaly in the NSE Finance Index returns.

Our results do confirm the April effect for NSE Finance index in India. The average return for March is low as compared to the April average return. This evidence is consistent with the 'tax-loss-selling' hypothesis. It appears that investors in India sell shares that have declined in values, and book losses to save taxes. This causes share prices to decline in March that results in lower returns.

7.3.26. NSE Fast Moving Consumer Goods Index

The following table exhibits whether monthly effect prevails in NSE FMCG index.

Table 7.26: Monthly Effect – NSE Fast Moving Consumer Goods Index

	Mean	Std. Deviation	Variance	Skewness	Kurtosis
April	3.6969	3.70536	13.73	-0.441	0.097
May	-0.543	7.65547	58.606	-1.294	1.609
June	1.3246	7.54947	56.995	-0.785	0.285
July	4.354	5.83357	34.031	1.493	3.466
August	0.7848	4.94629	24.466	-0.385	-1.03
September	5.1235	4.54349	20.643	-0.121	-1.241
October	-1.6787	6.78547	46.043	-0.599	0.767
November	3.8002	6.08054	36.973	0.611	-0.145
December	1.3869	4.05019	16.404	0.491	-0.417
January	-0.3029	5.36604	28.794	-0.774	0.003
February	0.1639	5.22397	27.29	1.239	2.856
March	3.0764	5.34304	28.548	-0.004	-0.791
Shapiro-Wilk test :0.000					
Source – Database collected from NSE web portal and computed.					

High mean returns were noticed during the month of September (5.1235) and low mean returns were found during the month of October (-1.6787). While comparing the variance, high level of volatility was noticed in the month of May (58.606) and low level of volatility was noticed in the month of April (13.730). Result of Skewness test disclosed the positive value and it was noticed during the month of July (1.493), November (0.611), December (0.491) and

February (1.239) returns, which implies that most of the July, November, December and February month returns were more than the average returns. The other Month's returns were found negative Skewness, which implies that most of the Other Month's returns were less than the average returns. The Kurtosis results of the NSE FMCG returns were found leptokurtic in the month of July (3.466) returns. Since, Kurtosis values are greater than 3, thus, it is inferred that the level of risk associated with the month of July returns of the NSE FMCG Index was high, which means investors may obtain either high level of profit or loss. The other month's returns were found platykurtic. Since, Kurtosis values are less than 3, thus, it is inferred that the level of risk associated with the other month's returns of the NSE FMCG Index was low, which means investors may obtain either low level of profit or loss.

As the calculated P value of the Shapiro-Wilk test is less than 0.01, it is clearly proved that the data are not normally distributed. Hence, there exists anomaly in the NSE FMCG Index returns.

Our results do confirm the April effect for NSE FMCG index in India. The average return for March is low as compared to the April average return. This evidence is consistent with the 'tax-loss-selling' hypothesis. It appears that investors in India sell shares that have declined in values, and book losses to save taxes. This causes share prices to decline in March that results in lower returns.

7.3.27. NSE IT Index

The following table exhibits whether monthly effect prevails in NSE IT index.

Table 7.27: Monthly Effect – NSE IT Index

	Mean	Median	Std. Deviation	Variance	Skewness	Kurtosis
April	1.2013	-0.1935	10.53981	111.088	0.037	-0.156
May	1.3258	-0.8611	8.66976	75.165	-0.025	0.131
June	1.9204	2.4005	6.70147	44.91	-1.458	3.918
July	2.3594	1.0678	9.10502	82.901	0.814	-0.285
August	1.3296	4.1335	7.88744	62.212	-1.804	3.316
September	0.743	4.1966	11.92533	142.213	-2.718	7.993
October	0.1719	-0.2793	6.5837	43.345	-0.255	0.06
November	0.2548	1.6261	7.85834	61.753	-0.382	-1.136
December	3.7777	6.375	6.99548	48.937	-0.767	-1.137
January	-1.6726	0.9342	10.34911	107.104	-1.642	3.521
February	0.8919	3.1058	5.50241	30.277	-0.771	-0.877
March	0.5915	1.4065	6.80049	46.247	-0.066	-0.855
Shapiro-Wilk test :0.000						
Source – Database collected from NSE web portal and computed.						

High mean returns were noticed during the month of December (3.7777) and low mean returns were found during the month of January (-1.6726). While comparing the variance, high level of volatility was noticed in the month of September (142.213) and low level of volatility was noticed in the month of February (30.277). Result of Skewness test disclosed the positive value and it was noticed during the month of April (0.037) and July (0.814) returns, which implies that most of the April and July month returns were more than the average returns. The other Month's returns were found negative Skewness, which implies that most of the Other Month's returns were less than the average returns. The Kurtosis results of the NSE IT returns were found leptokurtic on the month of June (3.918), August (3.316), September (7.993) and January (3.521) returns. Since, Kurtosis values are greater than 3, thus, it is inferred that the level of risk associated with the month of June, August, September and January returns of the NSE IT Index was high, which means investors may obtain either high level of profit or loss. The other month's returns were found platykurtic. Since, Kurtosis values are less than 3, thus, it is inferred that the level of risk associated with the other month's returns of the NSE IT Index was low, which means investors may obtain either low level of profit or loss.

As the calculated P value of the Shapiro-Wilk test is less than 0.01, it is clearly proved that the data are not normally distributed. Hence, there exists anomaly in the NSE IT Index returns.

Our results do confirm the April effect for NSE IT index in India. The average return for March is low as compared to the April average return. This evidence is consistent with the 'tax-loss-selling' hypothesis. It appears that investors in India sell shares that have declined in values, and book losses to save taxes. This causes share prices to decline in March that results in lower returns.

7.3.28. NSE Media Index

The following table exhibits whether monthly effect prevails in NSE Media index.

Table 7.28: Monthly Effect – NSE Media Index

	Mean	Std. Deviation	Variance	Skewness	Kurtosis
April	4.2232	6.49098	42.133	.451	-1.354
May	3.5225	15.91898	253.414	2.132	5.083
June	-.5983	9.68760	93.850	-.650	-.410
July	1.9022	5.75241	33.090	.696	-.641
August	-.9275	7.55792	57.122	.074	-1.616
September	4.0898	9.47559	89.787	-.908	2.581
October	-1.6414	11.90536	141.738	-2.124	5.491
November	1.3075	11.49610	132.160	-.273	.092
December	5.4680	9.84904	97.004	1.142	.968
January	-2.9696	10.41003	108.369	-.164	-1.567
February	-5.2817	4.18086	17.480	.326	-.656
March	1.7830	5.54367	30.732	-.781	.374
Shapiro-Wilk test :0.000					
Source – Database collected from NSE web portal and computed.					

High mean returns were noticed during the month of December (5.4680) and low mean returns were found during the month of February (-5.2817). While comparing the variance, high level of volatility was noticed in the month of May (253.414) and low level of volatility was noticed in the month of February (17.480).

Result of Skewness test disclosed the positive value and it was noticed during the month of April (0.451), May (2.132), July (.696), August (0.074), December (1.142) and February (0.326) returns, which implies that most of the April, May, July, August, December and February month returns were more than the average returns. The other Month's returns were found negative Skewness, which implies that most of the Other Month's returns were less than the average returns. The Kurtosis results of the NSE Media returns were found leptokurtic on the month of May (5.083) and October (5.491) returns. Since, Kurtosis values are greater than 3, thus, it is inferred that the level of risk associated with the month of May and October returns of the NSE Media Index was high, which means investors may obtain either high level of profit or loss. The other month's returns were found platykurtic. Since, Kurtosis values are less than 3, thus, it is inferred that the level of risk associated with the other month's returns of the NSE Media Index was low, which means investors may obtain either low level of profit or loss.

As the calculated P value of the Shapiro-Wilk test is less than 0.01, it is clearly proved that the data are not normally distributed. Hence, there exists anomaly in the NSE Media Index returns.

Our results do confirm the April effect for NSE Media index in India.The average return for March is low as compared to the April average return. This evidence is consistent with the 'tax-loss-selling' hypothesis. It appears that investors in India sell shares that have declined in values, and book losses to save taxes. This causes share prices to decline in March that results in lower returns.

7.3.29. NSE Metal Index

The following table exhibits whether monthly effect prevails in NSE Metal index.

Table 7.29: Monthly Effect – NSE Metal Index

	Mean	Std. Deviation	Variance	Skewness	Kurtosis
April	3.3892	10.13387	102.695	0.046	-0.735
May	1.8457	20.38719	415.637	1.57	2.759
June	-2.8871	8.24126	67.918	-1.415	2.997
July	3.1	11.07341	122.621	0.609	0.125
August	-0.1263	7.56764	57.269	0	-0.264
September	4.3647	12.93965	167.435	-1.133	1.199
October	-0.222	17.19219	295.571	-0.866	2.419
November	2.4685	13.89128	192.968	0.672	0.665
December	6.2668	8.22572	67.663	-0.904	-0.32
January	-1.9604	12.45614	155.155	0.622	1.705
February	-0.5881	7.41501	54.982	-0.516	-0.47
March	3.2994	14.24587	202.945	0.238	-0.867
Shapiro-Wilk test :0.000					
Source – Database collected from NSE web portal and computed.					

High mean returns were noticed during the month of December (6.2668) and low mean returns were found during the month of June (-2.8871). While comparing the variance, high level of volatility was noticed in the month of May (415.637) and low level of volatility was noticed in the month of February (54.982).

Result of Skewness test disclosed the positive value and it was noticed during the month of April (0.046), May (1.570), July (.609), November (0.672), January (0.622) and March (0.238) returns, which implies that most of the April, May, July, November, January and March month returns were more than the average returns. The other Month's returns were found negative Skewness, which implies that most of the Other Month's returns were less than the average returns. The Kurtosis results of the NSE Metal index returns were found platykurtic in all the months. Since, Kurtosis values are less than 3, thus, it is inferred that the level of risk associated with the all the months returns of the NSE Metal index was low, which means investors may obtain either low level of profit or loss.

As the calculated P value of the Shapiro-Wilk test is less than 0.01, it is clearly proved that the data are not normally distributed. Hence, there exists anomaly in the NSE Metal Index returns.

Our results do confirm the April effect for NSE Metal index in India. The average return for March is low as compared to the April average return. This evidence is consistent with the 'tax-loss-selling' hypothesis. It appears that investors in India sell shares that have declined in values, and book losses to save taxes. This causes share prices to decline in March that results in lower returns.

7.3.30. NSE Pharma Index

The following table exhibits whether monthly effect prevails in NSE Pharma index.

Table 7.30: Monthly Effect – NSE Pharma Index

	Mean	Std. Deviation	Variance	Skewness	Kurtosis
April	4.7784	5.31298	28.228	0.028	-1.073
May	0.4832	7.03654	49.513	-0.492	-0.044
June	0.311	5.09901	26	0.518	0.241
July	2.6918	4.25199	18.079	-0.048	-0.663
August	2.0809	4.8579	23.599	-0.092	-0.146
September	4.2138	7.38255	54.502	-1.126	2.184
October	-1.9857	8.98497	80.73	-1.854	3.583
November	3.336	4.21448	17.762	0.564	0.04
December	3.8465	5.17757	26.807	0.86	0.531
January	-2.9888	7.61819	58.037	-0.235	-1.008
February	0.5786	6.83565	46.726	0.421	-1.148
March	3.8045	5.48875	30.126	-1.093	0.393
Shapiro-Wilk test :0.000					
Source – Database collected from NSE web portal and computed.					

High mean returns were noticed during the month of April (4.7784) and low mean returns were found during the month of January (-2.9888). While comparing the variance, high level of volatility was noticed in the month of October (80.730) and low level of volatility was noticed in the month of November (17.762).

Result of Skewness test disclosed the positive value and it was noticed during the month of April (0.028), June (.518), November (0.564), December (0.860) and February (0.421) returns, which implies that most of the April, June, November, December and February month returns were more than the average returns. The other Month's returns were found negative Skewness, which implies that most of the Other Month's returns were less than the average returns. The Kurtosis results of the NSE Pharma index returns were found leptokurtic in the month of October (3.583) returns. Since, Kurtosis values are greater than 3, thus, it is inferred that the level of risk associated with the month of October returns of the NSE Pharma Index was high, which means investors may obtain either high level of profit or loss. The other month's returns were found platykurtic. Since, Kurtosis values are less than 3, thus, it is inferred that the level of risk associated with the other month's returns of the NSE Pharma Index was low, which means investors may obtain either low level of profit or loss.

As the calculated P value of the Shapiro-Wilk test is less than 0.01, it is clearly proved that the data are not normally distributed. Hence, there exists anomaly in the NSE Pharma Index returns.

Our results do confirm the April effect for NSE Pharma index in India. The average return for March is low as compared to the April average return. This evidence is consistent with the 'tax-loss-selling' hypothesis. It appears that investors in India sell shares that have declined in values, and book losses to save taxes. This causes share prices to decline in March that results in lower returns.

7.3.31. NSE Private Banks Index

The following table exhibits whether monthly effect prevails in NSE Private Bank index.

Table 7.31: Monthly Effect – NSE Private Banks Index

	Mean	Std. Deviation	Variance	Skewness	Kurtosis
April	6.1797	11.02917	121.642	1.388	2.256
May	5.1461	17.27172	298.312	1.801	4.006
June	-0.8158	10.31899	106.481	-1.642	3.136
July	3.1624	7.87288	61.982	-1.295	2.974
August	0.1695	7.48037	55.956	-0.009	-0.616
September	7.9162	9.11913	83.159	-0.532	-0.164
October	1.8734	13.8758	192.538	-0.795	0.132
November	1.8799	9.87832	97.581	-0.838	-0.711
December	2.7681	6.19599	38.39	1.104	3.452
January	1.0773	11.58327	134.172	0.74	0.187
February	-2.8257	7.00635	49.089	-0.215	-1.439
March	3.0464	11.11422	123.526	-1.025	1.476
Shapiro-Wilk test :0.000					
Source – Database collected from NSE web portal and computed.					

High mean returns were noticed during the month of September (7.9162) and low mean returns were found during the month of February (-2.8257). While comparing the variance, high level of volatility was noticed in the month of May (298.312) and low level of volatility was noticed in the month of December (38.390).

Result of Skewness test disclosed the positive value and it was noticed during the month of April (1.388), May (1.801), December (1.104) and January (0.740) returns, which implies that most of the April, May, December and January month returns were more than the average returns. The other Month's returns were found negative Skewness, which implies that most of the Other Month's returns were less than the average returns.

The Kurtosis results of the NSE Private Banks index returns were found leptokurtic on the month of May (4.006), June (3.136) and December (3.452) returns. Since, Kurtosis values are greater than 3, thus, it is inferred that the level of risk associated with the month of May, June and December returns of the NSE Private Banks Index was high, which means investors may obtain either high level of profit or loss.

The other month's returns were found platykurtic. Since, Kurtosis values are less than 3, thus, it is inferred that the level of risk associated with the other month's returns of the NSE Private Banks Index was low, which means investors may obtain either low level of profit or loss.

As the calculated P value of the Shapiro-Wilk test is less than 0.01, it is clearly proved that the data are not normally distributed. Hence, there exists anomaly in the NSE Private Banks Index returns.

Our results do confirm the April effect for NSE Private Banks index in India. The average return for March is low as compared to the April average return. This evidence is consistent with the 'tax-loss-selling' hypothesis. It appears that investors in India sell shares that have declined in values, and book losses to save taxes. This causes share prices to decline in March that results in lower returns.

7.3.32. NSE Public Sector Unit Banks Index

The following table exhibits whether monthly effect prevails in NSE PSU Bank index.

Table 7.32: Monthly Effect – NSE PSU Banks Index

	Mean	Std. Deviation	Variance	Skewness	Kurtosis
April	5.2748	9.37636	87.916	-0.480	-0.019
May	0.8151	20.44903	418.163	0.778	0.515
June	-2.5486	9.80317	96.102	-1.158	0.914
July	3.1675	11.51649	132.63	0.182	-0.745
August	-2.0133	9.36407	87.686	0.266	0.137
September	10.856	9.37826	87.952	-0.148	-1.229
October	-0.8346	10.39979	108.156	-0.380	0.407
November	5.6458	8.87335	78.736	0.501	0.997
December	3.4443	9.72616	94.598	0.420	-0.025
January	-3.0016	10.56674	111.656	2.232	6.389
February	-3.3788	7.62886	58.199	-0.004	-0.514
March	0.3713	12.54539	157.387	0.248	1.830
Shapiro-Wilk test :0.000					
Source – Database collected from NSE web portal and computed.					

High mean returns were noticed during the month of September (10.8560) and low mean returns were found during the month of February (-3.3788). While comparing the variance, high level of volatility was noticed in the month of May (418.163) and low level of volatility was noticed in the month of February (58.199).

Result of Skewness test disclosed the negative value and it was noticed during the month of April (-0.480), June (-1.158), September (-.148), October (-.380) and February (-.004) returns, which implies that most of the April, June, September, October and February month returns were less than the average returns. The other Month's returns were found positive Skewness, which implies that most of the Other Month's returns were more than the average returns. The Kurtosis results of the NSE PSU Banks returns were found leptokurtic in the month of January (6.389) returns. Since, Kurtosis values are greater than 3, thus, it is inferred that the level of risk associated with the month of January returns of the NSE PSU Banks Index was high, which means investors may obtain either high level of profit or loss. The other month's returns were found platykurtic. Since, Kurtosis values are less than 3, thus, it is inferred that the level of risk associated with the other month's returns of the NSE PSU Banks Index was low, which means investors may obtain either low level of profit or loss.

As the calculated P value of the Shapiro-Wilk test is less than 0.01, it is clearly proved that the data are not normally distributed. Hence, there exists anomaly in the NSE PSU Banks Index returns.

Our results do confirm the April effect for NSE PSU Banks index in India. The average return for March is low as compared to the April average return. This evidence is consistent with the 'tax-loss-selling' hypothesis. It appears that investors in India sell shares that have declined in values, and book losses to save taxes. This causes share prices to decline in March that results in lower returns.

7.3.33. NSE Realty Index

The following table exhibits whether monthly effect prevails in NSE Realty index.

Table 7.33: Monthly Effect – NSE Realty Index

	Mean	Std. Deviation	Variance	Skewness	Kurtosis
April	7.5588	15.71144	246.849	1.51	2.958
May	11.125	33.39688	1115.352	1.524	1.977
June	-7.0526	14.87458	221.253	-1.072	1.309
July	3.93	11.68422	136.521	0.073	-0.713
August	-5.5729	8.6358	74.577	1.572	3.049
September	3.6297	18.49456	342.049	-0.673	0.833
October	-3.4001	18.87097	356.114	-1.406	2.291
November	-5.3829	14.27365	203.737	-0.107	-1.705
December	8.2295	19.22366	369.549	1.517	2.734
January	-6.2695	19.69923	388.06	0.682	-1.101
February	-4.5322	9.72191	94.515	0.792	0.839
March	0.069	16.23517	263.581	0.276	-1.53
Shapiro-Wilk test :0.000					
Source – Database collected from NSE web portal and computed.					

High mean returns were noticed during the month of May (11.1250) and low mean returns were found during the month of June (-7.0526). While comparing the variance, high level of volatility was noticed in the month of May (1115.352) and low level of volatility was noticed in the month of August (74.577).

Result of Skewness test disclosed the negative value and it was noticed during the month of June (-1.072), September (-.673), October (-1.406) and November (-.107) returns, which implies that most of the June, September, October and November month returns were less than the average returns. The other Month's returns were found positive Skewness, which implies that most of the Other Month's returns were more than the average returns. The Kurtosis results of the NSE Realty index returns were found leptokurtic in the month of August (3.049) returns. Since, Kurtosis values are greater than 3, thus, it is inferred that the level of risk associated with the month of August returns of the NSE Realty Index was high, which means investors may obtain either high level of profit or loss. The other month's returns were found platykurtic. Since, Kurtosis values are less than 3, thus, it is inferred that the level of risk associated with the other month's returns of the NSE Realty Index was low, which means investors may obtain either low level of profit or loss.

As the calculated P value of the Shapiro-Wilk test is less than 0.01, it is clearly proved that the data are not normally distributed. Hence, there exists anomaly in the NSE Realty Index returns.

Our results do confirm the April effect for NSE Realty index in India. The average return for March is low as compared to the April average return. This evidence is consistent with the 'tax-loss-selling' hypothesis. It appears that investors in India sell shares that have declined in values, and book losses to save taxes. This causes share prices to decline in March that results in lower returns.

7.4. Conclusion

From the analysis, it is inferred that the Monthly Effect and April Effect exist in all BSE Sensex, 19 BSE sectoral indices, NSE Nifty and 12 NSE sectoral indices. Our results do confirm the April effect in India. The average return for March is low as compared to the April average return. This evidence is consistent with the 'tax-loss-selling' hypothesis. It appears that investors in India sell shares that have declined in values, and book losses to save taxes. This causes share prices to decline in March that results in lower returns. The next chapter discuss about Annual effect.

CHAPTER VIII

ANNUAL EFFECT IN INDIAN STOCK MARKET

8.1. Introduction

The stock returns vary from year to year due to excessive liquidation of securities by the investors considering the bank interest rate, arrival of new information in market leads to change in stock returns, portfolio rebalancing by institutions leads to change in stock returns, investors in order to reduce their tax-burden sell their loss making shares and buy back the share in future leads to fluctuation in share returns etc., Annual effect in which, stocks have generally tended to outperform at the over the year. It is referring to the time in calendar year when the present years come to an end and marks the beginning of the new year.

8.2. Tools for Analysis

The collected data have been analyzed by making use of Returns, Descriptive statistics such as Mean, Standard deviation, Variance, Skewness, Kurtosis, Shapiro-Wilk test and paired 't'test.

8.3. Annual Effect

The following subsections discuss about the Annual effect of BSE Sensex, 19 BSE sectoral indices, followed by NSE Nifty and 12 NSE sectoral indices.

8.3.1. Annual Effect BSE Sensex and Sectoral Indices

The following table tries to ascertain, whether Annual effect prevails in BSE Sensex and 19 sectoral indices.

Table 8.1: Annual Effect – BSE Sensex and Sectoral Indices

Sector	Mean	Std.Deviation	Variance	Skewness	Kurtosis	Shapiro-Wilk
Sensex	19.1819	35.47063	1258.165	-.425	.594	0.003
Auto	29.8201	63.24180	3999.525	1.931	5.708	0.011
Bank	25.5017	42.02090	1765.756	-.590	-.654	0.004
Basic Materials	22.3136	65.78434	4327.580	.997	1.796	0.002
Consumer Durables	34.5425	56.65171	3209.416	-.332	-.613	0.000
Consumer Goods	30.6471	57.65782	3324.425	-.084	-.785	0.002
Energy	18.3017	50.09839	2509.849	.714	.713	0.029
Finance	23.9105	47.63854	2269.430	-.353	-1.051	0.012
FMCG	19.4340	21.02563	442.077	.219	-.626	0.901
Health Care	20.3323	26.91823	724.591	-.271	.685	0.035
Industrial	24.4542	58.91478	3470.951	.080	-.455	0.002
IT	22.7915	46.21261	2135.605	.961	2.267	0.025
Metal	23.2672	81.93257	6712.947	1.741	3.581	0.002
Oil & Gas	17.6086	45.00193	2025.173	.749	1.079	0.015
Power	14.3782	53.85437	2900.293	.776	.535	0.076
Public Sector Unit	11.4475	39.45508	1556.703	.397	-.296	0.143
Realty	-.3212	54.93999	3018.402	.123	-1.289	0.001
Teck	18.7682	32.63980	1065.357	-.668	.676	0.001
Telecom	9.5018	36.54908	1335.835	.730	1.027	0.042
Utilities	16.1040	59.05228	3487.172	1.475	2.758	0.030

Source – Database collected from BSE web portal and computed.

High mean returns were noticed in the Consumer Durable sector (34.5425) and low mean returns were found in the Realty (-0.3212). Comparing the variance, high level of volatility was noticed in the Metal sector (6712.947) and low level of volatility was noticed in the FMCG sector (442.077).

Result of the Skewness test discloses that negative value were noticed on the Sensex index (-.425), Banking sector (-.590), Consumer Durables sector (-.332), Consumer Goods sector (-0.084), Finance sector (-.353), Health Care (-.271) and Technology sector (-.668) returns, which implies that most of the Sensex index, bankingsector, Consumer Durables sector, Consumer Goods sector, Finance Sector, Health Care sector and Technology sector returns were less than the average returns. The other sector returns were noticed positive Skewness, which implies that most of the other sectors returns were more than the average returns. The Kurtosis results of the BSE sector's annual returns were found leptokurtic on Auto sector (5.708) and Metal sector (3.581). Since, Kurtosis values are greater than 3, thus, it is inferred that the level of risk associated with Auto sector and Metal sector was high, which means investors may obtain either high level of profit or loss. The other sector results were found platykurtic. Since, Kurtosis values are less than 3, thus, it is inferred that the level of risk associated with the other sector was low, which means investors may obtain either low level of profit or loss. As the calculated P value of the Shapiro-Wilk testis greater than 0.05 for, FMCG (.901), Power (0.076) and PSU (.143) it is clearly proved that the data are normally distributed. Hence, there doesn't exists anomaly in the FMCG, Power and PSU sectors. As the calculated P value of the Shapiro-Wilk testof other sectors is less than 0.05, it is clearly proved that the data are not normally distributed. Hence, anomaly exists on other sectors.

8.3.2. Annual Effect NSE Nifty and Sectoral Indices

The following table tries to ascertain, Annual effect prevails in NSE Nifty and 12 sectoral indices.

Table 8.2: Annual Effect – NSE Nifty and Sectoral Indices

SECTOR	Mean	Std. Deviation	Variance	Skewness	Kurtosis	Shapiro-Wilk
Nifty	21.0445	35.33655	1248.671	-0.75	0.888	0.035
Auto	33.0728	63.91786	4085.493	1.565	4.036	0.002
Bank	26.5825	41.48963	1721.39	-0.675	-0.444	0.025
Energy	14.2105	39.52752	1562.425	0.672	1.081	0.001
Finance	28.5707	44.51141	1981.265	-0.566	-0.22	0.001
FMCG	22.8359	21.49991	462.246	-0.142	0.567	0.143
Media	23.6146	51.53544	2655.901	-0.663	-0.606	0.042
Metal	36.6325	87.17047	7598.691	1.11	1.085	0.002
Pharma	21.1032	24.49961	600.231	-0.573	0.035	0.000
Private banks	37.3595	55.13927	3040.339	-0.621	-0.833	0.029
PSU banks	20.8351	42.65545	1819.487	-0.384	-1.149	0.002
Realty	1.5916	59.27956	3514.066	0.017	-1.647	0.033

Source – Database collected from NSE web portal and computed.

High mean returns were noticed in the Private Banking sector (37.3595) and low mean returns were found in the Realty (1.5916). Comparing the variance, high level of volatility was noticed in the Metal sector (7598.691) and low level of volatility was noticed in the FMCG sector (462.246).

Result of the Skewness test discloses that positive value were noticed on the Auto sector (1.565), Energy sector (0.672), Metal sector (1.110) and Realty sector (0.017) returns, which implies that most of the Auto sector, Energy sector, Metal sector and Realty sector returns were more than the average returns. The other sector returns were noticed Negative Skewness, which implies that most of the other sectors returns were less than the average returns. The Kurtosis results of the NSE sector's annual returns were found leptokurtic on Auto sector (4.036), Since, Kurtosis values are greater than 3, thus, it is inferred that the level of risk associated with Auto sector was high, which means investors may obtain either high level of profit or loss.The other sector results were found platykurtic. Since, Kurtosis values are less than 3, thus, it is inferred that the level of risk associated with the other sector was low, which means investors may obtain either low level of profit or loss.

As the calculated P value of the Shapiro-Wilk testis greater than 0.05 for, FMCG (.143) it is clearly proved that the data are normally distributed.Hence, there does not exists anomaly inthe FMCGsector. Asthecalculated P value of the Shapiro-Wilk testof other sector is less than 0.05, it is clearly proved that the data are not normally distributed.Hence, anomaly exists on other sectors.

8.4. Conclusion

From the analysis, it is inferred that the annual effect exists in other sectors except in BSE FMCG, PSU, Power and NSE FMCG sectors. The next chapter discuss about Seasonality Effect in Shariah Index.

CHAPTER IX

SHARIAH INDEX IN INDIAN STOCK MARKET

9.1. Introduction

Islamic fund is fairly new phenomena in the financial system of India. Sharia is the Muslim or Islamic law which standardizes many aspects of a Muslim's life including the type of investments allowed. For instance, interests are considered according to the Riba rule therefore bonds are prohibited to investors following the Sharia law. A Shariah yielding fund is an investment vehicle fund structured in accordance to Shariah rules. To invest in common shares in companies engaged in halal business. Companies are also screened in order to check for Shariah compliant accounting principles. Because of the limited pool of companies, the funds can invest into, equity funds can have higher volatility compared to similar funds in the same space.

In BSE Sensex shariah index is computed only from the year 2014, whereas shariah index is computed since 2009 in NSE Nifty. Hence, in this chapter only shariah index of NSE Nifty alone discussed.

9.2. Tools for Analysis

The collected data have been analyzed by making use of Returns, Descriptive statistics such as Mean, Standard Deviation, Variance, Skewness, Kurtosis, Shapiro-Wilk test and OLS Regression.

9.3. Day of the Week Effect

The following table tries to ascertain, whether Day of the week effect prevails in NSE Shariah Index.

Table 9.1: Day of the Week Effect - Shariah Index

	MONDAY	TUESDAY	WEDNESDAY	THURSDAY	FRIDAY
Mean	.1038	.0953	.0775	.0342	.1105
Median	.0617	.1046	.0352	.0818	.0929
Std. Deviation	1.51838	1.00956	1.03691	1.11856	1.05872
Variance	2.305	1.019	1.075	1.251	1.121
Skewness	4.913	.288	.250	-.748	.302
Kurtosis	56.855	1.814	1.274	3.897	.687
Shapiro-Wilk	.000	.000	.000	.000	.000

Source - Database collected from NSE web portal and computed.

High mean returns were noticed during Friday (.1105) and low mean returns were found during Thursday (0.0342). While comparing to variance, high level of volatility was noticed on Monday (2.305) and low level of volatility was noticed on Tuesday (1.019).

Result of the Skewness test disclosed that negative value and it was noticed during Thursday returns (-.748), which implies that most of the Thursday returns were less than the average returns. The other day's returns were found positive skewness, which implies that most of the other day's returns were more than the average returns.

The Kurtosis result of the NSE Shariah index returns were found leptokurtic on Monday returns (56.855) and Thursday returns (3.897). Since, Kurtosis values are greater than 3, thus, it is inferred that the level of risk associated with the Monday and Tuesday returns of the NSE Shariah index was high, which means investors may obtain either high level of profit or loss. The other day's returns were found platykurtic. Since, Kurtosis values are less than 3, thus, it is inferred that the level of risk associated with the other day's returns of the NSE Shariah index was low, which means investors may obtain either low level of profit or loss.

As the calculated P value of the Shapiro-Wilk test is less than 0.01, it is clearly proved that the data are not normally distributed. Hence, anomaly exists in the NSE Shariah index returns.

To measure day of the week effect, OLS is employed. Friday return is introduced as dependent variable and the rest of the day, namely Monday, Tuesday, Wednesday and Thursday are considered as independent variables. The following table illustrates the determinants of Day of the week effect of NSE Shariah index.

Table 9.2: Determinants of Day of the Week Effect – Shariah Index

	Coefficient	***Std. Error***	***t-ratio***	***p-value***
Const	0.10827	0.0616538	1.7561	0.08010
Tuesday	0.054868	0.0599544	0.9152	0.36085
Wednesday	-0.0524195	0.0590068	-0.8884	0.37506
Thursday	-0.0312111	0.0548293	-0.5692	0.56962
Monday	0.0283911	0.0401307	0.7075	0.47983
R-squared	0.07923	Adjusted R-squared		-0.005394
F(4, 298)	0.594961	P-value(F)		0.666548
Source – Database collected from NSE web portal and computed.				

The result of OLS regression analyses disclose that the select independent variables collectively contribute to 7.92 per cent variation in Friday returns.

9.4. Semi Month Effect

The following table exhibits whether semi month effect prevails in NSE Shariah index.

Table 9.3: Semi Month Effect – Shariah Index

	Mean	Median	Std. Deviation	Variance	Skewness	Kurtosis	Shapiro-Wilk
First half	0.0592	0.0414	0.38473	0.148	0.997	5.981	0.000
Second half	0.103	0.0976	0.3595	0.129	1.314	7.177	0.000

Source – Database collected from NSE web portal and computed.

High mean returns were noticed during the second half of the month (0.103) and low mean returns were found during the first half of the month (0.0592). While comparing the variance, high level of volatility was noticed on the first half of the month (0.148) and low level of volatility was noticed in the second half of the month (0.129).

Result of the Skewness test disclosed that positive value were noticed during both the first half of the month (0.997) and the second half of the month (1.314) returns, which implies that most of the first and second half of the month returns were more than the average returns. The Kurtosis of the NSE Shariah index returns were found leptokurtic on both the First half of the month (5.981) and the second half of the month (7.177). Since, Kurtosis values are greater than 3, thus, it is inferred that the level of risk associated with the NSE Shariah index was high, which means investors may obtain either high level of profit or loss.

As the calculated P value of the Shapiro-Wilk test is less than 0.01, it is clearly proved that the data are not normally distributed. Hence, anomaly exists in the NSE Shariah index returns.

The following table depicts, whether first half and second half of the month returns differ in NSE Shariah Index.

Table 9.4: Semi Month Effect – Shariah Index

	Mean	N	Std. Deviation	Paired t value	P value
First half	.0592	75	.38473	0.749	0.456
Second half	.1030	75	.35950		

Source – Database collected from NSE web portal and computed.

As the calculated P value is greater than 0.05, it is inferred that NSE Shariah index returns does not differ between the first half and the second half of the month.

9.5. Turn of the Month Effect

The following table exhibits whether turn of the month effect prevails in NSE Shariah index.

Table 9.5: Turn of the Month Effect – Shariah Index

	Mean	Median	Std. Deviation	Variance	Skewness	Kurtosis	Shapiro-Wilk
First Half	0.2095	0.1786	0.44894	0.202	-0.125	-0.342	0.000
Rest of the Month	0.0463	0.0279	0.31046	0.096	0.695	1.794	0.000

Source – Database collected from NSE web portal and computed.

High mean returns were noticed during the First half of the month (0.2095) and low mean returns were found during the Rest of the month (0.0463). While comparing the variance, high level of volatility was noticed on the first half of the month (0.202) and low level of volatility was noticed in the rest of the month (0.096).

Result of the Skewness test disclosed that negative value were noticed during the first half of the month (-.125) returns, which implies that most of the first half of the month returns were less than the average returns. The rest of the month (0.695) returns was noticed positive Skewness, which implies that most of the rest of the month returns were more than the average returns. The Kurtosis of the NSE Shariah index returns were found platykurtic on both the First half of the month (-.342) and the rest of the month (1.794). Since, Kurtosis values are less than 3, thus, it is inferred that the level of risk associated with the NSE Shariah index was low, which means investors may obtain either low level of profit or loss.

As the calculated P value of the Shapiro-Wilk test is less than 0.01, it is clearly proved that the data are not normally distributed. Hence, anomaly exists in the NSE Shariah index returns.

The following table depicts, whether first half and rest of the month returns differ in NSE Shariah Index.

Table 9.6: Turn of the Month Effect – Shariah Index

	Mean	N	Std. Deviation	Paired t value	P value
First Half	.2095	74	.44894	2.655	0.010
Rest of the Month	.0463	74	.31046		

Source – Database collected from NSE web portal and computed.

As the calculated P value is less than 0.05, it is inferred that NSE Shariah index returns differs between the first half and rest of the month.

9.6. Monthly Effect

The following table exhibits whether monthly effect prevails in NSE Shariah index.

Table 9.7: Monthly Effect – Shariah Index

	Mean	Std. Deviation	Variance	Skewness	Kurtosis
April	2.2245	7.23608	52.361	2.054	4.183
May	3.6207	10.75974	115.772	2.022	4.327
June	3.7039	3.29857	10.881	0.408	0.011
July	1.1633	4.15627	17.275	1.058	0.805
August	-0.0132	4.0368	16.296	-0.667	1.04
September	4.9225	3.32064	11.027	-0.064	0.207
October	1.2664	5.53458	30.632	-0.284	-0.942
November	0.1884	4.57122	20.896	0.088	-0.178
December	1.4318	3.87508	15.016	-0.272	-1.716
January	-0.0653	6.969	48.567	-0.55	-1.545
February	0.506	3.29978	10.889	-0.083	-1.08
March	1.200	4.31645	18.632	0.203	-2.222
Shapiro-Wilk test :0.000					

Source – Database collected from NSE web portal and computed.

High mean returns were noticed during the month of September (4.9225) and low mean returns were found during the month of January (-0.0653). While comparing the variance, high level of volatility was noticed on the month of May (115.772) and low level of volatility was noticed in the month of June (10.881).

Result of Skewness test disclosed the positive value and it was noticed during the month of April (2.054), May (2.022), June (.408), July (1.058), November (0.088) and March (0.203) returns, which implies that most of the April, May, June, July, November and March month returns were more than the average returns. The other Month's returns were found negative Skewness, which implies that most of the Other Month's returns were less than the average returns. The Kurtosis results of the NSE Shariah index returns were found leptokurtic in the month of April (4.183) and May (4.327) returns. Since, Kurtosis values are greater than 3, thus, it is inferred that the level of risk associated with the month of April and May returns of the NSE Shariah index was high, which means investors may obtain either high level of profit or loss. The other month's returns were found platykurtic. Since, Kurtosis values are less than 3, thus, it is inferred that the level of risk associated with the other month's returns of the NSE Shariah index was low, which means investors may obtain either low level of profit or loss.

As the calculated P value of the Shapiro-Wilk test is less than 0.01, it is clearly proved that the data are not normally distributed. Hence, there exists anomaly in the NSE Shariah index returns.

Our results do confirm the April effect for NSE Shariah index in India. The average return for March is low as compared to the April average return. This evidence is consistent with the 'tax-loss-selling' hypothesis. It appears that investors in India sell shares that have declined in values, and book losses to save taxes. This causes share prices to decline in March that results in lower returns.

9.7. Conclusion

From the analysis, it is inferred that the day of the week effect, Monthly effect, Semi month effect and Turn of the month effect exists in NSE Shariah index. The next chapter discuss about Volatility in Indian stock market.

CHAPTER X

VOLATILITY IN INDIAN STOCK MARKET

10.1. Introduction

Fluctuations in stock prices is termed as volatility. A lower volatility means that a security's value does not fluctuate dramatically, but changes in value at a steady pace over a period of time. By computing beta volatility in stock market can be ascertained. Similarly, there are various Financial models for measuring stock market volatility.

In this chapter, Generalized Autoregressive Conditional Heteroscedasticity (GARCH) Model is applied for measuring volatility in Indian stock market.

10.2. Tools for Analysis

To measure whether volatility exist in Indian stock market, Generalized Autoregressive Conditional Heteroscedasticity (GARCH) model is applied.

ARCH models are employed commonly in modelling financial time series that exhibit time varying volatility clustering, i.e. periods of swings followed by periods of relative calm

Heteroscedasticity: In statistics, when the standard deviations of a variable, monitored over a specific amount of time, are non-constant. Conditional heteroscedasticity identifies non constant volatility when future periods of high and low volatility cannot be identified.

10.3. Volatility

The following list of Exhibits disclose volatility in Indian stock market. Exhibits are presented in the order of BSE Sensex, 19 BSE sectoral indices, NSE Nifty and 12 NSE sectoral indices.

The horizontal line denotes normal movement of stock price or Upper Control Limit. If the time series data of stock returns move along with horizontal line denotes there does not exist volatility in Indian stock market. If the stock returns moves above or below the horizontal line or Upper Control Limit denotes volatility exists in Indian stock market.

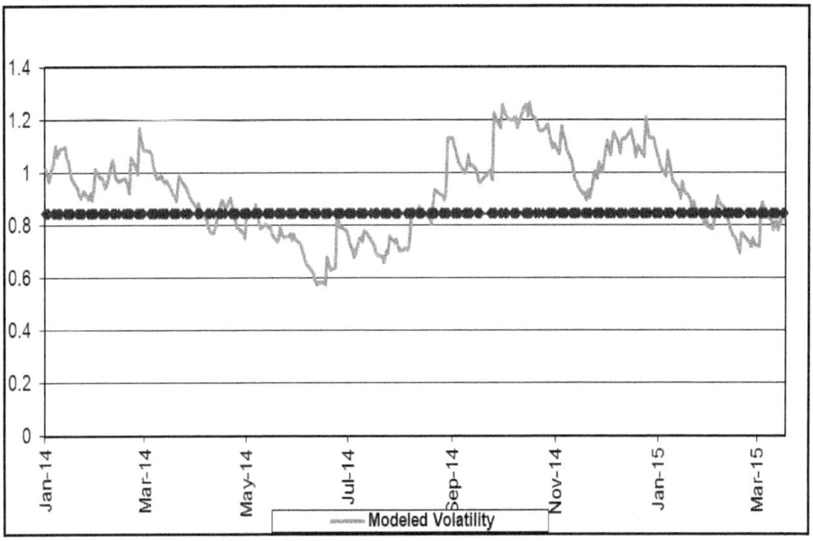

Exhibit 10.1: BSE Sensex Index

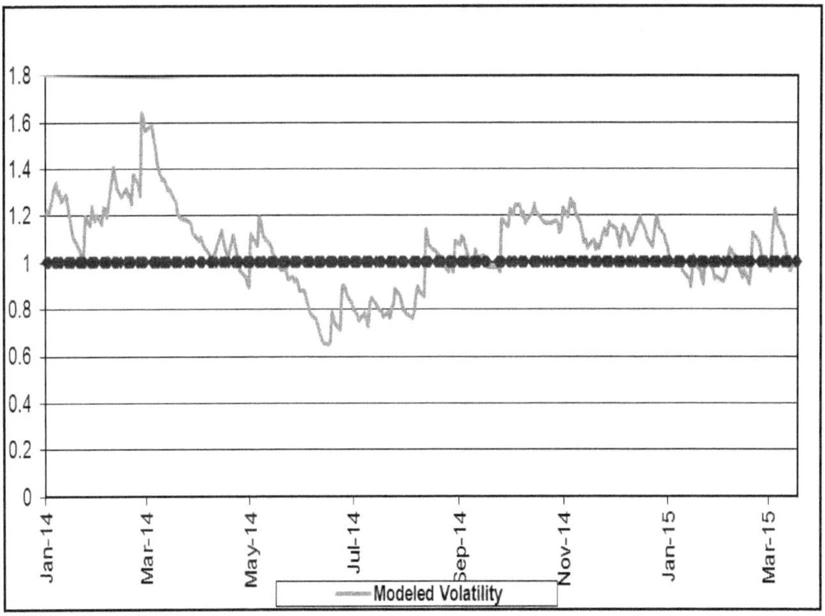

Exhibit 10.2: BSE Auto Index

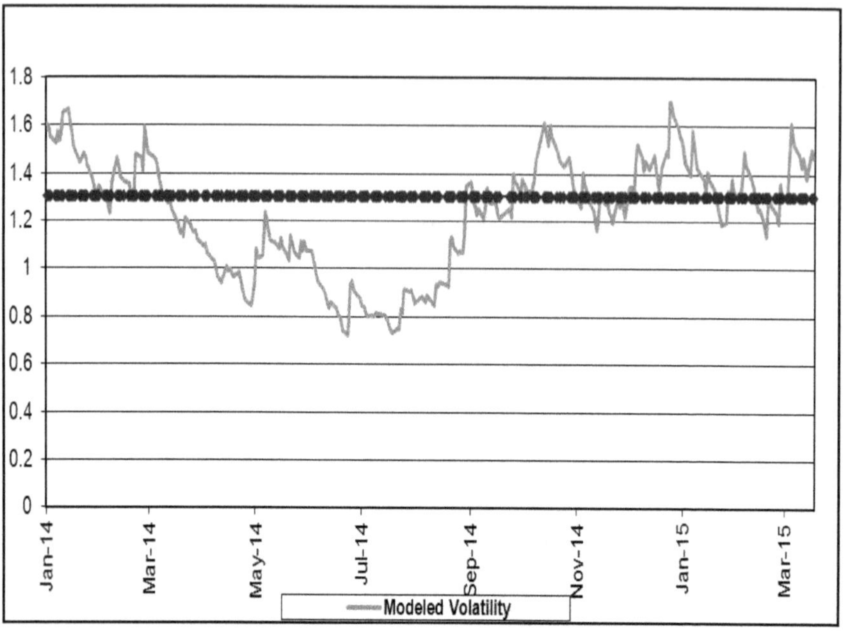

Exhibit 10.3: BSE Bank Index

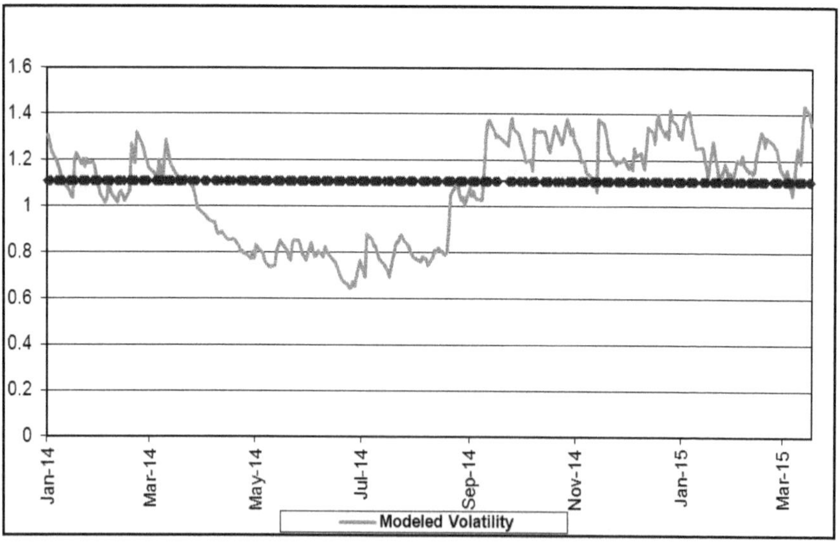

Exhibit 10.4: BSE Basic Materials Index

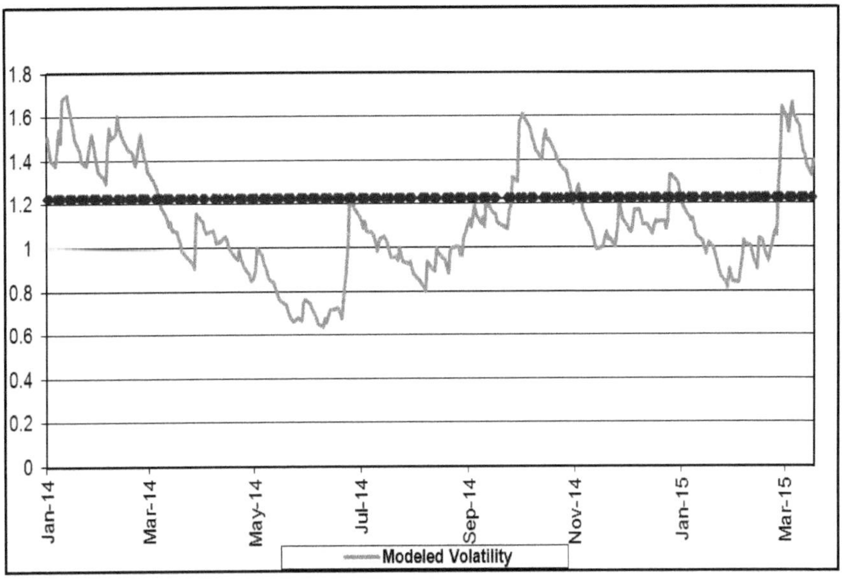

Exhibit 10.5: BSE Consumer Durables Index

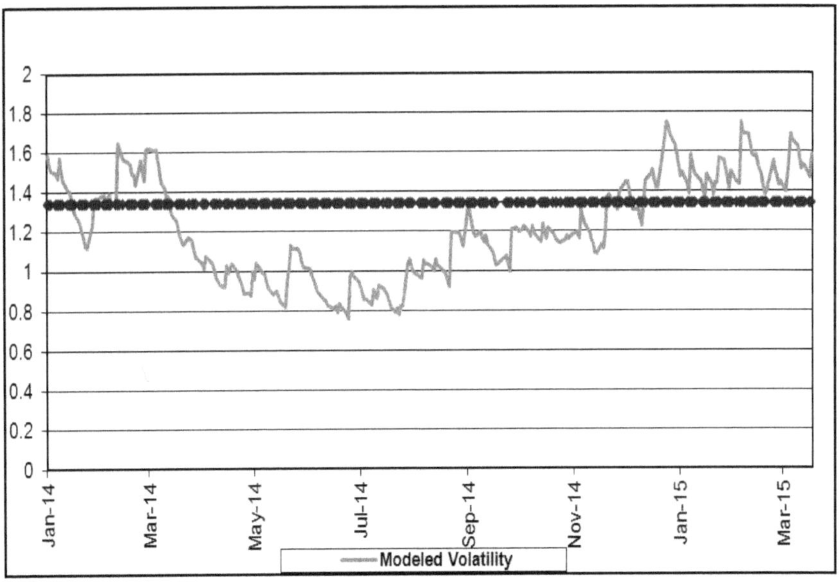

Exhibit 10.6: BSE Consumer Goods Index

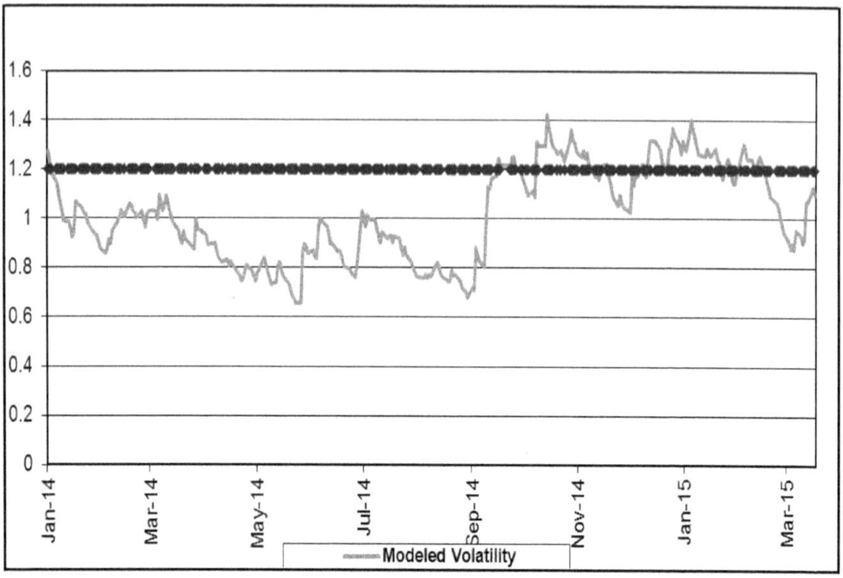

Exhibit 10.7: BSE Energy Index

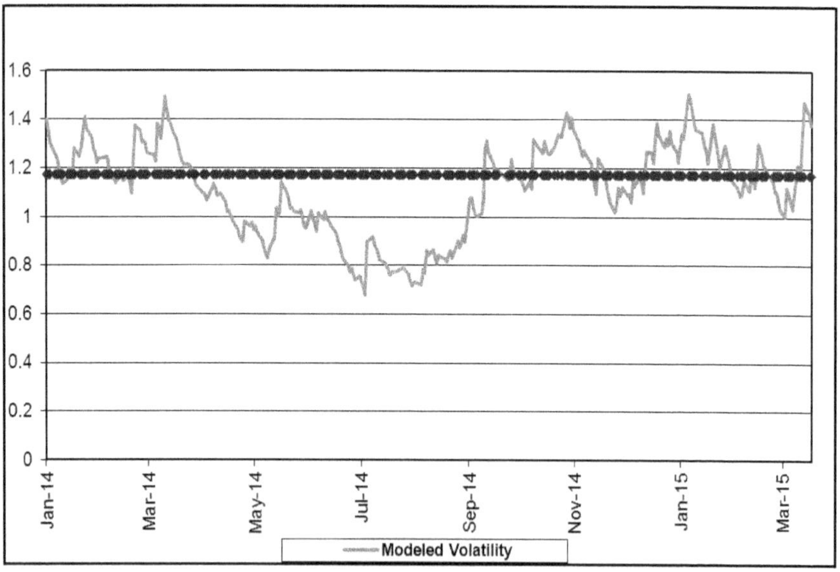

Exhibit 10.8: BSE Finance Index

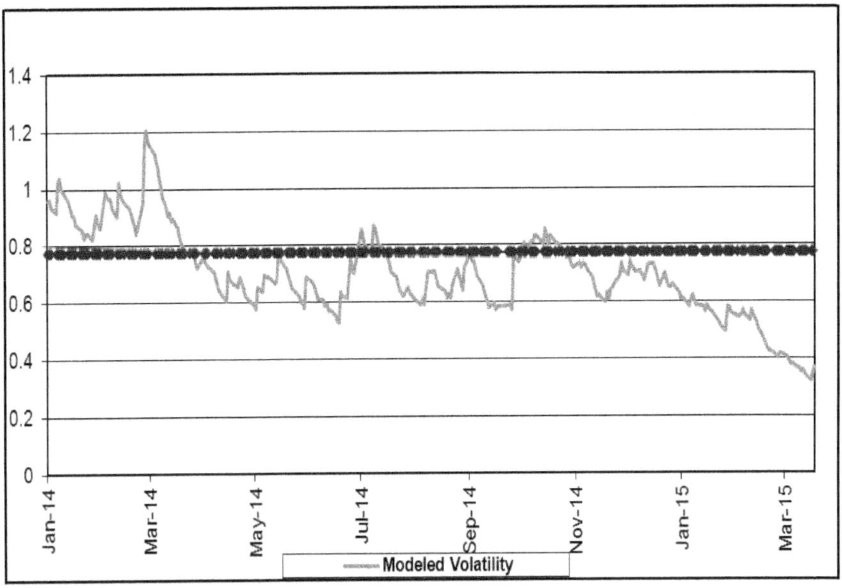

Exhibit 10.9: BSE Fast Moving Consumer Goods Index

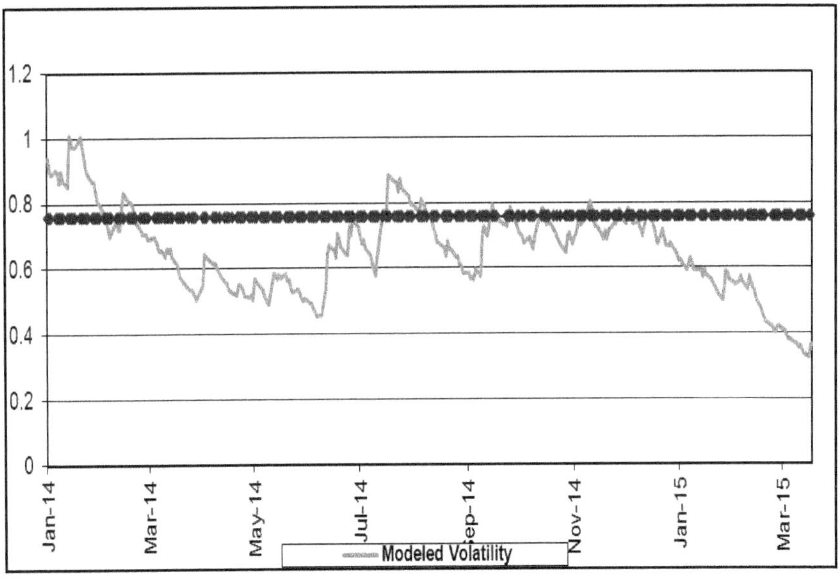

Exhibit 10.10: BSE Health Care Index

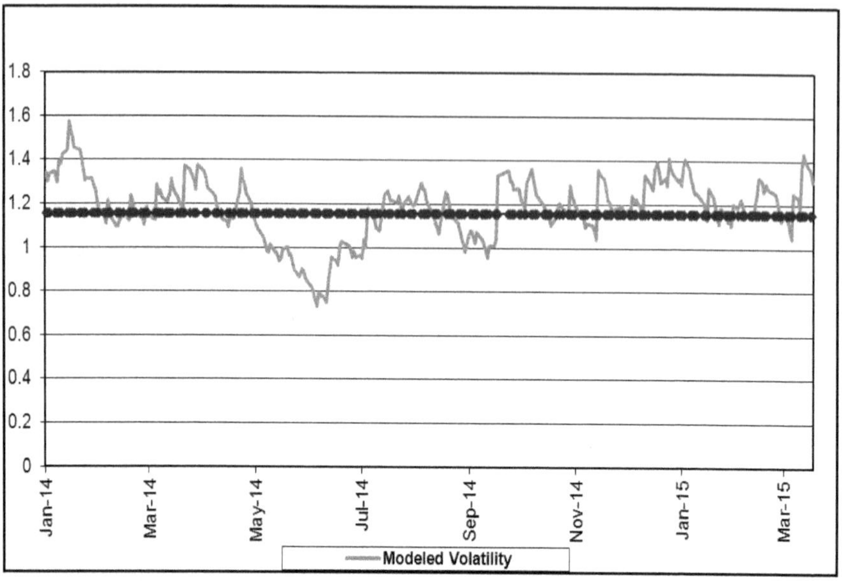

Exhibit 10.11: BSE Industrial Index

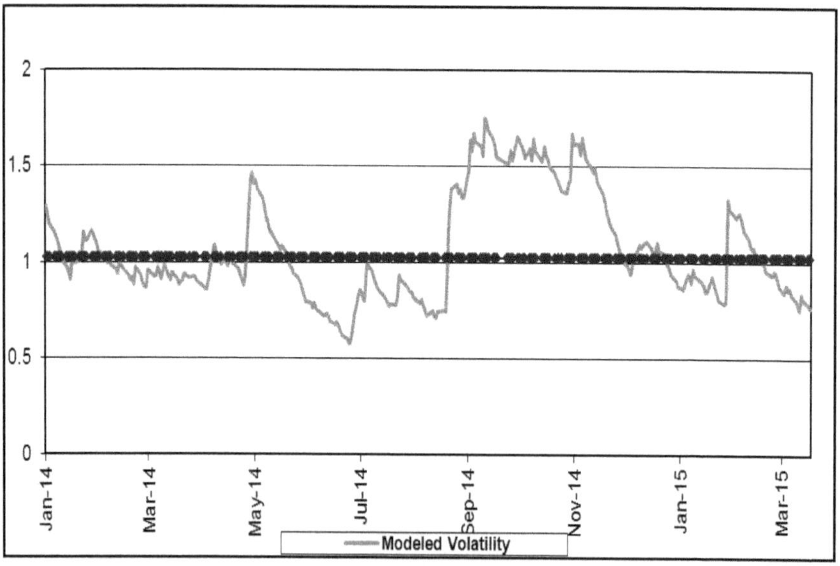

Exhibit 10.12: BSE IT Index

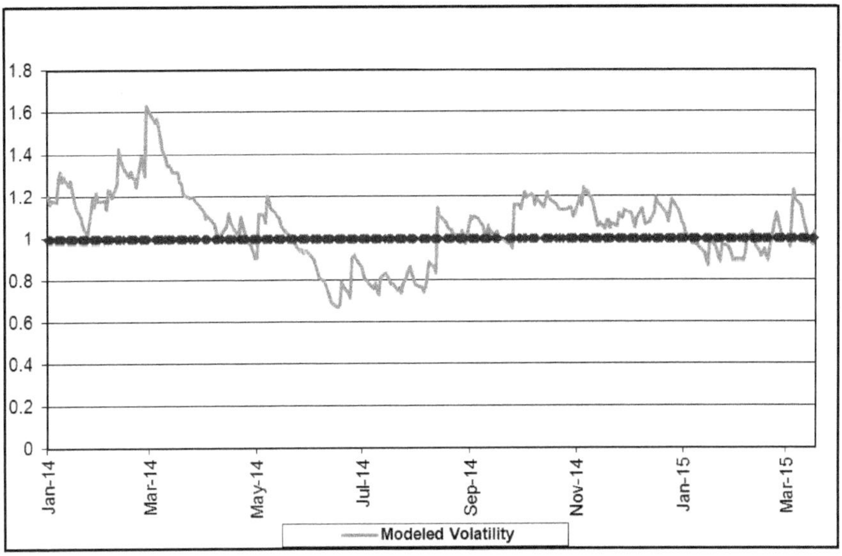

Exhibit 10.13: BSE Metal Index

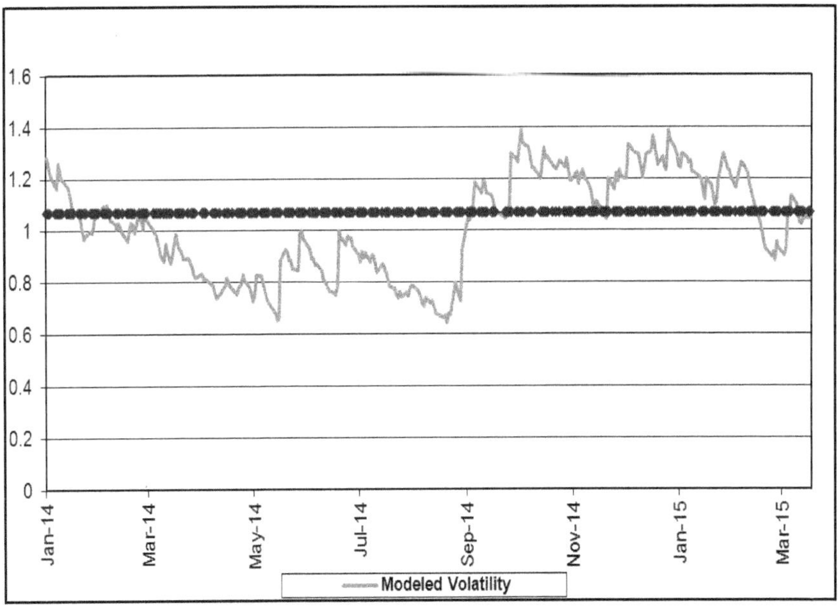

Exhibit 10.14: BSE Oil & Gas Index

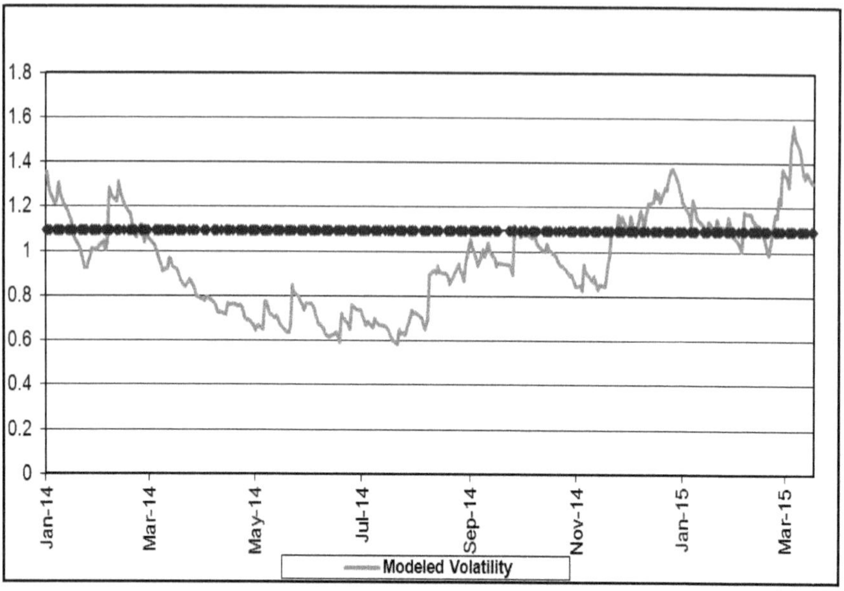

Exhibit 10.15: BSE Power Index

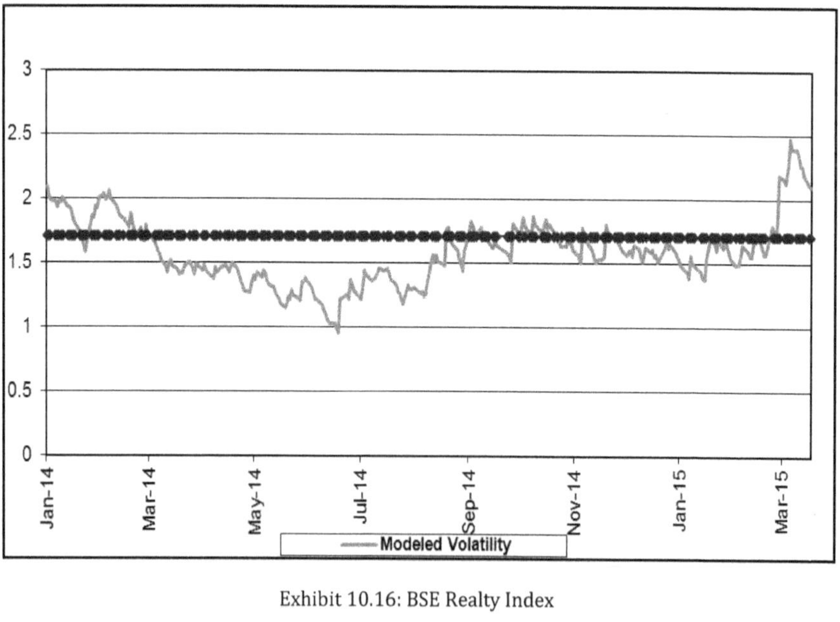

Exhibit 10.16: BSE Realty Index

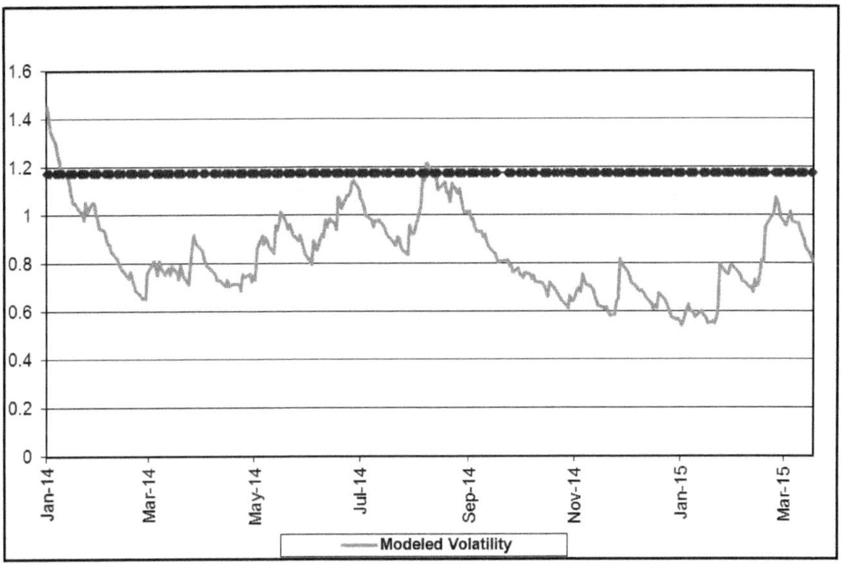

Exhibit 10.17: BSE Public Sector Unit Index

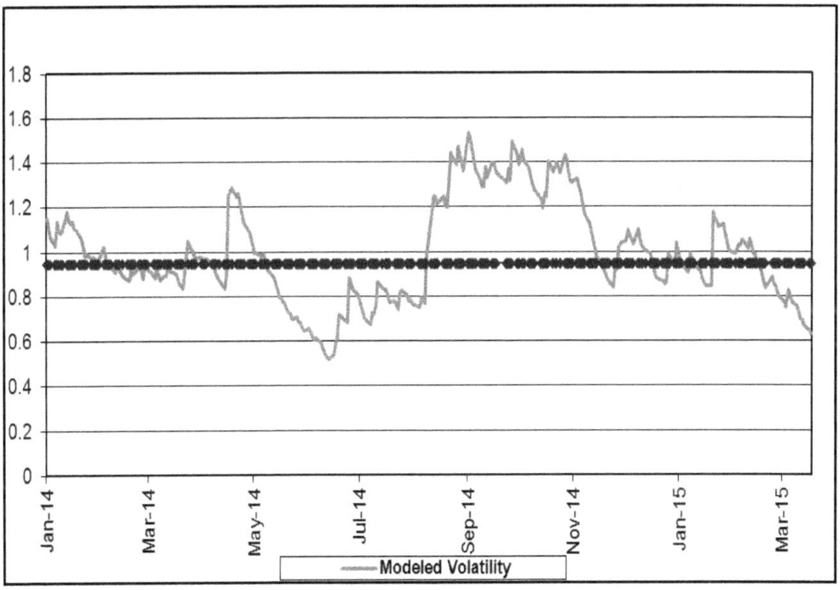

Exhibit 10.18: BSE Teck Index

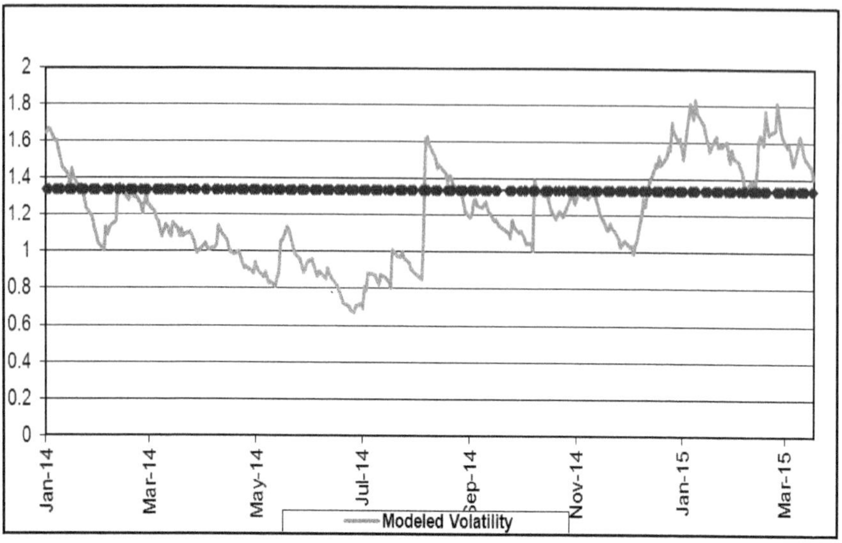

Exhibit 10.19: BSE Telecom Index

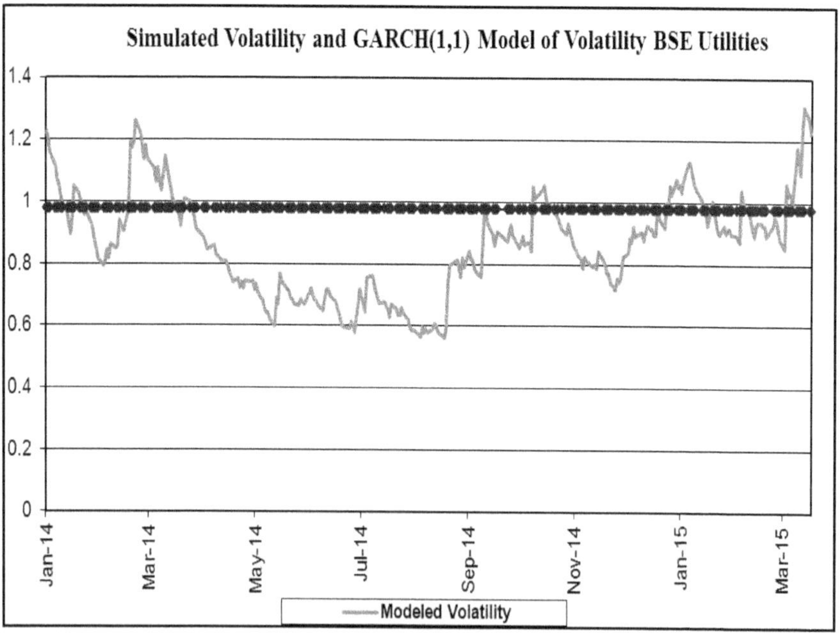

Exhibit 10.20: BSE Utilities Index

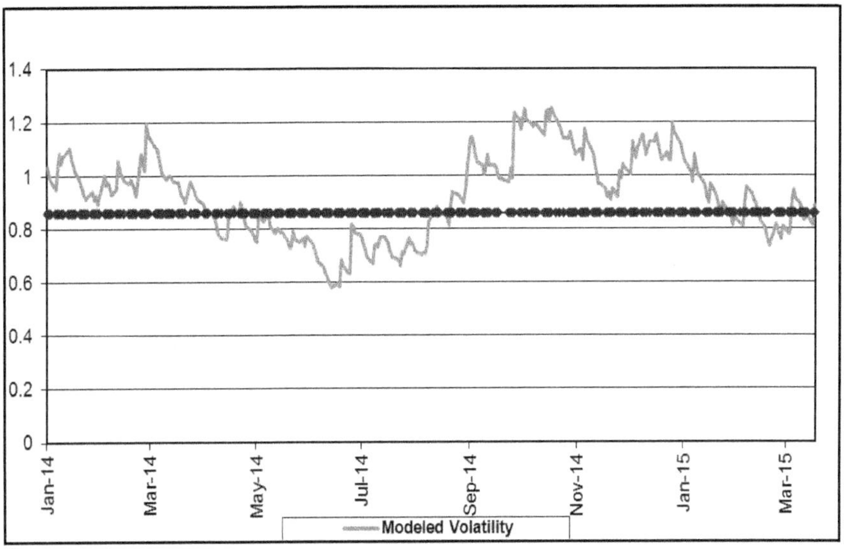

Exhibit 10.21: NSE Nifty Index

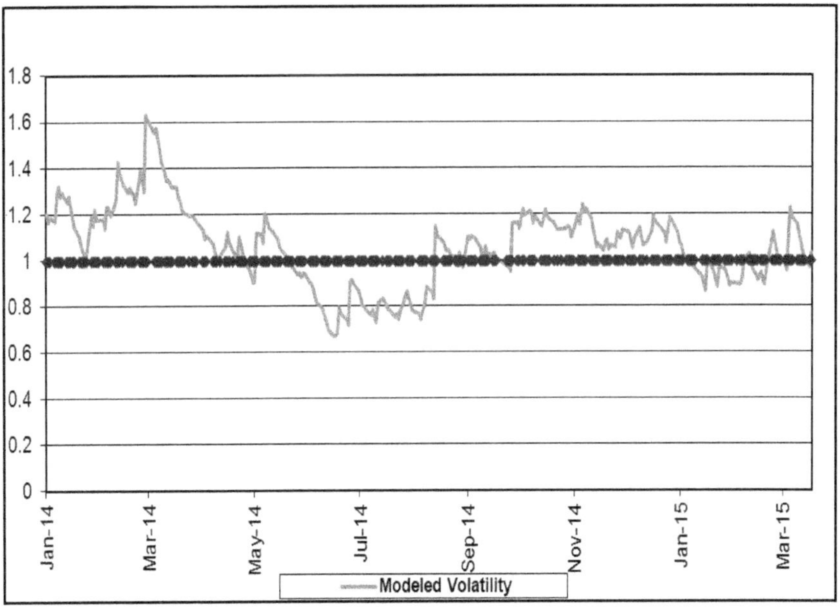

Exhibit 10.22: NSE Auto Index

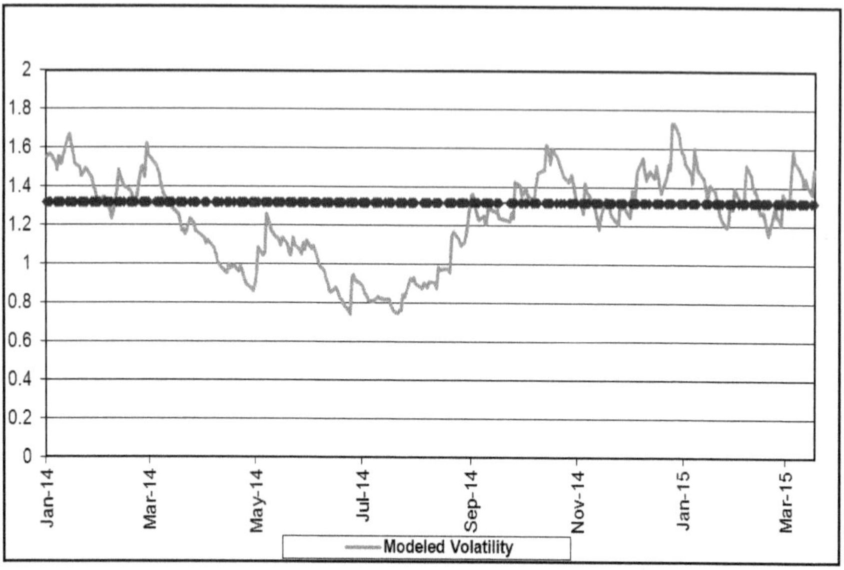

Exhibit 10.23: NSE Bank Index

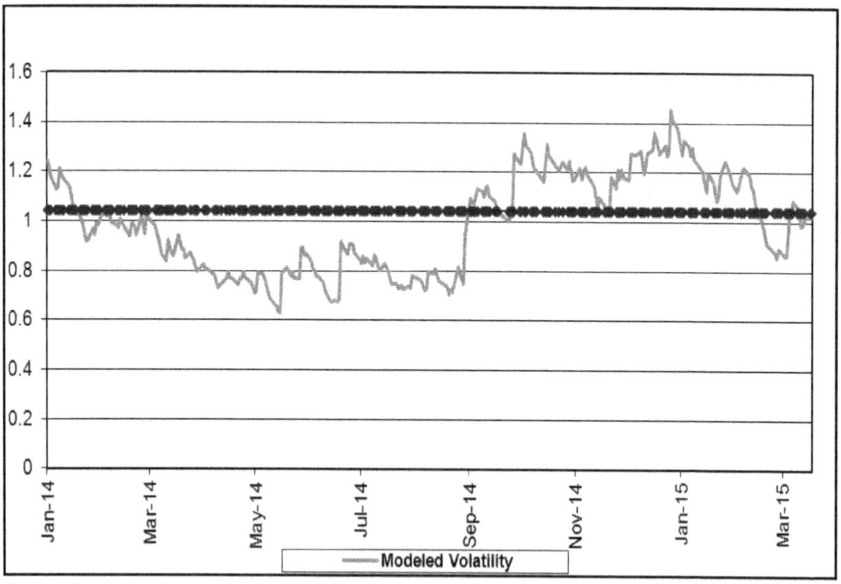

Exhibit 10.24: NSE Energy Index

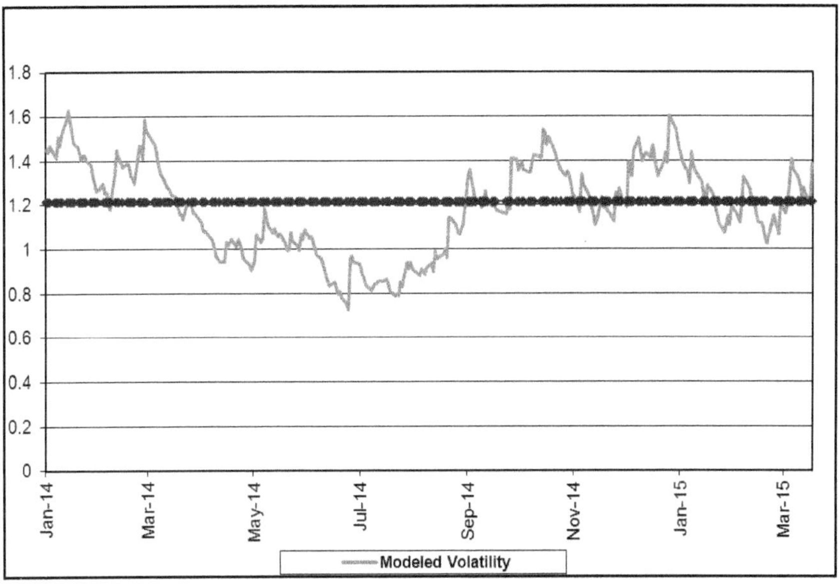

Exhibit 10.25: NSE Finance Index

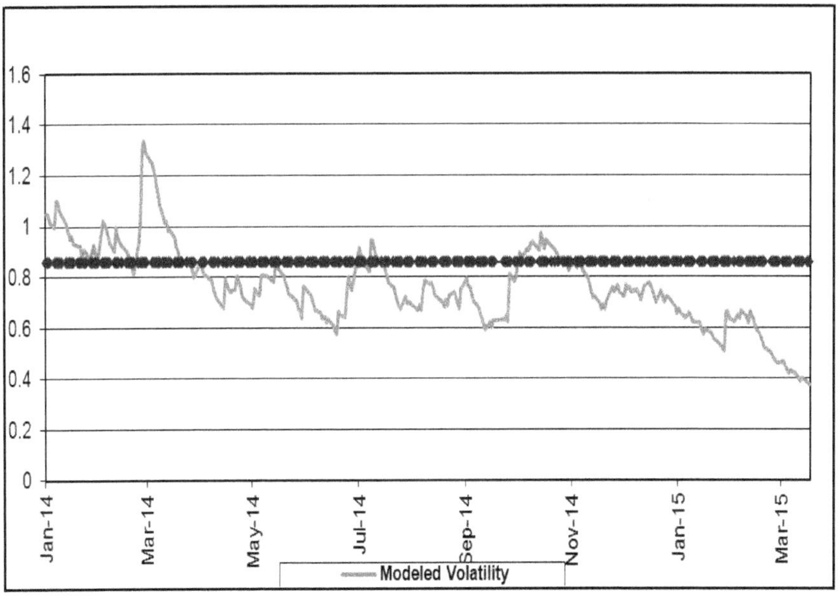

Exhibit 10.26: NSE Fast Moving Consumer Goods Index

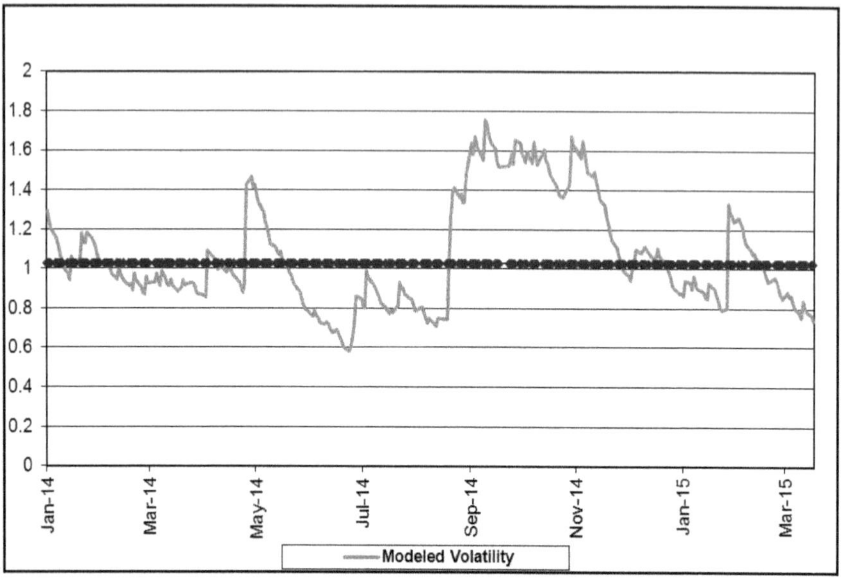

Exhibit 10.27: NSE IT Index

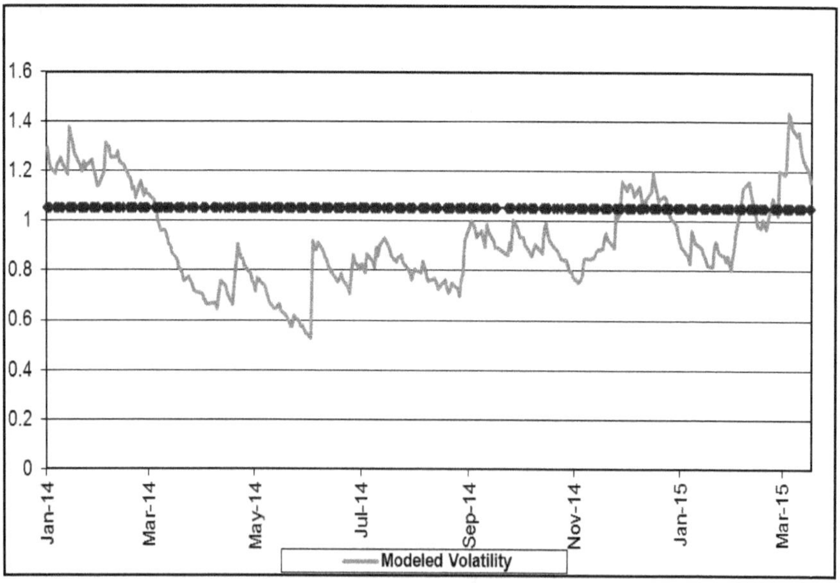

Exhibit 10.28: NSE Media Index

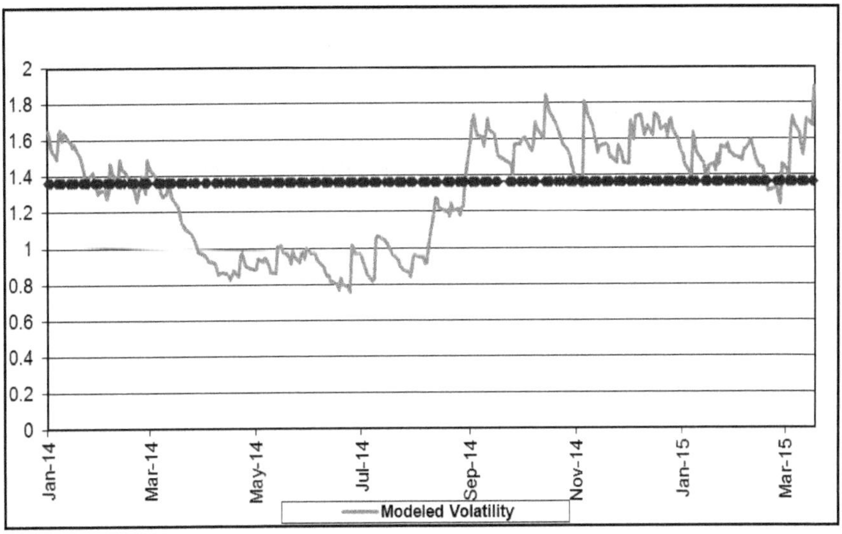

Exhibit 10.29: NSE Metal Index

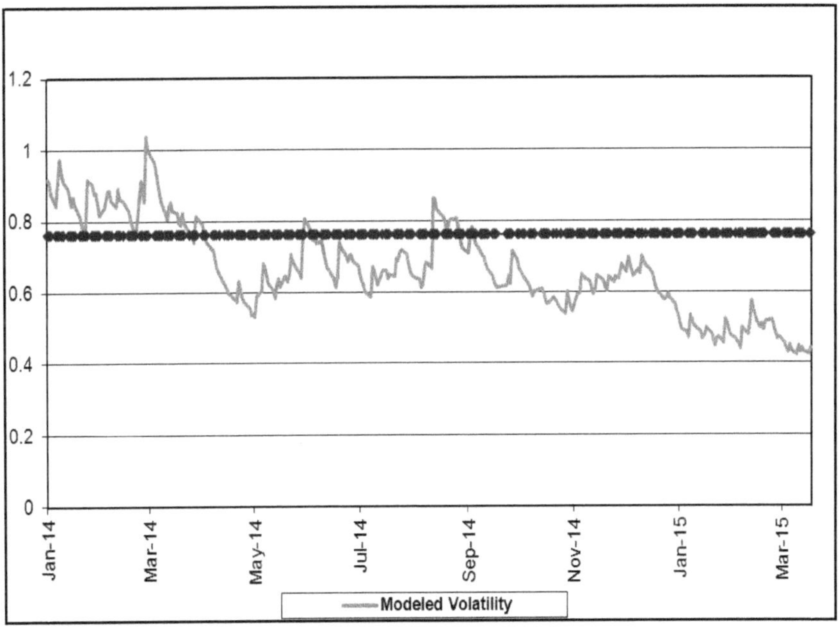

Exhibit 10.30: NSE Pharma Index

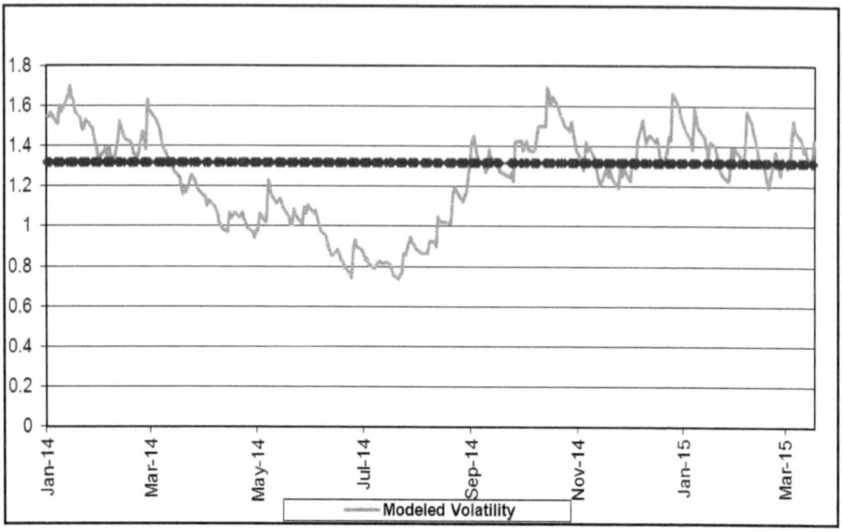

Exhibit 10.31: NSE Private Banks Index

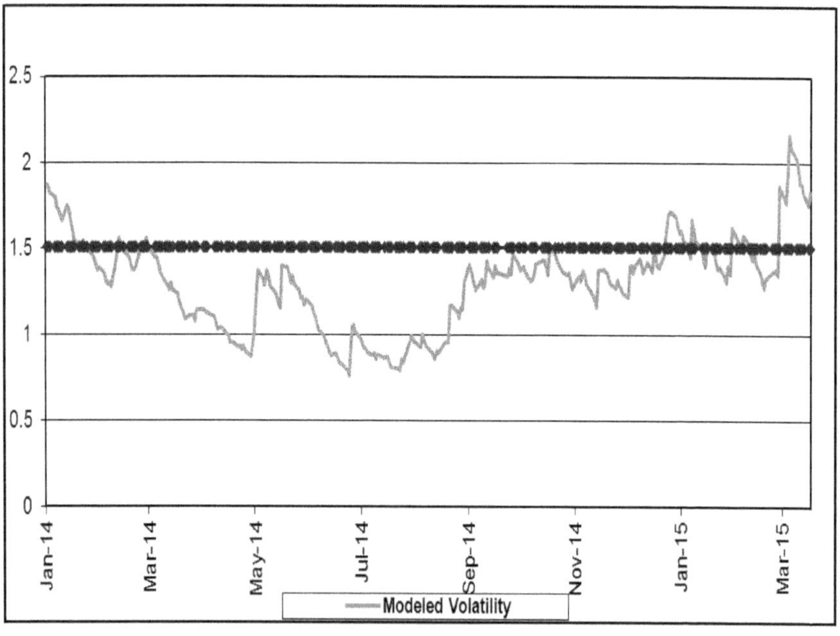

Exhibit 10.32: NSE Public Sector Unit Banks Index

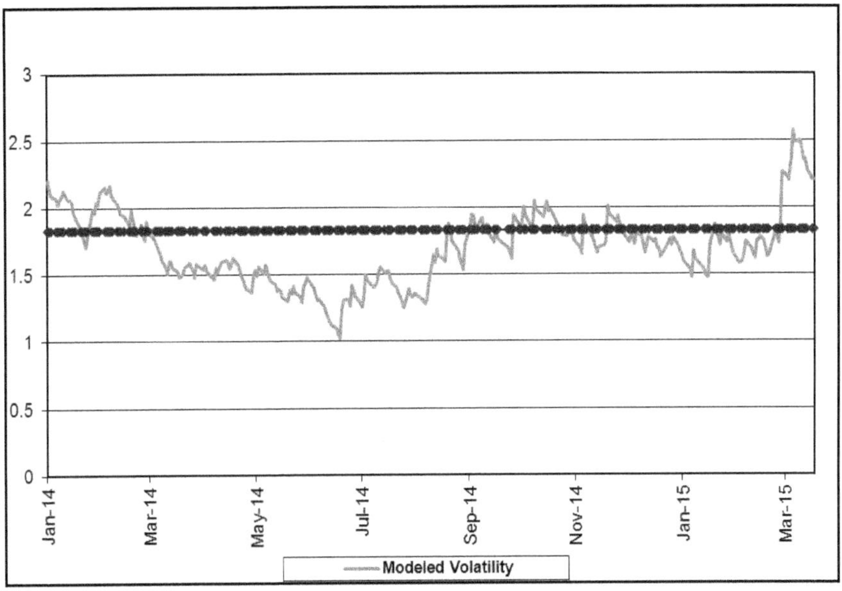

Exhibit 10.33: NSE Realty Index

As the stock market returns moves across the horizontal line or Upper Control Limit it is inferred that volatility exist in Indian stock market.

10.4. Conclusion

The above Exhibits clearly disclose that volatility prevails over the year in Indian stock market on BSE Sensex, 19 BSE sectoral indices, NSE Nifty and 12 NSE sectoral indices. The next chapter consolidates the summary of findings and suggestions.

CHAPTER XI

FINDINGS, SUGGESTION AND CONCLUSION

11.1. Introduction

Most of the individuals are not aware of the possibilities of investing shares. The current economic downturn in the India had a great impact on the stock marketplace prices. Many nations fear that they have to encounter an economic downturn in national economy, which leads to a scenario exactly where individuals fear about investing. When the total export falls, stock marketplace tends to take a dive. This influence on the stock market causes people to have a second thought prior to the trade stock. Present day stock marketplace is hence tending to fluctuate. Therefore, by following the economic downturn in India, investors act differently. There are various options that can be followed in the future to make revenue from stock marketplace. But the steps taken prior to investing in today's stock marketplace is highly essential when this is taken as a stage to success. They have to be very careful as there can be misleading and misconceptions that can end them up in difficulty. Never follow the views set by those who have no previous expertise in this situation blindly. It is usually advisable to follow the advices from those who have loved benefits from investing in a stock marketplace. The primary factors that have to be taken in this regard involve a correct updating with the latest information in stock marketplace. They can depend on greatest websites and brokers who by no means work merely for money. Timing is one of the most important factors in investing in the stock market. This fluctuation on rapid basis is cannot be fully reliant on this for money until and unless investors are stay in this area for a long time. The present study was undertaken with the objective of examining the Anomalies in Indian Stok Market. The objectives of the study are 1. To identify the existence of the Day of the Week Effect in Indian stock market. 2. To identify the presence of Semi- Month Effect in Indian stock market. 3. To identify the presence of Turn-of-the- Month effect in Indian stock market. 4. To identify the existence of Monthly/January Effect and Turn-of-the-year Effect in Indian stock market. 5. To study the Volatility Persistence in Indian Stock Market. 6. To identify the seasonality effect in Shariah index.

11.2. Day of the Week Effect

To measure the day of the week effect, returns, descriptive statistics like Mean, Standard deviation, Variance, Skewness, Kurtosis, Shapiro-wilk test and OLS regression are employed. The following paragraphs consolidates the result of the study.

11.2.1. BSE Sensex

High mean returns were noticed during Wednesday and low mean returns were found during Thursday. High level of volatility was noticed on Monday and low level of volatility was noticed on Thursday. Skewness test disclosed that positive value and it was noticed during Monday returns and Tuesday returns. Negative returns were noticed during other days. Kurtosis results were found leptokurtic in all the days of the week. Shapiro-Wilk test disclose that anomaly exist in the BSE SENSEX index returns. The result of OLS disclose that Monday return was found to be significant at 1 per cent level and Tuesday return is found to be significant at 5 per cent level. The regression coefficient indicates that Monday and Tuesday returns positively influences Friday returns. Around 27.79 per cent of variation in Friday return is due to select variables.

11.2.2. BSE Auto

High mean returns were noticed during Thursday and low mean returns were found during Monday. High level of volatility was noticed on Monday and low level of volatility was noticed on Wednesday. Skewness test disclosed the positive value and it was noticed during Tuesday. Negative returns were noticed during other days. Kurtosis results were found leptokurtic on Monday returns, Thursday returns and Friday returns. Other day's returns were found platykurtic. Shapiro-Wilk test disclose that anomaly exist in the BSE Auto index returns. The result of OLS disclose that Monday return was found to be significant at 1 per cent level and Tuesday return is found to be significant at 5 per cent level. The regression coefficient indicates that Tuesday returns positively influences Friday returns. Around 22.92 per cent of variation in Friday return is due to the select variables.

11.2.3. BSE Bank Index

High mean returns were noticed during Wednesday and low mean returns were found during Monday. High level of volatility was noticed on Monday and low level of volatility was noticed on Wednesday. Skewness test disclosed the negative value and it was noticed during Friday. Positive returns were noticed during other days. Kurtosis results were found leptokurtic on Monday returns, Tuesday returns and Friday returns. Other day's returns were found platykurtic. Shapiro-Wilk test disclose that anomaly exist in the BSE Bank index returns. The result of OLS disclose that Monday return was found to be significant at 1 per cent level and Tuesday return is found to be significant at 5 per cent level. The regression coefficient indicates that Monday and Tuesday returns positively influences Friday returns. Around 28.99 per cent of variation in Friday return is due to the select variables.

11.2.4. BSE Basic Material Index

High mean returns were noticed during Wednesday and low mean returns were found during Thursday. High level of volatility was noticed on Monday and low level of volatility was noticed on Tuesday. Skewness test disclosed that positive value and it was noticed during Wednesday returns. Negative returns were noticed during other days. Kurtosis results were found platykurtic on Tuesday returns. The other day's returns were found leptokurtic. Shapiro-Wilk test disclose that anomaly exist in the BSE Basic materials index returns. The result of OLS disclose that Monday and Thursday returns was found to be significant at 1 per cent level and Wednesday returns was found to be significant at 5 per cent level. The regression coefficient indicates that Monday, Wednesday and Thursday returns positively influences Friday returns. Around 61.83 per cent of variation in Friday return is due to the select variables.

11.2.5. BSE Consumer Durables Index

High mean returns were noticed during Monday and low mean returns were found during Thursday. High level of volatility was noticed on Monday and low level of volatility was noticed on Thursday. Skewness test disclosed that positive value and it was noticed during Tuesday returns. The other day's returns were found negative skewness. Kurtosis results were found platykurtic on Thursday returns. The other day's returns were found leptokurtic. Shapiro-Wilk test disclose that anomaly exist in the BSE Consumer Durables index returns. The result of OLS regression analysis disclose that the select independent variables collectively contribute to 7.74 per cent variation in Friday returns.

11.2.6. BSE Consumer Goods Index

High mean returns were noticed during Friday and low mean returns were found during Wednesday. High level of volatility was noticed on Monday and low level of volatility was noticed on Wednesday. Skewness test disclosed that positive value and it was noticed during Monday returns Tuesday returns and Thursday returns. Negative returns were noticed during other days. Kurtosis result were found leptokurtic on Monday returns and Thursday returns. The other day's returns were found platykurtic. Shapiro-Wilk test disclose that anomaly exist in the BSE Consumer Goods index returns. The result of OLS disclose that Monday return was found to be significant at 1 per cent level. The regression coefficient indicates that Monday returns positively influence Friday returns. Around 28.92 per cent of variation in Friday return is due to the select variable.

11.2.7. BSE Energy Index

High mean returns were noticed during Monday and low mean returns were found during Thursday. High level of volatility was noticed on Friday and low level of volatility was noticed on Tuesday and Wednesday. Result of the Skewness test disclosed that positive value and it was noticed during Monday returns, Wednesday returns and Friday returns. Negative returns were noticed during other days. Kurtosis results were found platykurtic on Wednesday returns. The other day's returns were found leptokurtic. Shapiro-Wilk test disclose that anomaly exist in the BSE Energy Sector Unit Index returns. The result of OLS regression analysis disclose that the select independent variables collectively contribute to 2.76 per cent variation in Friday returns.

11.2.8. BSE Finance Index

High mean returns were noticed during Monday and low mean returns were found during Friday. High level of volatility was noticed on Wednesday and low level of volatility was noticed on Friday. Skewness test disclosed that positive value and it was noticed during Monday returns, Wednesday returns and Thursday returns. Negative returns were noticed during other days. Kurtosis results were found platykurtic on Monday returns and Friday returns. The other day's returns were found leptokurtic. Shapiro-Wilk test disclose that anomaly exist in the BSE Finance Index returns. The result of OLS disclose that Thursday returns was found to be significant at 1 per cent level. The regression coefficient indicates that Thursday returns positively influences Friday returns. Around 27.99 per cent of variation in Friday return is due to the select variable.

11.2.9. BSE FMCG Index

High mean returns were noticed during Wednesday and low mean returns were found during Friday. High level of volatility was noticed on Monday and low level of volatility was noticed on Wednesday. Skewness test disclosed that positive value and it was noticed during Monday returns. Negative returns were noticed during other days. Kurtosis result were found platykurtic in Wednesday returns. The other day's returns were found leptokurtic. Shapiro-Wilk test disclose that anomaly exist in the BSE Fast Moving Consumer Goods index returns. The result of OLS disclose that Monday return was found to be significant at 1 per cent level and Tuesday and Wednesday return was found to be significant at 5 per cent level. The regression coefficient indicates that Monday, Tuesday and Wednesday returns positively influences Friday returns. Around 68.96 per cent of variation in Friday return is due to the select variables.

11.2.10. BSE Health Care Index

High mean returns were noticed during Wednesday and low mean returns were found during Thursday. High level of volatility was noticed on Friday and low level of volatility was noticed on Wednesday.

Skewness test disclosed that negative value and it was noticed all the days of the week. Kurtosis were found platykurtic in Monday returns and Tuesday returns. The other day's returns were found leptokurtic. Shapiro-Wilk test disclose that anomaly exist in the BSE Health Care Index returns. The result of OLS regression analysis disclose that the select independent variables collectively contribute to 7.35 per cent variation in Friday returns.

11.2.11. BSE IT Index

High mean returns were noticed during Wednesday and low mean returns were found during Friday. High level of volatility was noticed on Wednesday and low level of volatility was noticed on Friday. Skewness test disclosed that positive value and it was noticed during Tuesday returns and Wednesday returns. Negative returns were noticed during other days. Kurtosis result were found leptokurtic on all the days of the week. Shapiro-Wilk test disclose that anomaly exist in the BSE IT Index returns. The result of OLS disclose that Thursday return was found to be significant at 1 per cent level and Tuesday return was found to be significant at 5 per cent level. The regression coefficient indicates that Thursday and Tuesday returns positively influences Friday returns. Around 34.97 per cent of variation in Friday return is due to the select variables.

11.2.12. BSE Industrial Index

High mean returns were noticed during Monday and low mean returns were found during Friday. High level of volatility was noticed on Wednesday and low level of volatility was noticed on Friday. Skewness test disclosed that positive value and it was noticed during Wednesday returns. Negative returns were noticed during other days. Kurtosis results were found platykurtic on Thursday returns and Friday returns. The other day's returns were found leptokurtic. Shapiro-Wilk test disclose that anomaly exist in the BSE Industrial Index returns. The result of OLS disclose that Tuesday returns was found to be significant at 5 per cent level and Thursday returns was found to be significant at 1 per cent level. The regression coefficient indicates that Tuesday and Thursday returns positively influences Friday returns. Around 44.10 per cent of variation in Friday return is due to the select variables.

11.2.13. *BSE Metal Index*

High mean returns were noticed during Friday and low mean returns were found during Tuesday. High level of volatility was noticed on Monday and low level of volatility was noticed on Wednesday. Skewness test disclosed that positive value and it was noticed during Monday returns and Tuesday returns. Negative returns were noticed during other days. Kurtosis results were found leptokurtic on Monday returns and Friday returns. The other day's returns were found platykurtic. Shapiro-Wilk test disclose that anomaly exist in the BSE Metal Index returns. The result of OLS disclose that Tuesday returns was found to be significant at 1 per cent level. The regression coefficient indicates that Tuesday returns positively influences Friday returns. Around 19.56 per cent of variation in Friday return is due to the select variable.

11.2.14. *BSE Oil & Gas Index*

High mean returns were noticed during Wednesday and low mean returns were found during Thursday. High level of volatility was noticed on Monday and low level of volatility was noticed on Tuesday. Skewness test disclosed that positive value and it was noticed during Monday returns and Wednesday returns. Negative returns were noticed during other days. Kurtosis results were found platykurtic on Thursday returns. The other day's returns were found leptokurtic. Shapiro-Wilk test disclose that anomaly exist in the BSE Oil & Gas Index returns. The result of OLS disclose that Monday returns was found to be significant at 1 per cent level. The regression coefficient indicates that Monday returns positively influences Friday returns. Around 35.90 per cent of variation in Friday return is due to the select variable.

11.2.15. *BSE Power Index*

High mean returns were noticed during Friday and low mean returns were found during Thursday. High level of volatility was noticed on Monday and low level of volatility was noticed on Wednesday. Skewness test disclosed that negative value and it was noticed during the Thursday returns and Friday returns. Positive returns were noticed during other days. Kurtosis result were found leptokurtic on all the days of the week. Shapiro-Wilk test disclose that anomaly exist in the BSE Power Index returns. The result of OLS regression analysis disclose that the select independent variables collectively contribute to 2.76 per cent variation in Friday returns.

11.2.16. *BSE Public Sector Index*

High mean returns were noticed during Wednesday and low mean returns were found during Tuesday. High level of volatility was noticed on Monday and low level of volatility was noticed on

Wednesday. Skewness test disclosed that positive value and it was noticed during Monday returns and Wednesday returns. Negative returns were noticed during other days. Kurtosis results were found platykurtic on Thursday returns. The other day's returns were found leptokurtic. Shapiro-Wilk test disclose that anomaly exist in the BSE Public Sector Unit Index returns. The result of OLS disclose that Monday returns was found to be significant at 1 per cent level and Tuesday and Wednesday returns was found to be significant at 5 per cent level. The regression coefficient indicates that Monday, Tuesday and Wednesday returns positively influences Friday returns. Around 68.96 per cent of variation in Friday return is due to the select variables.

11.2.17. BSE Realty Index

High mean returns were noticed during Wednesday and low mean returns were found during Friday. High level of volatility was noticed on Monday and low level of volatility was noticed on Wednesday. Skewness test disclosed that positive value and it was noticed during Monday returns and Tuesday returns. Negative returns were noticed during other days. Kurtosis results were found platykurtic on Tuesday returns and Thursday returns. The other day's returns were found leptokurtic. Shapiro-Wilk test disclose that anomaly exist in the BSE Realty Index returns. The result of OLS disclose that Tuesday returns was found to be significant at 5 per cent level and Wednesday returns was found to be significant at 1 per cent level. The regression coefficient indicates that Tuesday and Wednesday returns positively influences Friday returns. Around 28.86 per cent of variation in Friday return is due to the select variables.

11.2.18. BSE Teck Index

High mean returns were noticed during Wednesday and low mean returns were found during Thursday. High level of volatility was noticed on Monday and low level of volatility was noticed on Wednesday. Skewness test disclosed that positive value and it was noticed during Monday returns and Tuesday returns. Negative returns were noticed during other days. Kurtosis results were found platykurtic on Wednesday returns and Thursday returns. The other day's returns were found leptokurtic. Shapiro-Wilk test disclose that anomaly exist in the BSE Teck Index returns. The result of OLS disclose that Monday returns was found to be significant at 5 per cent level. The regression coefficient indicates that Monday returns positively influences Friday returns. Around 16.19 per cent of variation in Friday return is due to the select variable.

11.2.19. BSE Telecom Index

High mean returns were noticed during Monday and low mean returns were found during Friday. High level of volatility was noticed on Wednesday and low level of volatility was noticed on Monday. Skewness test disclosed that positive value and it was noticed during Wednesday returns. Negative returns were noticed during other days. Kurtosis results were found leptokurtic on Tuesday and Wednesday returns. The other day's returns were found platykurtic. Shapiro-Wilk test disclose that anomaly exist in the BSE Telecom Index returns. The result of OLS disclose that Thursday returns was found to be significant at 5 per cent level. The regression coefficient indicates that Thursday returns positively influences Friday returns. Around 13.35 per cent of variation in Friday return is due to the select variable.

11.2.20. BSE Utilities Index

High mean returns were noticed during Wednesday and low mean returns were found during Thursday. High level of volatility was noticed on Monday and low level of volatility was noticed on Thursday. Skewness test disclosed that positive value and it was noticed during Wednesday returns. Negative returns were noticed during other days. Kurtosis results were found platykurtic on Thursday returns. The other day's returns were found leptokurtic. Shapiro-Wilk test disclose that anomaly exist in the BSE Utilities Index returns. The results of OLS disclose that Monday returns was found to be significant at 1 per cent level and Thursday returns was found to be significant at 5 per cent level. The regression coefficient indicates that Monday and Thursday returns positively influences Friday returns. Around 29.86 per cent of variation in Friday return is due to the select variables.

11.2.21. NSE Nifty Index

High mean returns were noticed during Friday and low mean returns were found during Wednesday. High level of volatility was noticed on Monday and low level of volatility was noticed on Thursday. Skewness test disclosed that negative value and it was noticed during the Thursday returns and Friday returns. Positive returns were noticed during other days. Kurtosis results were found platykurtic on Thursday returns. The other day's returns were found leptokurtic. Shapiro-Wilk test disclose that anomaly exist in the NSE Nifty index returns. The result of OLS disclose that Monday returns was found to be significant at 5 per cent level. The regression coefficient indicates that Monday returns positively influences Friday returns. Around 12.76 per cent of variation in Friday return is due to the select variable.

11.2.22. *NSE Auto Index*

High mean returns were noticed during Friday and low mean returns were found during Tuesday. High level of volatility was noticed on Monday and low level of volatility was noticed on Wednesday. Skewness test disclosed that positive value and it was noticed during Monday returns and Tuesday returns. Negative returns were noticed during other days. Kurtosis results were found leptokurtic on Monday returns and Friday returns. The other day's returns were found platykurtic. Shapiro-Wilk test disclose that anomaly exist in the NSE Auto index returns. The result of OLS disclose that Tuesday returns was found to be significant at 5 per cent level. The regression coefficient indicates that Tuesday returns positively influences Friday returns. Around 19.55 per cent of variation in Friday return is due to the select variable.

11.2.23. *NSE Bank Index*

High mean returns were noticed during Friday and low mean returns were found during Wednesday. High level of volatility was noticed on Monday and low level of volatility was noticed on Thursday. Skewness test disclosed that negative value and it was noticed during the Thursday and Friday returns. Positive returns were noticed during other days. Kurtosis results were found platykurtic on Wednesday returns and Thursday returns. The other day's returns were found leptokurtic. Shapiro-Wilk test disclose that anomaly exist in the NSE Bank index returns. The result of OLS disclose that Monday returns was found to be significant at 5 per cent level. The regression coefficient indicates that Monday returns positively influences Friday returns. Around 15.76 per cent of variation in Friday return is due to the select variable.

11.2.24. *NSE Energy Index*

High mean returns were noticed during Tuesday and low mean returns were found during Thursday. High level of volatility was noticed on Monday and low level of volatility was noticed on Thursday. Skewness test disclosed that positive value and it was noticed during Wednesday returns. Negative returns were noticed during other days. Kurtosis results were found platykurtic on Thursday returns.

The other day's returns were found leptokurtic. Shapiro-Wilk test disclose that anomaly exist in the NSE Energy index returns. The result of OLS disclose that Monday returns was found to be significant at 1 per cent level. The regression coefficient indicates that Monday returns positively influences Friday returns. Around 27.38 per cent of variation in Friday return is due to the select variable.

11.2.25. *NSE Finance Index*

High mean returns were noticed during Monday and low mean returns were found during Wednesday. High level of volatility was noticed on Monday and low level of volatility was noticed on Thursday. Skewness test disclosed that negative value and it was noticed during the Thursday returns and Friday returns. Positive returns were noticed during other days. Kurtosis results were found platykurtic on Thursday returns. The other day's returns were found leptokurtic. Shapiro-Wilk test disclose that anomaly exist in the NSE Finance index returns. The result of OLS disclose that Monday returns was found to be significant at 5 per cent level. Around 27.60 per cent of variation in Friday return is due to the select variable.

11.2.26. *NSE FMCG Index*

High mean returns were noticed during Thursday and low mean returns were found during Friday. High level of volatility was noticed on Monday and low level of volatility was noticed on Wednesday. Skewness test disclosed that positive value and it was noticed during Wednesday returns and Friday returns. Negative returns were noticed during other days. Kurtosis results were found platykurtic on Wednesday returns and Friday returns. The other day's returns were found leptokurtic. Shapiro-Wilk test disclose that anomaly exist in the NSE FMCG index returns. The result of OLS regression analysis disclose that the select independent variables collectively contribute to 2.34 per cent variation in Friday returns.

11.2.27. *NSE IT Index*

High mean returns were noticed during Wednesday and low mean returns were found during Monday. High level of volatility was noticed on Monday and low level of volatility was noticed on Wednesday. Skewness test disclosed that positive value and it was noticed during Monday returns and Tuesday returns. Negative returns were noticed during other days. Kurtosis results were found platykurtic on Wednesday returns and Thursday returns. The other day's returns were found leptokurtic. Shapiro-Wilk test disclose that anomaly exist in the NSE IT index returns. The result of regression analysis disclose that the select independent variables collectively contribute to 9.12 per cent variation in Friday returns.

11.2.28. *NSE Media Index*

High mean returns were noticed during Wednesday and low mean returns were found during Tuesday. High level of volatility was noticed on Monday and low level of volatility was noticed on Friday. Skewness test disclosed that positive value and it was noticed during Monday returns and Wednesday returns. Negative returns were noticed during other days. Kurtosis results were found platykurtic on Friday returns. The other day's returns were found leptokurtic. Shapiro-Wilk test disclose that anomaly exist in the NSE Media index returns. The result of OLS regression analysis disclose that the select independent variables collectively contribute to19.71 per cent variation in Friday returns.

11.2.29. NSE Metal Index

High mean returns were noticed during Friday and low mean returns were found during Wednesday. High level of volatility was noticed on Monday and low level of volatility was noticed on Thursday. Skewness test disclosed that positive value and it was noticed during Tuesday returns. Negative returns were noticed during other days. Kurtosis results were found platykurtic on Wednesday returns. The other day's returns were found leptokurtic. Shapiro-Wilk test disclose that anomaly exist in the NSE Metal index returns. The result of OLS disclose that Tuesday returns was found to be significant at 5 per cent level. The regression coefficient indicates that Tuesday returns positively influences Friday returns. Around 12.50 per cent of variation in Friday return is due to the select variable.

11.2.30. NSE Pharma Index

High mean returns were noticed during Friday and low mean returns were found during Tuesday. High level of volatility was noticed on Monday and low level of volatility was noticed on Wednesday. Skewness test disclosed that negative value and it was noticed all the days of the week. Kurtosis results were found leptokurtic on Monday returns and Tuesday returns. The other day's returns were found platykurtic. Shapiro-Wilk test disclose that anomaly exist in the NSE Pharma index returns. The result of OLS regression analysis disclose that the select independent variables collectively contribute to11.03 per cent variation in Friday returns.

11.2.31. NSE Private Bank Index

High mean returns were noticed during Friday and low mean returns were found during Tuesday. High level of volatility was noticed on Monday and low level of volatility was noticed on Wednesday. Skewness test disclosed that negative value and it was noticed during Tuesday and Friday returns. Positive returns were noticed during other days. Kurtosis results NSE Private Bank Index returns were found leptokurtic on Monday returns and Friday returns. The other day's returns were found platykurtic. Shapiro-Wilk test disclose that anomaly exist in the NSE Private Bank index returns. The result of OLS disclose that Wednesday returns was found to be significant at 5 per cent level. The regression coefficient indicates that Wednesday returns positively influences Friday returns. Around 14.93 per cent of variation in Friday return is due to the select variable.

11.2.32. NSE Public Sector Bank Index

High mean returns were noticed during Friday and low mean returns were found during Tuesday. High level of volatility was noticed on Monday and low level of volatility was noticed on Thursday. Skewness test disclosed that negative value and it was noticed during Thursday returns and Friday returns. Positive returns were noticed during other days. Kurtosis results were found platykurtic on Wednesday returns and Thursday returns. The other day's returns were found leptokurtic. Shapiro-Wilk test disclose that anomaly exist in the NSE PSU Bank index returns. The result of OLS disclose that Monday and Wednesday returns was found to be significant at 5 per cent level. The regression coefficient indicates that Monday and Wednesday returns positively influences Friday returns. Around 22.46 per cent of variation in Friday return is due to the select variables.

11.2.33. NSE Realty Index

High mean returns were noticed during Friday and low mean returns were found during Thursday. High level of volatility was noticed on Monday and low level of volatility was noticed on Thursday. Skewness test disclosed that negative value and it was noticed during Monday returns and Thursday returns. Positive returns were noticed during other days. Kurtosis results were found leptokurtic on Monday returns and Thursday returns. The other day's returns were found platykurtic. Shapiro-Wilk test disclose that anomaly exist in the NSE Realty index returns. The result of OLS disclose that Wednesday returns was found to be significant at 5 per cent level. The regression coefficient indicates that Wednesday returns positively influences Friday returns. Around 15.51 per cent of variation in Friday return is due to the select variable.

11.3. Semi Month Effect

To measure the Semi Month effect, returns, descriptive statistics like Mean, Standard deviation, Variance, Skewness, Kurtosis, Shapiro-wilk test and paired 't' test are employed. The following paragraphs consolidates the result of the study.

11.3.1. BSE Sensex Index

High mean returns were noticed during the second half of the month and low mean returns were found during the first half of the month. High level of volatility was noticed on the first half of the month and low level of volatility was noticed in the second half of the month. Skewness test disclosed that negative value were noticed during the first half of the month returns. The second half of the month returns was noticed positive Skewness. Kurtosis results were found leptokurtic on First half of the month. The second half of the month returns were found platykurtic. Shapiro-Wilk test disclose that anomaly exist in the BSE Sensex index returns. Paired 't' test result of the BSE Sensex index returns does not differ between the first half and the second half of the month.

11.3.2. BSE Auto Index

High mean returns were noticed during the first half of the month and low mean return were found during the second half of the month. High level of volatility was noticed on the second half of the month and low level of volatility was noticed in the first half of the month. Skewness test disclosed that positive value were noticed during both the first half of the month and the second half of the month. Kurtosis results were found platykurtic on First half of the month. The second half of the month returns were found leptokurtic. Shapiro-Wilk test disclose that anomaly exist in the BSE AUTO index returns. Paired 't' test result of the BSE Auto index returns does not differ between the first half and the second half of the month.

11.3.3. BSE Bank Index

High mean returns were noticed during the first half of the month and low mean return were found during the second half of the month. High level of volatility was noticed on the second half of the month and low level of volatility was noticed in the first half of the month. Skewness test disclosed that positive value were noticed during both the first half of the month and the second half of the month returns. Kurtosis results were found leptokurtic on First half of the month. The second half of the month returns were found platykurtic. Shapiro-Wilk test disclose that anomaly exist in the BSE Bank index returns. Paired 't' test result of the BSE Bank index returns does not differ between the first half and the second half of the month.

11.3.4. BSE Basic Materials Index

High mean returns were noticed during the first half of the month and low mean return were found during the second half of the month. High level of volatility was noticed on the second half of the month and low level of volatility was noticed in the first half of the month. Skewness test disclosed that negative value were noticed during both the first half of the month and the second half of the month returns. Kurtosis results were found platykurtic on First half of the month. The second half of the month returns were found leptokurtic. Shapiro-Wilk test disclose that anomaly exist in the BSE Basic Materials index returns. Paired 't' test result of the BSE Basic Materials index returns does not differ between the first half and the second half of the month.

11.3.5. BSE Consumer Durables Index

High mean returns were noticed during the first half of the month and low mean return were found during the second half of the month. High level of volatility was noticed on the first half of the month and low level of volatility was noticed in the second half of the month. Skewness test disclosed that negative value were noticed during the first half of the month. The second half of the month returns was noticed positive Skewness. Kurtosis results were found leptokurtic on both the First half of the month and the second half of the month. Shapiro-Wilk test disclose that anomaly exist in the BSE Consumer Durables index returns. Paired 't' test result of the BSE Consumer Durables index returns does not differ between the first half and the second half of the month.

11.3.6. BSE Consumer Goods Index

High mean returns were noticed during the first half of the month and low mean return were found during the second half of the month. High level of volatility was noticed on the second half of the month and low level of volatility was noticed in the first half of the month. Skewness test disclosed that negative value were noticed during the first half of the month returns. The second half of the month returns was noticed positive Skewness. Kurtosis results were found leptokurtic on both the First half of the month and the second half of the month. Shapiro-Wilk test disclose that anomaly exist in the BSE Consumer Goods index returns. Paired 't' test result of the BSE Consumer Goods index returns does not differ between the first half and the second half of the month.

11.3.7. BSE Energy Index

High mean returns were noticed during the first half of the month and low mean return were found during the second half of the month. High level of volatility was noticed on the second half of the month and low level of volatility was noticed in the first half of the month. Skewness test disclosed that negative value were noticed during the second half of the month returns. The first half of the month returns was noticed positive Skewness. Kurtosis results were found platykurtic on First half of the month. The second half of the month returns were found leptokurtic. Shapiro-Wilk test disclose that anomaly exist in the BSE Energy index returns. Paired 't' test result of the BSE Energy index returns does not differ between the first half and the second half of the month.

11.3.8. BSE Finance Index

High mean returns were noticed during the first half of the month and low mean return were found during the second half of the month. High level of volatility was noticed on the second half of the month and low level of volatility was noticed in the first half of the month.

Skewness test disclosed that negative value were noticed during both the first half of the month and the second half of the month returns. Kurtosis results were found platykurtic on both the First half of the month and the second half of the month. Shapiro-Wilk test disclose that anomaly exist in the BSE Finance index returns. Paired 't' test result of the BSE Finance index returns does not differ between the first half and the second half of the month.

11.3.9. BSE FMCG Index

High mean returns were noticed during the first half of the month and low mean return were found during the second half of the month. High level of volatility was noticed on the first half of the month and low level of volatility was noticed in the second half of the month. Skewness test disclosed that negative value were noticed during both the first half of the month and the second half of the month returns. Kurtosis results were found platykurtic on both the First half of the month and the second half of the month. Shapiro-Wilk test disclose that anomaly exist in the BSE FMCG index returns. Paired 't' test result of the BSE FMCG index returns does not differ between the first half and the second half of the month.

11.3.10. BSE Health Care Index

High mean returns were noticed during the first half of the month and low mean return were found during the second half of the month. High level of volatility was noticed on the second half of the month and low level of volatility was noticed in the first half of the month. Skewness test disclosed that negative value were noticed during both the first half of the month and the second half of the month returns. Kurtosis Results were found platykurtic on both the First half of the month and the second half of the month. Shapiro-Wilk test disclose that anomaly exist in the BSE Health care index returns. Paired 't' test result of the BSE Health care index returns differs between the first half and the second half of the month.

11.3.11. BSE Industrial Index

High mean returns were noticed during the first half of the month and low mean return were found during the second half of the month. High level of volatility was noticed on the second half of the month and low level of volatility was noticed in the first half of the month. Skewness test disclosed that negative value were noticed during both the first half of the month and the second half of the month returns. Kurtosis results were found platykurtic on First half of the month. The second half of the month returns were found leptokurtic. Shapiro-Wilk test disclose that anomaly exist in the BSE Industrial index returns. Paired 't' test result of the BSE Industrial index returns does not differ between the first half and the second half of the month.

11.3.12. BSE IT Index

High mean returns were noticed during the first half of the month and low mean return were found during the second half of the month. High level of volatility was noticed on the second half of the month and low level of volatility was noticed in the first half of the month. Skewness test disclosed that positive value were noticed during the first half of the month. The second half of the month returns was noticed negative Skewness. Kurtosis results were found platykurtic on both the First half of the month and the second half of the month. Shapiro-Wilk test disclose that anomaly exist in the BSE Industrial index returns. Paired 't' test result of the BSE IT index returns differs between the first half and the second half of the month.

11.3.13. BSE Metal Index

High mean returns were noticed during the first half of the month and low mean return were found during the second half of the month. High level of volatility was noticed on the second half of the month and low level of volatility was noticed in the first half of the month. Skewness test disclosed that positive value were noticed during the second half of the month returns. The first half of the month returns was noticed negative Skewness. Kurtosis results were found platykurtic on both the First half of the month and the second half of the month. Shapiro-Wilk test disclose that anomaly exist in the BSE Metal index returns. Paired 't' test result of the BSE Metal index returns does not differ between the first half and the second half of the month.

11.3.14. BSE Oil and Gas Index

High mean returns were noticed during the first half of the month and low mean return were found during the second half of the month. High level of volatility was noticed on the first half of the month and low level of volatility was noticed in the second half of the month. Skewness test disclosed that positive value were noticed during the second half of the month returns. The first half of the month returns was noticed negative Skewness. Kurtosis results were found leptokurtic on First half of the month. The second half of the month returns were found platykurtic. Shapiro-Wilk test disclose that anomaly exist in the BSE Oil and Gas index returns. Paired 't' test result of the BSE Oil and Gas index returns does not differ between the first half and the second half of the month.

11.3.15. BSE Power Index

High mean returns were noticed during the first half of the month and low mean return were found during the second half of the month. High level of volatility was noticed on the first half of the month and low level of volatility was noticed in the second half of the month.

Skewness test disclosed that positive value were noticed during both the first half of the month and the second half of the month returns. Kurtosis results were found platykurtic on First half of the month. The second half of the month returns were found leptokurtic. Shapiro-Wilk test disclose that anomaly exist in the BSE Power index returns. Paired 't' test result of the BSE Power index returns does not differ between the first half and the second half of the month.

11.3.16. BSE PSU Index

High mean returns were noticed during the first half of the month and low mean return were found during the second half of the month. High level of volatility was noticed on the second half of the month and low level of volatility was noticed in the first half of the month. Skewness test disclosed that positive value were noticed during the second half of the month returns. The first half of the month returns was noticed negative Skewness. Kurtosis results were found leptokurtic on both the First half of the month and the second half of the month. Shapiro-Wilk test disclose that anomaly exist in the BSE PSU index returns. Paired 't' test result of the BSE PSU index returns does not differ between the first half and the second half of the month.

11.3.17. BSE Realty Index

High mean returns were noticed during the first half of the month and low mean return were found during the second half of the month. High level of volatility was noticed on the first half of the month and low level of volatility was noticed in the second half of the month. Skewness test disclosed that positive value were noticed during both the first half of the month and the second half of the month returns. Kurtosis results were found leptokurtic on both the First half of the month and the second half of the month. Shapiro-Wilk test disclose that anomaly exist in the BSE Realty index returns. Paired 't' test result of the BSE Realty index returns differs between the first half and the second half of the month.

11.3.18. BSE Teck Index

High mean returns were noticed during the first half of the month and low mean return were found during the second half of the month. High level of volatility was noticed on the first half of the month and low level of volatility was noticed in the second half of the month. Skewness test disclosed that negative value were noticed during both the first half of the month and the second half of the month returns. Kurtosis results were found platykurtic on both the First half of the month and the second half of the month. Shapiro-Wilk test disclose that anomaly exist in the BSE TECK index returns. Paired 't' test result of the BSE TECK index returns does not differ between the first half and the second half of the month.

11.3.19. BSE Telecom Index

High mean returns were noticed during the first half of the month and low mean return were found during the second half of the month. High level of volatility was noticed on the second half of the month and low level of volatility was noticed in the first half of the month. Skewness test disclosed that negative value were noticed during both the first half of the month and the second half of the month returns. Kurtosis results were found platykurtic on both the First half of the month and the second half of the month. Shapiro-Wilk test disclose that anomaly exist in the BSE Telecom index returns. Paired 't' test result of the BSE Telecom index returns does not differ between the first half and the second half of the month.

11.3.20. BSE Utilities Index

High mean returns were noticed during the first half of the month and low mean return were found during the second half of the month. High level of volatility was noticed on the first half of the month and low level of volatility was noticed in the second half of the month. Skewness test disclosed that positive value were noticed during the first half of the month returns. The second half of the month returns was noticed negative Skewness. Kurtosis results were found leptokurtic on First half of the month. The second half of the month returns were found platykurtic. Shapiro-Wilk test disclose that anomaly exist in the BSE Utilities index returns. Paired 't' test result of the BSE Telecom index returns does not differ between the first half and the second half of the month.

11.3.21. NSE Nifty Index

High mean returns were noticed during the second half of the month and low mean return were found during the first half of the month. High level of volatility was noticed on the first half of the month and low level of volatility was noticed in the second half of the month. Skewness test disclosed that positive value were noticed during the first half of the month. The second half of the month returns was noticed negative Skewness. Kurtosis results were found leptokurtic on both the First half of the month and the second half of the month. Shapiro-Wilk test disclose that anomaly exist in the NSE Nifty index returns. Paired 't' test result of the NSE Nifty index returns does not differ between the first half and the second half of the month.

11.3.22. NSE Auto Index

High mean returns were noticed during the first half of the month and low mean return were found during the second half of the month. High level of volatility was noticed on the second half of the month and low level of volatility was noticed in the second half of the month.

Skewness test disclosed that positive value were noticed during the second half of the month returns. The first half of the month returns was noticed negative Skewness. Kurtosis results were found platykurtic on both the First half of the month and the second half of the month. Shapiro-Wilk test disclose that anomaly exist in the NSE Auto index returns. Paired 't' test result of the NSE Auto index returns does not differ between the first half and the second half of the month.

11.3.23. NSE Bank Index

High mean returns were noticed during the first half of the month and low mean return were found during the second half of the month. High level of volatility was noticed on the second half of the month and low level of volatility was noticed in the second half of the month. Skewness test disclosed that positive value were noticed during the second half of the month returns. The first half of the month returns was noticed negative Skewness. Kurtosis results were found leptokurtic on First half of the month. The second half of the month returns were found platykurtic. Shapiro-Wilk test disclose that anomaly exist in the NSE Bank index returns. Paired 't' test result of the NSE Bank index returns does not differ between the first half and the second half of the month.

11.3.24. NSE Energy Index

High mean returns were noticed during the first half of the month and low mean return were found during the second half of the month. High level of volatility was noticed on the second half of the month and low level of volatility was noticed in the second half of the month. Skewness test disclosed that positive value were noticed during the second half of the month returns. The first half of the month returns was noticed negative Skewness. Kurtosis Results were found leptokurtic on both the First half of the month and the second half of the month. Shapiro-Wilk test disclose that anomaly exist in the NSE Energy index returns. Paired 't' test result of the NSE Energy index returns does not differ between the first half and the second half of the month

11.3.25. NSE Finance Index

High mean returns were noticed during the first half of the month and low mean return were found during the second half of the month. High level of volatility was noticed on the first half of the month and low level of volatility was noticed in the second half of the month. Skewness test disclosed that positive value were noticed during both the first half of the month and the second half of the month returns. Kurtosis results were found leptokurtic on First half of the month. The second half of the month returns were found platykurtic. Shapiro-Wilk test disclose that anomaly exist in the NSE Finance index returns. Paired 't' test result of the NSE Finance index returns does not differ between the first half and the second half of the month.

11.3.26. NSE FMCG Index

High mean returns were noticed during the second half of the month and low mean return were found during the first half of the month. High level of volatility was noticed on the first half of the month and low level of volatility was noticed in the second half of the month. Skewness test disclosed that positive value were noticed during the second half of the month returns. The first half of the month returns was noticed negative Skewness. Kurtosis results were found platykurtic on both the First half of the month and the second half of the month. Shapiro-Wilk test disclose that anomaly exist in the NSE FMCG index returns. Paired 't' test result of the NSE FMCG index returns does not differ between the first half and the second half of the month.

11.3.27. NSE IT Index

High mean returns were noticed during the second half of the month and low mean return were found during the first half of the month. High level of volatility was noticed on the first half of the month and low level of volatility was noticed in the second half of the month. Skewness test disclosed that negative value were noticed during both the first half of the month and the second half of the month returns. The Kurtosis results were found platykurtic on both the First half of the month and the second half of the month. Shapiro-Wilk test disclose that anomaly exist in the NSE IT index returns. Paired 't' test result of the NSE IT index returns does not differ between the first half and the second half of the month.

11.3.28. NSE Media Index

High mean returns were noticed during the second half of the month and low mean return were found during the first half of the month. High level of volatility was noticed on the first half of the month and low level of volatility was noticed in the second half of the month. Skewness test disclosed that positive value were noticed during both the first half of the month and the second half of the month returns. Kurtosis results were found leptokurtic on First half of the month. The second half of the month returns were found platykurtic. Shapiro-Wilk test disclose that anomaly exist in the NSE Media index returns. Paired 't' test result of the NSE Media index returns does not differ between the first half and the second half of the month.

11.3.29. NSE Metal Index

High mean returns were noticed during the first half of the month and low mean return were found during the second half of the month. High level of volatility was noticed on the first half of the month and low level of volatility was noticed in the second half of the month. Skewness test disclosed that positive value were noticed during the second half of the month returns. The first half of the month returns was noticed negative Skewness. Kurtosis results were found leptokurtic on First half of the month. The second half of the month returns were found platykurtic. Shapiro-Wilk test disclose that anomaly exist in the NSE Metal index returns. Paired 't' test result of the NSE Metal index returns does not differ between the first half and the second half of the month.

11.3.30. NSE Pharma Index

High mean returns were noticed during the first half of the month and low mean return were found during the second half of the month. High level of volatility was noticed on the second half of the month and low level of volatility was noticed in the first half of the month. Skewness test disclosed that negative value were noticed during both the first half of the month and the second half of the month returns. Kurtosis results were found platykurtic on both the First half of the month and the second half of the month. Shapiro-Wilk test disclose that anomaly exist in the NSE Pharma index returns. Paired 't' test result of the NSE Pharma index returns does not differ between the first half and the second half of the month.

11.3.31. NSE Private Bank Index

High mean returns were noticed during the first half of the month and low mean return were found during the second half of the month. High level of volatility was noticed on the second half of the month and low level of volatility was noticed in the first half of the month. Skewness test disclosed that positive value were noticed during the first half of the month returns. The second half of the month returns was noticed negative Skewness. Kurtosis results were found leptokurtic on First half of the month. The second half of the month returns were found platykurtic. Shapiro-Wilk test disclose that anomaly exist in the NSE Private Bank index returns. Paired 't' test result of the NSE Private Bank index returns does not differ between the first half and the second half of the month.

11.3.32. NSE Public Sector Unit Bank Index

High mean returns were noticed during the first half of the month and low mean return were found during the second half of the month. High level of volatility was noticed on the second half of the month and low level of volatility was noticed in the first half of the month. Skewness test disclosed that positive value were noticed during the second half of the month returns. The first half of the month returns was noticed negative Skewness. Kurtosis results were found platykurtic on both the First half of the month and the second half of the month. Shapiro-Wilk test disclose that anomaly exist in the NSE PSU index returns. Paired 't' test result of the NSE PSU index returns does not differ between the first half and the second half of the month.

11.3.33. NSE Realty Index

High mean returns were noticed during the first half of the month and low mean return were found during the second half of the month. High level of volatility was noticed on the second half of the month and low level of volatility was noticed in the first half of the month. Skewness test disclosed that positive value were noticed during both the first half of the month and the second half of the month returns. Kurtosis results were found leptokurtic on both the First half of the month and the second half of the month. Shapiro-Wilk test disclose that anomaly exist in the NSE Realty index returns. Paired 't' test result of the NSE Realty index returns differs between the first half and the second half of the month.

11.4. Turn of the Month Effect

To measure the Turn of the Month effect, returns, descriptive statistics like Mean, Standard deviation, Variance, Skewness, Kurtosis, Shapiro-wilk test and paired 't' test are employed. The following paragraphs consolidates the result of the study.

11.4.1. BSE Sensex Index

High mean returns were noticed during the First half of the month and low mean returns were found during the rest of the month. High level of volatility was noticed on the First half of the month and low level of volatility was noticed in rest of the month. Skewness test disclosed that negative returns were noticed during the First half of the month and rest of the month returns. Kurtosis results were found platykurtic in the first half of the month. The rest of the month return were found leptokurtic. Shapiro-Wilk test disclose that anomaly exist in the BSE Sensex returns. Paired 't' test result of the BSE Sensex index returns differs between the first half and rest of the month.

11.4.2. BSE Auto Index

High mean returns were noticed during the First half of the month and low mean returns were found during the rest of the month. High level of volatility was noticed on the First half of the month and low level of volatility was noticed in rest of the month. Skewness test disclosed that negative returns were noticed during the First half of the month and rest of the month returns. Kurtosis results were found platykurtic in the first half of the month The rest of the month return were found leptokurtic. Shapiro-Wilk test disclose that anomaly exist in the BSE Auto index returns. Paired 't' test result of the BSE Auto index returns differs between the first half and rest of the month.

11.4.3. BSE Bank Index

High mean returns were noticed during the First half of the month and low mean returns were found during the rest of the month. High level of volatility was noticed on the First half of the month and low level of volatility was noticed in rest of the month. Skewness test disclosed that negative returns were noticed during the First half of the month and rest of the month returns. Kurtosis results were found platykurtic in both the First half of the month and the rest of the month. Shapiro-Wilk test disclose that anomaly exist in the BSE Bank index returns. Paired 't' test result of the BSE Bank index returns differs between the first half and rest of the month.

11.4.4. BSE Basic Materials Index

High mean returns were noticed during the Rest of the month and low mean returns were found during the First half of the month. High level of volatility was noticed on the First half of the month and low level of volatility was noticed in rest of the month. Skewness test disclosed that negative returns were noticed during the First half of the month and rest of the month returns. The Kurtosis results were founded leptokurtic in both the First half of the month and rest of the month. Shapiro-Wilk test disclose that anomaly exist in the BSE Basic Materials index returns. Paired 't' test result of the BSE Basic Materials index returns does not differ between the first half and the rest of the month.

11.4.5. BSE Consumer Durables Index

High mean returns were noticed during the First half of the month and low mean returns were found during the rest of the month. High level of volatility was noticed on the First half of the month and low level of volatility was noticed in rest of the month. Skewness test disclosed that negative returns were noticed during the First half of the month and rest of the month returns. Kurtosis results were founded platykurtic in both the First half of the month and rest of the month. Shapiro-Wilk test disclose that anomaly exist in the BSE Consumer Durables index returns. Paired 't' test result of the BSE Consumer Durables index returns differs between the first half and rest of the month.

11.4.6. BSE Consumer Goods Index

High mean returns were noticed during the First half of the month and low mean returns were found during the rest of the month. High level of volatility was noticed on the First half of the month and low level of volatility was noticed in rest of the month. Skewness test disclosed that negative returns were noticed during the First half of the month and rest of the month returns. Kurtosis results were founded platykurtic in both the First half of the month and rest of the month. Shapiro-Wilk test disclose that anomaly exist in the BSE Consumer Goods index returns. Paired 't' test result of the BSE Consumer Goods index returns differs between the first half and rest of the month.

11.4.7. BSE Energy Index

High mean returns were noticed during the rest of the month and low mean returns were found during the first half of the month. High level of volatility was noticed on the First half of the month and low level of volatility was noticed in rest of the month. Skewness test disclosed that negative returns were noticed during the First half of the month and rest of the month returns. Kurtosis results were found leptokurtic in both the First half of the month and the rest of the month. Shapiro-Wilk test disclose that anomaly exist in the BSE Energy index returns. Paired 't' test result of the BSE Energy index returns does not differ between the first half and the rest of the month.

11.4.8. BSE Finance Index

High mean returns were noticed during the rest of the month and low mean returns were found during the first half of the month. High level of volatility was noticed on the First half of the month and low level of volatility was noticed in rest of the month. Skewness test disclosed that negative returns were noticed during the First half of the month and rest of the month returns. Kurtosis results were found leptokurtic in both the First half of the month and the rest of the month. Shapiro-Wilk test disclose that anomaly exist in the BSE Finance index returns. Paired 't' test result of the BSE Finance index returns does not differ between the first half and the rest of the month.

11.4.9. BSE FMCG Index

High mean returns were noticed during the First half of the month and low mean returns were found during the rest of the month. High level of volatility was noticed on the First half of the month and low level of volatility was noticed in rest of the month. Skewness test disclosed that negative returns were noticed during the First half of the month and rest of the month

returns. Kurtosis were found leptokurtic in the First half of the month. The rest of the month return were found platykurtic. Shapiro-Wilk test disclose that anomaly exist in the BSE FMCG index returns. Paired 't' test result of the BSE FMCG index returns does not differ between the first half and the rest of the month.

11.4.10. BSE Health Care Index

High mean returns were noticed during the First half of the month and low mean returns were found during the rest of the month. High level of volatility was noticed on the First half of the month and low level of volatility was noticed in rest of the month. Skewness test disclosed that negative returns were noticed during the First half of the month and rest of the month returns. Kurtosis results were found leptokurtic in both the First half of the month and the rest of the month. Shapiro-Wilk test disclose that anomaly exist in the BSE Health Care index returns. Paired 't' test result of the BSE Health Care index returns does not differ between the first half and the rest of the month.

11.4.11. BSE IT Index

High mean returns were noticed during the First half of the month and low mean returns were found during the rest of the month. High level of volatility was noticed on the First half of the month and low level of volatility was noticed in rest of the month. Skewness test disclosed that negative returns were noticed during the First half of the month and rest of the month returns. Kurtosis results were found platykurtic in both the First half of the month and the rest of the month. Shapiro-Wilk test disclose that anomaly exist in the BSE IT index returns. Paired 't' test result of the BSE IT index returns does not differ between the first half and the rest of the month.

11.4.12. BSE Industrial Index

High mean returns were noticed during the rest of the month and low mean returns were found during the first half of the month. High level of volatility was noticed on the First half of the month and low level of volatility was noticed in rest of the month. Skewness test disclosed that negative returns were noticed during the First half of the month and rest of the month returns. Kurtosis results BSE Industrial index returns were found leptokurtic in both the First half of the month and the rest of the month. Shapiro-Wilk test disclose that anomaly exist in the BSE Industrial index returns. Paired 't' test result of the BSE Industrial index returns does not differ between the first half and the rest of the month.

11.4.13. *BSE Metal Index*

High mean returns were noticed during the First half of the month and low mean returns were found during the rest of the month. High level of volatility was noticed on the First half of the month and low level of volatility was noticed in rest of the month. Skewness test disclosed that negative returns were noticed during the First half of the month and rest of the month returns. Kurtosis results BSE Metal index returns were found leptokurtic in both the First half of the month and the rest of the month. Shapiro-Wilk test disclose that anomaly exist in the BSE Metal index returns. Paired 't' test result of the BSE Metal index returns differs between the first half and rest of the month.

11.4.14. *BSE Oil and Gas Index*

High mean returns were noticed during the First half of the month and low mean returns were found during the rest of the month. High level of volatility was noticed on the First half of the month and low level of volatility was noticed in rest of the month. Skewness test disclosed that negative returns were noticed during the First half of the month and rest of the month returns. Kurtosis results were found platykurtic in the First half of the month. The rest of the month return were found leptokurtic. Shapiro-Wilk test disclose that anomaly exist in the BSE Oil and Gas index returns. Paired 't' test result of the BSE Oil and Gas index returns differs between the first half and rest of the month.

11.4.15. *BSE Power Index*

High mean returns were noticed during the First half of the month and low mean returns were found during the first half of the month. High level of volatility was noticed on the First half of the month and low level of volatility was noticed in rest of the month. Skewness test disclosed that positive returns were noticed in the first half of the month returns. The rest of the month returns found Negative Skewness. Kurtosis results were found leptokurtic in the rest of the month The first half of the month return were found platykurtic. Shapiro-Wilk test disclose that anomaly exist in the BSE Power index returns. Paired 't' test result of the BSE Power index returns differs between the first half and rest of the month.

11.4.16. *BSE Public Sector Unit Index*

High mean returns were noticed during the First half of the month and low mean returns were found during the rest of the month. High level of volatility was noticed on the First half of the month and low level of volatility was noticed in rest of the month. Skewness test disclosed that negative returns were noticed during the First half of the month and rest of the month

returns. Kurtosis results were found platykurtic in the First half of the month. The rest of the month return were found leptokurtic. Shapiro-Wilk test disclose that anomaly exist in the BSE PSU index returns. Paired 't' test result of the BSE PSU index returns differs between the first half and rest of the month.

11.4.17. BSE Realty Index

High mean returns were noticed during the First half of the month and low mean returns were found during the first half of the month. High level of volatility was noticed on the First half of the month and low level of volatility was noticed in rest of the month. Skewness test disclosed that negative returns were noticed in the first half of the month returns. The rest of the month returns found positive Skewness. Kurtosis results were found platykurtic in both the First half of the month and the rest of the month. Shapiro-Wilk test disclose that anomaly exist in the BSE Realty index returns. Paired 't' test result of the BSE Realty index returns differs between the first half and rest of the month.

11.4.18. BSE Teck Index

High mean returns were noticed during the First half of the month and low mean returns were found during the rest of the month. High level of volatility was noticed on the First half of the month and low level of volatility was noticed in rest of the month. Skewness test disclosed that negative returns were noticed during the First half of the month and rest of the month returns. Kurtosis results were found platykurtic in both the First half of the month and the rest of the month. Shapiro-Wilk test disclose that anomaly exist in the BSE Teck index returns. Paired 't' test result of the BSE Teck index returns differs between the first half and rest of the month.

11.4.19. BSE Telecom Index

High mean returns were noticed during the rest of the month and low mean returns were found during the first half of the month. High level of volatility was noticed on the First half of the month and low level of volatility was noticed in rest of the month. Skewness test disclosed that negative returns were noticed during the First half of the month and rest of the month returns. Kurtosis results were found leptokurtic in the rest of the month. The first half of the month return were found platykurtic. Shapiro-Wilk test disclose that anomaly exist in the BSE Telecom index returns. BSE Telecom index returns does not differ between the first half and the rest of the month.

11.4.20. *BSE Utilities Index*

High mean returns were noticed during the Rest of the month and low mean returns were found during the First half of the month. High level of volatility was noticed on the First half of the month and low level of volatility was noticed in rest of the month. Skewness test disclosed that positive returns were noticed during the First half of the month and rest of the month returns. The Kurtosis results were founded leptokurtic in both the First half of the month and rest of the month the rest of the month returns. Shapiro-Wilk test disclose that anomaly exist in the BSE Utilities index returns. Paired 't' test result of the BSE Utilities index returns does not differ between the first half and the rest of the month.

11.4.21. *NSE Nifty Index*

High mean returns were noticed during the First half of the month and low mean returns were found during the rest of the month. High level of volatility was noticed on the First half of the month and low level of volatility was noticed in rest of the month. Skewness test disclosed that negative returns were noticed during the First half of the month and rest of the month returns. Kurtosis results NSE Nifty index returns were founded leptokurtic in both the First half of the month and rest of the month. Shapiro-Wilk test disclose that anomaly exist in the NSE Nifty index returns. Paired 't' test result of the NSE Nifty index differs between the first half and rest of the month.

11.4.22. *NSE Auto Index*

High mean returns were noticed during the First half of the month and low mean returns were found during the rest of the month. High level of volatility was noticed on the First half of the month and low level of volatility was noticed in rest of the month. Skewness test disclosed that negative returns were noticed during the First half of the month and rest of the month returns. Kurtosis results were found platykurtic in the first half of the month. The rest of the month return were found leptokurtic. Shapiro-Wilk test disclose that anomaly exist in the NSE Auto index returns. Paired 't' test result of the NSE Auto index returns differs between the first half and rest of the month.

11.4.23. *NSE Bank Index*

High mean returns were noticed during the First half of the month and low mean returns were found during the rest of the month. High level of volatility was noticed on the First half of the month and low level of volatility was noticed in rest of the month. Skewness test disclosed that negative returns were noticed during the First half of the month and rest of the month

returns. Kurtosis results NSE Bank index returns were founded platykurtic in both the First half of the month and rest of the month. Shapiro-Wilk test disclose that anomaly exist in the NSE Bank index returns. Paired 't' test result of the NSE Bank index returns differs between the first half and rest of the month.

11.4.24. NSE Energy Index

High mean returns were noticed during the First half of the month and low mean returns were found during the rest of the month. High level of volatility was noticed on the First half of the month and low level of volatility was noticed in rest of the month. Skewness test disclosed that negative returns were noticed during the First half of the month and rest of the month returns. Kurtosis results were found platykurtic in the first half of the month. The rest of the month return were found leptokurtic. Shapiro-Wilk test disclose that anomaly exist in the NSE Energy index returns. Turn of the month effect prevails in the NSE Energy index. Paired 't' test result of the NSE Energy index returns differs between the first half and rest of the month.

11.4.25. NSE Finance Index

High mean returns were noticed during the First half of the month and low mean returns were found during the rest of the month. High level of volatility was noticed on the First half of the month and low level of volatility was noticed in rest of the month. Skewness test disclosed that negative returns were noticed during the First half of the month and rest of the month returns. Kurtosis results NSE Finance index returns were founded platykurtic in both the First half of the month and rest of the month. Shapiro-Wilk test disclose that anomaly exist in the NSE Finance index returns. Paired 't' test result of the NSE Finance index returns differs between the first half and rest of the month.

11.4.26. NSE FMCG Index

High mean returns were noticed during the First half of the month and low mean returns were found during the rest of the month. High level of volatility was noticed on the First half of the month and low level of volatility was noticed in rest of the month. Skewness test disclosed that negative returns were noticed during the First half of the month and rest of the month returns. Kurtosis results were founded platykurtic in both the First half of the month and rest of the month. Shapiro-Wilk test disclose that anomaly exist in the NSE FMCG index returns. Paired 't' test result of the NSE FMCG returns does not differs between the first half and rest of the month.

11.4.27. NSE IT Index

High mean returns were noticed during the First half of the month and low mean returns were found during the rest of the month. High level of volatility was noticed on the First half of the month and low level of volatility was noticed in rest of the month. Skewness test disclosed that negative returns were noticed during the First half of the month and rest of the month returns. Kurtosis results NSE IT index returns were founded platykurtic in both the First half of the month and rest of the month. Shapiro-Wilk test disclose that anomaly exist in the NSE IT index returns. Paired 't' test result of the NSE IT index returns differs between the first half and rest of the month.

11.4.28. NSE Media Index

High mean returns were noticed during the First half of the month and low mean returns were found during the rest of the month. High level of volatility was noticed on the First half of the month and low level of volatility was noticed in rest of the month. Skewness test disclosed that negative returns were noticed during the First half of the month and rest of the month returns. Kurtosis results NSE Media index return were found platykurtic in the first half of the month. The rest of the month return were found leptokurtic. A Shapiro-Wilk test disclose that anomaly exist in the NSE Media index returns. Paired 't' test result of the NSE Media index returns differs between the first half and rest of the month.

11.4.29. NSE Metal Index

High mean returns were noticed during the First half of the month and low mean returns were found during the rest of the month. High level of volatility was noticed on the First half of the month and low level of volatility was noticed in rest of the month. Skewness test disclosed that negative returns were noticed during the First half of the month and rest of the month returns. Kurtosis results were founded leptokurtic in both the First half of the month and rest of the month. Shapiro-Wilk test disclose that anomaly exist in the NSE Metal index returns. Paired 't' test result of the NSE Metal index returns differs between the first half and rest of the month.

11.4.30. NSE Pharma Index

High mean returns were noticed during the First half of the month and low mean returns were found during the rest of the month. High level of volatility was noticed on the First half of the month and low level of volatility was noticed in rest of the month. Skewness test disclosed that negative returns were noticed during the First half of the month and rest of the month

returns. Kurtosis results were found platykurtic in the first half of the month The rest of the month return were found leptokurtic. Shapiro-Wilk test disclose that anomaly exist in the NSE Pharma index returns. Paired 't' test result of the NSE Pharma index returns differs between the first half and rest of the month.

11.4.31. NSE Private Banks Index

High mean returns were noticed during the First half of the month and low mean returns were found during the rest of the month. High level of volatility was noticed on the First half of the month and low level of volatility was noticed in rest of the month. Skewness test disclosed that negative returns were noticed in the first half of the month returns. The rest of the month returns found positive Skewness. Kurtosis results were found platykurtic in both the First half of the month and rest of the month. Shapiro-Wilk test disclose that anomaly exists in the NSE Private Banks index returns. Paired 't' test result of the NSE Private Banks index returns differs between the first half and rest of the month.

11.4.32. NSE Public Sector Unit Bank Index

High mean returns were noticed during the First half of the month and low mean returns were found during the rest of the month. High level of volatility was noticed on the First half of the month and low level of volatility was noticed in rest of the month. Skewness test disclosed that negative returns were noticed during the First half of the month and rest of the month returns. Kurtosis results were found platykurtic in the first half of the month. The rest of the month return were found leptokurtic. Shapiro-Wilk test disclose that anomaly exist in the NSE PSU Bank index returns. Paired 't' test result of the NSE PSU Bank index returns differs between the first half and rest of the month.

11.4.33. NSE Realty Index

High mean returns were noticed during the First half of the month and low mean returns were found during the rest of the month. High level of volatility was noticed on the First half of the month and low level of volatility was noticed in rest of the month. Skewness test disclosed that negative returns were noticed during the First half of the month and rest of the month returns. Kurtosis results NSE Realty index returns were founded platykurtic in both the First half of the month and rest of the month. Shapiro-Wilk test disclose that anomaly exist in the NSE Realty index returns. Paired 't' test result of the NSE Realty index returns differs between the first half and rest of the month.

11.5. Monthly Effect

To measure the Monthly effect, returns, descriptive statistics like Mean, Standard deviation, Variance, Skewness, Kurtosis and Shapiro-wilk test are employed. The following paragraphs consolidates the result of the study.

11.5.1. BSE Sensex Index

High mean returns were noticed during the month of September and low mean returns were found during the month of January. High level of volatility was noticed on the month of May and low level of volatility was noticed in the month of December. Skewness test disclosed the positive value and it was noticed during the month of April and May returns. Negative returns were noticed during other months. Kurtosis results were found leptokurtic in the month of June returns. The other month's returns were found platykurtic. Shapiro-Wilk test disclose that anomaly exist in the BSE Sensex index returns. April effect exists in BSE Sensex index.

11.5.2. BSE Auto Index

High mean returns were noticed during the month of September and low mean returns were found during the month of January. High level of volatility was noticed on the month of May and low level of volatility was noticed in the month of December. Skewness test disclosed the negative value and it was noticed during the month of June, September, October, November and December. Positive returns were noticed during other months. Kurtosis results were found leptokurtic on the month of July and October returns. The other month's returns were found platykurtic. Shapiro-Wilk test disclose that anomaly exist in the BSE Auto index returns. April effect exists in BSE Auto index.

11.5.3. BSE Bank Index

High mean returns were noticed during the month of September and low mean returns were found during the month of February. High level of volatility was noticed on the month of May and low level of volatility was noticed in the month of February. Skewness test disclosed the positive value and it was noticed during the month of April, May, August, December and January returns. Negative returns were noticed during other months. Kurtosis results were found leptokurtic on the month of June and January returns. The other month's returns were found platykurtic. Shapiro-Wilk test disclose that anomaly exist in the BSE Bank index returns. April effect exists in BSE Bank index.

11.5.4. BSE Basic Materials Index

High mean returns were noticed during the month of April and low mean returns were found during the month of March. High level of volatility was noticed on the month of May and low level of volatility was noticed in the month of December. Skewness test disclosed the positive value and it was noticed during the month of April, May, June, December, February and March returns. Negative returns were noticed during other months. Kurtosis results were found leptokurtic on the month of July and October returns. The other month's returns were found platykurtic. Shapiro-Wilk test disclose that anomaly exist in the BSE Basic Materials index returns. April effect exists in BSE Basic Materials index.

11.5.5. BSE Consumer Durables Index

High mean returns were noticed during the month of May and low mean returns were found during the month of January. High level of volatility was noticed on the month of May and low level of volatility was noticed in the month of April. Skewness test disclosed the positive value and it was noticed during the month of April, May, July, November, December and February returns. Negative returns were noticed during other months. Kurtosis results were found leptokurtic on the month of May, September, October and March returns. The other month's returns were found platykurtic. Shapiro-Wilk test disclose that anomaly exist in the BSE Consumer Durables index returns. April effect exists in BSE Consumer Durables index.

11.5.6. BSE Consumer Goods Index

High mean returns were noticed during the month of September and low mean returns were found during the month of January. High level of volatility was noticed on the month of May and low level of volatility was noticed in the month of August. Skewness test disclosed the positive value and it was noticed during the month of April, May, July, November and January returns. Negative returns were noticed during other months. Kurtosis results were found leptokurtic in the month of June returns. The other month's returns were found platykurtic. Shapiro-Wilk test disclose that anomaly exist in the BSE Consumer Goods index returns. April effect exists in BSE Consumer Goods index.

11.5.7. BSE Energy Index

High mean returns were noticed during the month of April and low mean returns were found during the month of November. High level of volatility was noticed on the month of October and low level of volatility was noticed in the month of February.

Skewness test disclosed the negative value and it was noticed during the month of June, October, December, January and February returns. Positive returns were noticed during other months. Kurtosis results result were found the platykurtic in all the months. Shapiro-Wilk test disclose that anomaly exist in the BSE Energy index returns. April effect exists in BSE Energy Goods index.

11.5.8. BSE Finance Index

High mean returns were noticed during the month of September and low mean returns were found during the month of February. High level of volatility was noticed on the month of May and low level of volatility was noticed in the month of December. Skewness test disclosed the positive value and it was noticed during the month of April, May, December and January returns. Negative returns were noticed during other months. Kurtosis results were found leptokurtic on the month of May returns. The other month's returns were found platykurtic. Shapiro-Wilk test disclose that anomaly exist in the BSE Finance index returns. April effect exists in BSE Finance index.

11.5.9. BSE FMCG Index

High mean returns were noticed during the month of September and low mean returns were found during the month of October. High level of volatility was noticed on the month of May and low level of volatility was noticed in the month of December. Skewness test disclosed the positive value and it was noticed during the month of July, September, November, December, February and March returns. Negative returns were noticed during other months. Kurtosis results were found leptokurtic in the month of July returns. The other month's returns were found platykurtic. Shapiro-Wilk test disclose that anomaly exist in the BSE FMCG index returns. April effect exists in BSE FMCG index.

11.5.10. BSE Health Care Index

High mean returns were noticed during the month of April and low mean returns were found during the month of January. High level of volatility was noticed on the month of October and low level of volatility was noticed in the month of July. Skewness test disclosed the positive value and it was noticed during the month of June, November, December, and February returns. Negative returns were noticed during other months. Kurtosis results were found leptokurtic in the month of October returns. The other month's returns were found platykurtic. Shapiro-Wilk test disclose that anomaly exist in the BSE Health Care index returns. April effect exists in BSE Health Care index.

11.5.11. *BSE Industrial Index*

High mean returns were noticed during the month of April and low mean returns were found during the month of January. High level of volatility was noticed on the month of May and low level of volatility was noticed in the month of July. Skewness test disclosed the positive value and it was noticed during the month of April, May, July, January, and February returns. Negative returns were noticed during other months. Kurtosis results were found leptokurtic on the month of April and May returns. The other month's returns were found platykurtic. Shapiro-Wilk test disclose that anomaly exist in the BSE Industrial index returns. April effect exists in BSE Industrial index.

11.5.12. *BSE IT Index*

High mean returns were noticed during the month of July and low mean returns were found during the month of January. High level of volatility was noticed on the month of April and low level of volatility was noticed in the month of February. Skewness test disclosed the positive value and it was noticed during the month of April, May, July and October returns. Negative returns were noticed during other months. Kurtosis results were found leptokurtic in the month of June and September returns. The other month's returns were found platykurtic. Shapiro-Wilk test disclose that anomaly exist in the BSE IT index returns. April effect exists in BSE IT index.

11.5.13. *BSE Metal Index*

High mean returns were noticed during the month of December and low mean returns were found during the month of June. High level of volatility was noticed on the month of May and low level of volatility was noticed in the month of August. Skewness test disclosed the positive value and it was noticed during the month of April, May, July, August, January and March returns. Negative returns were noticed during other months. Kurtosis results were found leptokurtic on the month of May and June returns. The other month's returns were found platykurtic. Shapiro-Wilk test disclose that anomaly exist in the BSE Metal index returns. April effect exists in BSE Metal index.

11.5.14. *BSE Oil and Gas Index*

High mean returns were noticed during the month of April and low mean returns were found during the month of February. High level of volatility was noticed on the month of May and low level of volatility was noticed in the month of February. Skewness test disclosed the negative value and it was noticed during the month of June, October, December and January returns. Positive returns were noticed during other months. The Kurtosis results were found the platykurtic in all the months. Shapiro-Wilk test disclose that anomaly exist in the BSE Oil and Gas index returns. April effect exists in BSE Metal index.

11.5.15. BSE Power Index

High mean returns were noticed during the month of September and low mean returns were found during the month of February. High level of volatility was noticed on the month of May and low level of volatility was noticed in the month of August. Skewness test disclosed the negative value and it was noticed during the month of June, September, December and March returns. Positive returns were noticed during other months. Kurtosis results were found leptokurtic in the month of June returns. The other month's returns were found platykurtic. Shapiro-Wilk test disclose that anomaly exist in the BSE Power index returns. April effect exists in BSE Power index.

11.5.16. BSE PSU Index

High mean returns were noticed during the month of September and low mean returns were found during the month of January. High level of volatility was noticed on the month of May and low level of volatility was noticed in the month of August. Skewness test disclosed the negative value and it was noticed during the month of June, September, October, November, January and February returns. Positive returns were noticed during other months. Kurtosis results were found the platykurtic in all the months. Shapiro-Wilk test disclose that anomaly exist in the BSE PSU index returns. April effect exists in BSE PSU index.

11.5.17. BSE Realty Index

High mean returns were noticed during the month of April and low mean returns were found during the month of June. High level of volatility was noticed on the month of May and low level of volatility was noticed in the month of August. Skewness test disclosed the negative value and it was noticed during the month of June, September and October returns. Positive returns were noticed during other months. Kurtosis results were found platykurtic in all the months. Shapiro-Wilk test disclose that anomaly exist in the BSE Realty index returns. April effect exists in BSE Realty index.

11.5.18. BSE Teck Index

High mean returns were noticed during the month of July and low mean returns were found during the month of January. High level of volatility was noticed on the month of April and low level of volatility was noticed in the month of February. Skewness test disclosed the positive value and it was noticed during the month of April, May, July, and March returns.

Negative returns were noticed during other months. Kurtosis results were found leptokurtic on the month of June and September returns. The other month's returns were found platykurtic. Shapiro-Wilk test disclose that anomaly exist in the BSE TECK index returns. April effect exists in BSE TECK index.

11.5.19. BSE Telecom Index

High mean returns were noticed during the month of July and low mean returns were found during the month of February. High level of volatility was noticed on the month of October and low level of volatility was noticed in the month of February. Skewness test disclosed the positive value and it was noticed during the month of May, July and November returns. Negative returns were noticed during other months. Kurtosis results were found leptokurtic in the month of June returns. The other month's returns were found platykurtic. Shapiro-Wilk test disclose that anomaly exist in the BSE Telecom index returns. April effect exists in BSE Telecom index.

11.5.20. BSE Utilities Index

High mean returns were noticed during the month of April and low mean returns were found during the month of March. High level of volatility was noticed on the month of May and low level of volatility was noticed in the month of February. Skewness test disclosed the negative value and it was noticed during the month of June, October and January returns. Positive returns were noticed during other months. Kurtosis results were found leptokurtic on the month of July, October and December returns. The other month's returns were found platykurtic. Shapiro-Wilk test disclose that anomaly exist in the BSE Utilities index returns. April effect exists in BSE Utilities index.

11.5.21. NSE Nifty Index

High mean returns were noticed during the month of September and low mean returns were found during the month of January. High level of volatility was noticed on the month of May and low level of volatility was noticed in the month of February. Skewness test disclosed the positive value and it was noticed during the month of April, May and July returns. Negative returns were noticed during other months. Kurtosis results were found leptokurtic in the month of June returns. The other month's returns were found platykurtic. Shapiro-Wilk test disclose that anomaly exist in the NSE Nifty Index returns. April effect exists in NSE Nifty index.

11.5.22. NSE Auto Index

High mean returns were noticed during the month of September and low mean returns were found during the month of January. High level of volatility was noticed in the month of May and low level of volatility was noticed in the month of April. Skewness test disclosed the positive value and it was noticed during the month of April, May, July, August and March returns. Negative returns were noticed during other months. Kurtosis results were found leptokurtic in the month of July and October returns. The other month's returns were found platykurtic. Shapiro-Wilk test disclose that anomaly exist in the NSE Auto Index returns. April effect exists in NSE Auto index.

11.5.23. NSE Bank Index

High mean returns were noticed during the month of September and low mean returns were found during the month of February. High level of volatility was noticed in the month of May and low level of volatility was noticed in the month of February. Skewness test disclosed the positive value and it was noticed during the month of April, May, August, December and January returns. Negative returns were noticed during other months. Kurtosis results were found leptokurtic in the month of January returns. The other month's returns were found platykurtic. Shapiro-Wilk test disclose that anomaly exist in the NSE Bank Index returns. April effect exists in NSE Bank index.

11.5.24. NSE Energy Index

High mean returns were noticed during the month of September and low mean returns were found during the month of February. High level of volatility was noticed in the month of May and low level of volatility was noticed in the month of February. Skewness test disclosed the negative value and it was noticed during the month of June, October, December, January and February returns. Positive returns were noticed during other months. Kurtosis results were found platykurtic in all the months. Shapiro-Wilk test disclose that anomaly exist in the NSE Energy Index returns. April effect exists in NSE Energy index.

11.5.25. NSE Finance Index

High mean returns were noticed during the month of September and low mean returns were found during the month of February. High level of volatility was noticed in the month of May and low level of volatility was noticed in the month of December. Skewness test disclosed the positive value and it was noticed during the month of April, May, August, December and January returns. Negative returns were noticed during other months. Kurtosis results were found leptokurtic in the month of June returns. The other month's returns were found platykurtic. Shapiro-Wilk test disclose that anomaly exist in the NSE Finance Index returns. April effect exists in NSE Finance index.

11.5.26. NSE FMCG Index

High mean returns were noticed during the month of September and low mean returns were found during the month of October. High level of volatility was noticed in the month of May and low level of volatility was noticed in the month of April. Skewness test disclosed the positive value and it was noticed during the month of July, November, December and February returns. Negative returns were noticed during other months. Kurtosis results were found leptokurtic in the month of July returns The other month's returns were found platykurtic. Shapiro-Wilk test disclose that anomaly exist in the NSE FMCG Index returns. April effect exists in NSE FMCG index.

11.5.27. NSE IT Index

High mean returns were noticed during the month of December and low mean returns were found during the month of January. High level of volatility was noticed in the month of September and low level of volatility was noticed in the month of February. Skewness test disclosed the positive value and it was noticed during the month of April and July returns. The other Month's returns were found negative Skewness. The Kurtosis results were found leptokurtic on the month of June, August, September and January returns. The other month's returns were found platykurtic. Shapiro-Wilk test disclose that anomaly exist in the NSE IT Index returns. April effect exists in NSE IT index.

11.5.28. NSE Media Index

High mean returns were noticed during the month of December and low mean returns were found during the month of February. High level of volatility was noticed in the month of May and low level of volatility was noticed in the month of February. Skewness test disclosed the positive value and it was noticed during the month of April, May, July, August, December and February returns. Negative returns were noticed during other months. Kurtosis results NSE Media returns were found leptokurtic on the month of May and October returns. The other month's returns were found platykurtic. Shapiro-Wilk test disclose that anomaly exist in the NSE Media Index returns. April effect exists in NSE Media index.

11.5.29. NSE Metal Index

High mean returns were noticed during the month of December and low mean returns were found during the month of June. High level of volatility was noticed in the month of May and low level of volatility was noticed in the month of February. Skewness test disclosed the positive value and it was noticed during the month of April, May, July, August, November, January and March returns. Negative returns were noticed during other months. Kurtosis results were found platykurtic in all the months. Shapiro-Wilk test disclose that anomaly exist in the NSE Metal Index returns. April effect exists in NSE Metal index.

11.5.30. NSE Pharma Index

High mean returns were noticed during the month of April and low mean returns were found during the month of January. High level of volatility was noticed in the month of October and low level of volatility was noticed in the month of November. Result of Skewness test disclosed the positive value and it was noticed during the month of April, June, November, December and February returns. Negative returns were noticed during other months. Kurtosis results were found leptokurtic in the month of October returns. The other month's returns were found platykurtic. Shapiro-Wilk test disclose that anomaly exist in the NSE Pharma Index returns. April effect exists in NSE Pharma index.

11.5.31. NSE Private Banks Index

High mean returns were noticed during the month of September and low mean returns were found during the month of February. High level of volatility was noticed in the month of May and low level of volatility was noticed in the month of December. Skewness test disclosed the positive value and it was noticed during the month of April, May, December and January returns. Negative returns were noticed during other months. Kurtosis results were found leptokurtic on the month of May, June and December returns. The other month's returns were found platykurtic. Shapiro-Wilk test disclose that anomaly exist in the NSE Private Banks Index returns. April effect exists in NSE Private Banks index.

11.5.32. NSE Public Sector Unit Bank Index

High mean returns were noticed during the month of September and low mean returns were found during the month of February. High level of volatility was noticed in the month of May and low level of volatility was noticed in the month of February. Skewness test disclosed the negative value and it was noticed during the month of April, June, September, October and February returns. Positive returns were noticed during other months. Kurtosis results were found leptokurtic in the month of January returns. The other month's returns were found platykurtic. Shapiro-Wilk test disclose that anomaly exist in the NSE PSU Banks Index returns. April effect exists in NSE PSU Bank index.

11.5.33. NSE Realty Index

High mean returns were noticed during the month of May and low mean returns were found during the month of June. High level of volatility was noticed in the month of May and low level of volatility was noticed in the month of August. Skewness test disclosed the negative value and it was noticed during the month of June, September, October and November returns. Positive returns were noticed during other months. Kurtosis results NSE Realty index returns were found leptokurtic in the month of August returns. The other month's returns were found platykurtic. Shapiro-Wilk test disclose that anomaly exist in the NSE Realty Index returns. April effect exists in NSE Realty index.

11.6. Annual Effect in Indian Stock Market

To measure the Annual Effect in Indian stock market, returns, descriptive statistics like Mean, Standard deviation, Variance, Skewness, Kurtosis and Shapiro-wilk test are employed. The following paragraphs consolidates the result of the study.

11.6.1. Annual Effect BSE Sensex and Sectoral Indices

High mean returns were noticed in the Consumer Durable sector and low mean returns were found in the Realty. High level of volatility was noticed in the Metal sector and low level of volatility was noticed in the FMCG sector. Skewness test discloses that negative value were noticed on the Sensex index, Bank sector, Consumer Durables sector, Consumer Goods sector, Finance sector, Health Care and Technology sector returns. The other sector returns were noticed positive Skewness. Kurtosis results were found leptokurtic on Auto sector and Metal sector. The other sector results were found platykurtic. Shapiro-Wilk test disclose that doesn't exist anomaly in the FMCG, Power and PSU sectors. Hence, anomaly exists on other sectors.

11.6.2. Annual Effect NSE Nifty and Sectoral Indices

High mean returns were noticed in the Private Banking sector and low mean returns were found in the Realty. High level of volatility was noticed in the Metal sector and low level of volatility was noticed in the FMCG sector. Skewness test discloses that positive value were noticed on the Auto sector, Energy sector, Metal sector and Realty sector returns. The other sector returns were noticed Negative Skewness, which implies that most of the other sectors returns were less than the average returns. Kurtosis results were found leptokurtic on Auto sector. The other sector results were found platykurtic. Shapiro-Wilk test disclose that does not exist anomaly in the FMCG sector. Hence, anomaly exists on other sectors.

11.7. Shariah Index in Indian Stock Market

To measure the Seasonality Effect in Shariah Index, returns, descriptive statistics like Mean, Standard deviation, Variance, Skewness, Kurtosis, Shapiro-wilk test, OLS regression and Paired 't' test are employed. The following paragraphs consolidates the result of the study.

11.7.1. Day of the Week Effect - Shariah Index

High mean returns were noticed during Friday and low mean returns were found during Thursday. High level of volatility was noticed on Monday and low level of volatility was noticed on Tuesday. Skewness test disclosed that negative value and it was noticed during Thursday returns. The Kurtosis result of the NSE Shariah index returns were found leptokurtic on Monday returns and Thursday returns. The other day's returns were found platykurtic. Shapiro-Wilk test disclose that anomaly exist in the NSE Shariah index returns. The result of OLS regression analyses disclose that the select independent variables collectively contribute to 7.92 per cent variation in Friday returns.

11.7.2. Monthly Effect- Shariah Index

High mean returns were noticed during the month of September and low mean returns were found during the month of January. High level of volatility was noticed on the month of May and low level of volatility was noticed in the month of June. Skewness test disclosed the positive value and it was noticed during the month of April, May, June, July, November and March. The other Month's returns were found negative Skewness. The Kurtosis results NSE Shariah index returns were found leptokurtic in the month of April and May returns. The other month's returns were found platykurtic. Shapiro-Wilk test disclose that anomaly exist in the NSE Shariah index returns. April effect exists in NSE Shariah index.

11.7.3. Semi Month Efect- Shariah Index

High mean returns were noticed during the second half of the month and low mean returns were found during the first half of the month. High level of volatility was noticed on the first half of the month and low level of volatility was noticed in the second half of the month. Skewness test disclosed that positive value were noticed during both the first half of the month and the second half of the month returns. The Kurtosis results were found leptokurtic on both the First half of the month and the second half of the month. Shapiro-Wilk test disclose that anomaly exist in the NSE Shariah index returns. Paired 't' test result of the NSE Shariah index returns does not differ between the first half and the second half of the month.

11.7.4. Turn of the Month Effect- Shariah Index

High mean returns were noticed during the First half of the month and low mean returns were found during the Rest of the month. High level of volatility was noticed on the first half of the month and low level of volatility was noticed in the rest of the month. Skewness test disclosed that negative value were noticed during the first half of the month returns. The rest of the month returns was noticed positive Skewness. The Kurtosis results were found platykurtic on both the First half of the month and the rest of the month. Shapiro-Wilk test disclose that anomaly exist in the NSE Shariah index returns. Paired 't' test result of the NSE Shariah index returns differs between the first half and rest of the month.

11.8. Volatility in Indian Stock Market

To measure the Volatility in Indian Stock Market. Generalized Autoregressive Conditional Heteroscedasticity is employed. The following paragraphs consolidates the result of the study.

11.8.1. Volatility

Volatility prevails over the year in Indian stock market on all the sectors BSE Sensex, 19 BSE sectoral indices, NSE Nifty and 12 NSE sectoral indices.

11.9. Suggestions

11.9.1. Day of the week Effect

Investors who base their decision based on day of the week effect are advised to buy and sell shares based on the following.

- High level return is noticed on Wednesday and low level of return noticed on Friday for FMCG, IT and Realty sectors. Hence, investors are advised to buy BSE FMCG, IT and Realty shares on Friday and to sell on Wednesday.
- High level return is noticed on Friday and low level of return noticed on Thursday for Power sectors. Hence, investors are advised to buy BSE Power sector shares buy on Thursday and to sell on Friday.
- High level return is noticed on Wednesday and low level of return noticed on Tuesday for PSU sectors. Hence, investors are advised to buy BSE PSU sector shares buy on Tuesday and to sell on Wednesday.
- High level return is noticed on Friday and low level of return noticed on Tuesday for Metal sectors. Hence, investors are advised to buy BSE Metal shares buy on Tuesday and to sell on Friday.

- High level return is noticed on Friday and low level of return noticed on Wednesday for Consumer Goods sectors. Hence, investors are advised to buy BSE Consumer Goods shares buy on Wednesday and to sell on Friday.
- High level return is noticed on Wednesday and low level of return noticed on Monday for Bank sectors. Hence, investors are advised to buy BSE Bank shares buy on Monday and to sell on Wednesday.
- High level return is noticed on Wednesday and low level of return noticed on Thursday for Basic Materials, Health Care, Oil and Gas, Teck and Utilities sectors. Hence, investors are advised to buy BSE Basic Materials, Health Care, Oil and Gas, Teck and Utilities shares on Thursday and to sell on Wednesday.
- High level return is noticed on Monday and low level of return noticed on Thursday for Consumer Durables and Energy sectors. Hence, investors are advised to buy BSE Consumer Durables and Energy shares on Thursday and to sell on Monday.
- High level return is noticed on Monday and low level of return noticed on Friday for Finance and Telecom sectors. Hence, investors are advised to buy Finance and Telecom shares on Friday and to sell on Monday.
- High level return is noticed on Thursday and low level of return noticed on Monday for Auto sectors. Hence, investors are advised to buy BSE Auto shares on Monday and to sell on Thursday.
- High level return is noticed on Friday and low level of return noticed on Thursday for Realty sectors. Hence, investors are advised to buy NSE Energy shares on Thursday and to sell on Friday.
- High level return is noticed on Wednesday and low level of return noticed on Monday for IT sectors. Hence, investors are advised to buy NSE IT shares on Monday and to sell on Wednesday.
- High level return is noticed on Wednesday and low level of return noticed on Tuesday for Media sectors. Hence, investors are advised to buy NSE Media shares on Tuesday and to sell on Wednesday.
- High level return is noticed on Friday and low level of return noticed on Wednesday for Bank sectors. Hence, investors are advised to buy NSE Bank shares on Wednesday and to sell on Friday.
- High level return is noticed on Tuesday and low level of return noticed on Thursday for Energy sectors. Hence, investors are advised to buy NSE Energy shares on Thursday and to sell on Tuesday.

- High level return is noticed on Thursday and low level of return noticed on Friday for FMCG sectors. Hence, investors are advised to buy NSE FMCG shares on Friday and to sell on Thursday.
- High level return is noticed on Friday and low level of return noticed on Tuesday for Auto, Pharma, PSU BANKS and Private Banks sectors. Hence, investors are advised to buy NSE Auto, Pharma, PSU BANKS and Private Banks sectors shares on Tuesday and to sell on Friday.
- High level return is noticed on Friday and low level of return noticed on Wednesday for NSE Bank and Metal sectors. Hence, investors are advised to buy NSE Bank and Metal sectors shares on Wednesday and to sell on Friday.

11.9.2. Semi Month Effect

Investors who base their decision based on semi month effect are advised to buy and sell shares based on the following.

- High level return is noticed on First half of the month and low level of return noticed on Second half of the month for all the BSE sectors. Hence, investors are advised to buy for all the BSE sector shares on second half of the month and to sell on First half of the Month.
- High level return is noticed on Second half of the month and low level of return noticed on First half of the month for the FMCG, IT and Media sectors. Hence, investors are advised to buy for FMCG, IT and Media shares on First half of the month and to sell on Second half of the Month. Other sectors High level return is noticed on First half of the month and low level of return noticed on Second half of the month for the other sectors. Hence, investors are advised to buy for Auto, Metal, Pharma, Bank, Energy, Finance, PSU Banks, Private Banks and Realty shares on second half of the month and to sell on First half of the Month.

11.9.3. Turn of the Month Effect

Investors who base their decision based on turn of the month effect are advised to buy and sell shares based on the following.

- High level return is noticed on Rest of the month and low level of return noticed on First half of the month for Basic Materials, Energy, Finance, Industrial, Telecom and Utilities. Hence, investors are advised to buy for BSE Basic Materials, Energy, Finance, Industrial, Telecom and Utilities sectors shares on First half of the month and to sell on Rest of the Month. Other sectors High level return is noticed on First half of the month and low level of return noticed on rest of the month for the other sectors. Hence, investors are advised to buy for Auto, Bank. Consumer Goods, Consumer Durables, FMCG, Health Care, IT, PSU, Metal, Oil & Gas, Power, Realty and Tech shares on rest of the month and to sell on First half of the Month.

- High level return is noticed on First half of the month and low level of return noticed on rest of the month for all the NSE sectors. Hence, investors are advised to buy for all the NSE sector shares on rest of the month and to sell on First half of the Month.

11.9.4. Monthly Effect

Investors who base their decision based on monthly effect are advised to buy and sell shares based on the following.

- High level return is noticed on December and low level of return noticed on June for Metal sector. Hence, investors are advised to buy for BSE Realty sector shares on June and to sell on December.
- High level return is noticed on July and low level of return noticed on January for Teck sector. Hence, investors are advised to buy for BSE Teck sector shares on January and to sell on July.
- High level return is noticed on July and low level of return noticed on February for Telecom sector. Hence, investors are advised to buy for BSE Telecom sector shares on February and to sell on July.
- High level return is noticed on May and low level of return noticed on January for Consumer Durables sector. Hence, investors are advised to buy for BSE Consumer Durables sector shares on January and to sell on May.
- High level return is noticed on July and low level of return noticed on January for IT sector. Hence, investors are advised to buy for BSE IT sector shares on January and to sell on July.
- High level return is noticed on April and low level of return noticed on March for Basic Materials and Utilities sectors. Hence, investors are advised to buy for BSE Basic Materials and Utilities sectors shares on March and to sell on April.
- High level return is noticed on April and low level of return noticed on January for Health Care and Industrial sectors. Hence, investors are advised to buy for Health Care and Industrial sectors shares on January and to sell on April.
- High level return is noticed on April and low level of return noticed on June for Realty sector. Hence, investors are advised to buy for BSE Realty sector shares on June and to sell on April.

- High level return is noticed on April and low level of return noticed on November for Energy sector. Hence, investors are advised to buy for BSE Energy sector shares on November and to sell on April.
- High level return is noticed on September and low level of return noticed on January for Auto, Consumer Goods and PSU sectors. Hence, investors are advised to buy for BSE Auto, Consumer Goods and PSU sectors shares on January and to sell on September.
- High level return is noticed on September and low level of return noticed on February for Bank, Finance and Power sectors. Hence, investors are advised to buy for BSE Bank, Finance and Power sectors shares on February and to sell on September.
- High level return is noticed on September and low level of return noticed on October for FMCG sectors. Hence, investors are advised to buy for BSE FMCG sectors shares on October and to sell on September.
- High level return is noticed on April and low level of return noticed on January for Pharma sector. Hence, investors are advised to buy for NSE Pharma sector shares on January and to sell on April.
- High level return is noticed on May and low level of return noticed on June for Realty sector. Hence, investors are advised to buy for NSE Realty sector shares on June and to sell on May.
- High level return is noticed on December and low level of return noticed on June for Metal sector. Hence, investors are advised to buy for NSE Metal sector shares on June and to sell on December.
- High level return is noticed on December and low level of return noticed on January for IT sector. Hence, investors are advised to buy for NSE IT sector shares on January and to sell on December.
- High level return is noticed on December and low level of return noticed on February for Media sector. Hence, investors are advised to buy for NSE Media sector shares on February and to sell on December.
- High level return is noticed on September and low level of return noticed on January for Auto sector. Hence, investors are advised to buy for NSE Auto sector shares on January and to sell on September.
- High level return is noticed on September and low level of return noticed on February for Bank, Energy, Finance, PSU Banks and Private Banks sectors. Hence, investors are advised to buy for NSE Bank, Energy, Finance, PSU Banks and Private Banks sectors shares on February and to sell on September.

- High level return is noticed on September and low level of return noticed on October for FMCG sector. Hence, investors are advised to buy for NSE FMCG sector shares on October and to sell on September.

11.9.5. Shariah Index in Indian Stock Market

Investors who base their decision based on Seasonality Effect in Shariah Index are advised to buy and sell shares based on the following.

- High level returns noticed on Friday and low level returns noticed on Thursday for NSE Shariah index. Hence, investors are advised to buy NSE Shariah shares on Thursday and to sell on Friday.
- High level returns noticed on during the month of September and low level returns noticed on during the month of January for NSE Shariah index. Hence, investors are advised to buy NSE Shariah shares on January and to sell on September.
- High level return is noticed on second half of the month and low level of return noticed on first half of the month for NSE Shariah index. Hence, investors are advised to buy for the NSE Shariah index shares on First half of the month and to sell on second half of the Month.
- High level return is noticed on First half of the month and low level of return noticed on rest of the month for NSE Shariah index. Hence, investors are advised to buy for all the NSE Shariah index shares on rest of the month and to sell on First half of the Month.

11.9.6. Annual Effect in Indian Stock Market

- High returns are noticed at Banking and FMCG sectors. Hence, investors may prefer to invest at banking and FMCG sector for longer period of time.
- The above outcome is based on a statistical tool used for analyzing the anomalies in the BSE Sensex, 19 BSE sectoral indices, NSE Nifty and 12 NSE sectoral indices. There are various other factors to be considered before investing. We also suggest that the same can be applied in small stocks and extend the same on blue-chips based on the risks and rewards.
- It is necessary for the Indian Investors to carefully study the publically available information, because it plays a major role in analyzing the Market Efficiency and changes in the market. The present study would be useful to the native and foreign investors, traders and arbitrageurs who formulate profitable trading strategies in the stock market

11.10. Conclusion

The research of the study raises questions on the efficient market hypothesis which states that stock prices are random, and that investors cannot make abnormal profits using historical prices. The day of the week effect patterns in return and volatility can enable investors to take advantage of relatively regular market shifts by designing and implementing trading strategies, which account for such predictable patterns. The existent theories are inadequate in modelling stock market. The stock market is full of anomalies. If the market is not efficient, then investors can make profit by analysing the historic data. By digging in to vast data you can unearth many inefficiencies which can be to make in to high returns. By finding these inefficiencies you can make the system more efficient.

11.11. Scope for Further Research

A study, with similar objectives, could be made with reference to Spot, Futures, and Commodity and Derivative Markets. A study could be made with Other Calendar Effects like Week of the Month Effect, Month of the Quarter Effects, Turn of the Year Effect, Summer Effect, Hour of the Day Effect. A study may be conducted to investigate the Calendar Effect of the Trading Days across the individual securities. A comparative study, with similar objectives, could be made to study the in between ideas of Indian Stock Market and indices of other Stock Markets foreign indices etc. The intra-day stock price can be examined to investigate the behaviour of share prices. A comparative examination for the presence of Calendar anomalies can be done on international level. Further research on the above mentioned research issues should be undertaken to strengthen the existing literature as it will be highly useful for academicians, investment managers and policy makers.

www.ingramcontent.com/pod-product-compliance
Lightning Source LLC
Chambersburg PA
CBHW071435230926
51846CB00001B/237
* 9 7 8 9 3 8 6 6 3 8 4 1 0 *